Praise for Livin

"This fresh, potent approach to Reiki is unlike any other…Follow Melissa's wisdom to create a life imbued with soul-on-fire passion and purpose."

—Cyndi Dale, author of *Raise Clairaudient Energy*

"Melissa Tipton is a genius. *Living Reiki* is not only life changing, it's also engaging, accessible, and a joy to read. And it's not just for Reiki practitioners! It's illuminating reading for absolutely everyone who is interested in energy, manifestation, complementary medicine, or personal power. I wholeheartedly recommend it."

—Tess Whitehurst, author of *The Good Energy Book*

LIVING
REIKI

About the Author

Melissa Tipton is a tarot reader, Reiki Master, licensed massage therapist, and witch. She has been practicing yoga for over a decade and discovered that it complements witchcraft very well.

LIVING
REIKI

Heal Yourself &
Transform Your Life

MELISSA TIPTON

Llewellyn Worldwide
Woodbury, Minnesota

FIRST EDITION
First Printing, 2019

Book design by Bob Gaul
Cover design by Ellen Lawson
Editing by Laura Kurtz
Interior art by Llewellyn art department

Llewellyn Publications is a registered trademark of Llewellyn Worldwide Ltd.

Library of Congress Cataloging-in-Publication Data

Names: Tipton, Melissa, author.
Title: Living Reiki : heal yourself & transform your life / Melissa Tipton.
Description: First edition. | Woodbury, Minnesota : Llewellyn Publishing, [2019] | Includes bibliographical references.
Identifiers: LCCN 2018042900 (print) | LCCN 2018044320 (ebook) | ISBN 9780738759883 () | ISBN 9780738759432 (alk. paper)
Subjects: LCSH: Reiki (Healing system)
Classification: LCC RZ403.R45 (ebook) | LCC RZ403.R45 T57 2019 (print) | DDC 615.8/52—dc23
LC record available at https://lccn.loc.gov/2018042900

Llewellyn Worldwide Ltd. does not participate in, endorse, or have any authority or responsibility concerning private business transactions between our authors and the public.

All mail addressed to the author is forwarded, but the publisher cannot, unless specifically instructed by the author, give out an address or phone number.

Any internet references contained in this work are current at publication time, but the publisher cannot guarantee that a specific location will continue to be maintained. Please refer to the publisher's website for links to authors' websites and other sources.

Llewellyn Publications
A Division of Llewellyn Worldwide Ltd.
2143 Wooddale Drive
Woodbury, MN 55125-2989
www.llewellyn.com

Printed in the United States of America

Contents

Introduction

Welcome to the path of the healer. You are embarking on a journey that will take you deep into the mysteries of Reiki and self-transformation, blending the two in a potent elixir of healing, an elixir that, if taken with an open heart by the soul of the seeker, will unite you with your True Self. Amidst the busyness of our lives, it's easy to forget that we live in a universe that is positively humming with magic. We're too busy paying the bills that we forget to pay attention to our soul. We're so wrapped up in the anxieties and worries of life that we no longer remember what it feels like to be wrapped up in the Divine. And yet, we don't have to quit our jobs, walk out on our families, or trek up a mountain to find something more, something deeper. We can find it right where we are, and indeed, we *must* find it where we are. As Doreen Valiente wrote in her poem "The Charge of the Goddess," "if that which you seek, you find not within yourself, you will never find it without. For behold, I have been with you from the beginning, and I am that which is attained at the end of desire."

We are what we seek, and in the very stuff of our lives—the beautiful mess of it all—we find liberation and awakening. When we allow ourselves to spiral inward, it is here, deep in our core, that we understand why we came into this life, what we as a unique being are here to do, and a fire is sparked. A fire that will not allow us to be waylaid, a lantern amidst the distractions. With this light to guide the way, our lives are radically transformed, and we embrace our birthright as natural healers.

Your Healing Apprenticeship

Inside each and every one of us lies a vast store of untapped wisdom, seeds of potential waiting for the right conditions to germinate. It is time. The time is now. Our world is badly in need of healing, and we each must start with the only person we can ever truly change: our self. The more each of us shifts into our power, reclaiming our original wisdom and weaving a web of healing, the greater our communal strength becomes, the stronger the web, the deeper the healing, the bigger the ripples of change.

The form of Reiki I practice, Life Alchemy Reiki, is a path that emphasizes *self*-transformation. This is the foundation of the entire practice, for if *you* have forgotten your wholeness, how can you ever hope to remind others of theirs? This is not a path of "fixing" yourself or "fixing" other people, as that approach starts with a faulty assumption of brokenness. Instead, we seek to reinstill our trust in the unshakeable reality that we are already Whole. We are already enough. We have simply forgotten. So, let us remember. Let's embark on this journey together, learning the ways of the Reiki healer, blending them with the magic and power of self-transformation.

Who Is This Book For?

This path is open to all who feel called to learn the ways of the healer, whether you are just beginning or have walked the healing path for years and yearn to go deeper. In my practice as a massage therapist, Reiki Master, and tarot reader, I am privileged to front-row seats to my clients' amazing spiritual, mental, and physical shifts, and it truly is a magical thing to behold. The number one block to these shifts, hands down, is the false belief that we're not worthy, and I've seen time and time again that once this belief is released, spontaneous self-healing can occur. Dis-ease can be thought of as existing out of alignment with who we truly are—in other words, out of alignment with the truth that we are *already* whole, that we are already one with a state of health. When we are separated from this truth, we get stuck in seeing ourselves as broken, and we believe that the only way to earn our return to wholeness is by eating a certain way, exercising enough, getting another certification, landing the right job, finding the perfect partner—and the list goes on. *And on.* We're stuck in a loop of not enoughness, and in order to heal this dis-ease, in order to return to a state of *ease*, we must remember our True Self.

The tools and techniques presented in this course are designed to help you shed, layer by layer, the filters and obstructions created by the ego, which are obscuring your True Self from view. The more you release these obstructions, the more you are able to see how wonderfully unique, how incredibly magical you *already* are, and from this new vantage point you'll have increased clarity on what you came into this life to do. Each and every one of us channels Divine energy uniquely—no two people will channel this energy in the same way, so you *cannot* be replaced in the unfolding of the cosmos. No one else can weave your magic for you. The world needs the gifts that you, and you alone, possess.

If you are being called to walk the path of healing, let this book be a companion on your quest. In its pages, you will learn about the practice of Reiki, moving through three levels of training, each level punctuated by an attunement or initiation. Many of us receive our Reiki attunements in the context of weekend workshops or brief online courses. In modern life, we have so few initiatory experiences, so few rites of passage, yet without these mindful ways of marking and celebrating our life transitions, it's often difficult to fully integrate the changes we seek. We might have a luminously transcendent experience on Saturday, and then feel hit by the tsunami wave of "normal" life come Monday, quickly getting sucked under by our routines and feeling progressively more disconnected from the wisdom we unearthed during the workshop. The Life Alchemy path is one of weaving the magic of transformation into the very stuff of life. You don't have to wait until you can get away for a retreat to do this work; it happens right here, right now. The practices build upon each other, each level culminating in a Reiki attunement, of which you will receive three in total (Levels One, Two, and Three) over the course of your studies. If you have already been attuned in another lineage, you can use the practices at your own pace to deepen your understanding and practice of Reiki. Beginners and more advanced practitioners alike may elect to use the text while taking my online or in-person Life Alchemy course, receiving your Life Alchemy attunements (available distantly or in-person) as you reach the appropriate junctures in the lessons, or you can use it in tandem with any Reiki course of your choosing as a means of deepening the experience. The practices are designed to help you internalize the principles of both Reiki and self-transformation in new ways using meditation, ritual, and other techniques to move beyond an intellectual understanding to an embodied wisdom.

This course of study asks for fearless self-inquiry; we are calling on the powers of Reiki and self-transformation in order to know ourselves more deeply, and it is *this* process that ignites our inner healer more than any course, book, or attunement ever will. Without intimate knowledge of our True Self, we're like a rudderless ship without a map, but through the magic of Reiki and self-transformation, we can pick up the subtle currents that are ready to guide us back home. This journey will take us far from the shores of the familiar, and we'll be asked to shed our preconceived ideas and leave the posturing of the ego behind. For, if it is radical transformation we seek, we must be radical in our approach. We must be willing to push our own limits, stretch the bounds of our minds, and expand our view of what is possible. If the call is alive within you, and you can feel, in your very bones, that it is time, the time is now, then let us begin. Let us pass through the veil of the known and unravel the hidden mysteries and the secret ways of the healer within.

−1−
REIKI AND SELF-TRANSFORMATION

The Japanese word Reiki roughly translates to "spiritual energy" or "universal energy" with "rei" meaning "spiritual" or "universal" and "ki" meaning "energy." In other cultures, this ki or energy goes by other names, such as chi (Chinese), prana (Hindu), manu (shamanic Hawaiian), rauch (Hebrew), and so forth. Essentially, it's the energy that makes life possible. When I learned the translation of "universal energy," my first question was, "Well, if it's universal, why do I need to get an attunement in order to use it?" My confusion was rooted in the difference between what the word Reiki means in Japanese and its usage in the West. In the West, Reiki is used to describe a specific healing modality, but in Japan, this method of healing is often denoted with more precise names, such as Reiki Ryoho, Reiki-ho, or Usui Reiki Ryoho, because again, Reiki simply means spiritual or universal energy in Japanese. This very broad term is akin to saying that you're interested in movement versus specifying what kind of movement, such as yoga or ballet, and in regards to a Reiki attunement, it makes more sense when you think of an attunement as an initiation into a specific type of movement, like being trained in ballet or yoga, as opposed to simply having the innate ability to move. A Reiki attunement initiates you into a specific lineage and tradition that utilizes universal, spiritual energy.

If we look closer at the name Reiki Ryoho, a translation by Reiki scholar/practitioner Frans Stiene gives us important clues as to the deeper meaning and purpose of Reiki (Steine 2015, 15). Stiene argues that Reiki can be interpreted to mean your True Self, because Reiki, or spiritual energy, *is* our True Self. "Ryoho," which can be parsed as ryô, meaning "to cure or heal" and hô, meaning "method, teachings, truth," gives us the interpretation "teachings to cure and heal one's True Self." As Stiene writes, "Of course [this is] a metaphor: to heal one's True Self. [The truth is that there is] nothing to heal—we just need to remember our True Self." We'll return to this concept of remembering our True Self quite a bit in future chapters, but first, let's talk about where Reiki as we know it today originated.

A Brief History of Reiki

Mikao Usui (1865–1926) is credited with developing the healing system of Reiki, and while there is a great deal of myth and legend surrounding his life, I'm going to stick to the story as presented by Hiroshi Doi, a renowned Reiki practitioner and scholar. He went to great lengths to track down historical documents and to speak to people who studied under Usui in order to piece together as close to first-hand information as possible. In short, his version seems to contain far less B.S. than other stories I've read.

In a nutshell, Mikao Usui was born in Japan, and as a dedicated student-practitioner of Buddhism, he was very interested in answering the age-old question, "Why are we here?" His studies led him to surmise that the ultimate purpose of life is to attain *An-shin Ritsu-mei,* which Doi defines as, "You should leave what you cannot change to the universe and keep peaceful Kokoro without worrying about anything at all"[1] (Doi 2014, 35). In other words, chill out; do your best, then surrender the things you can't control to the universe instead of worrying your life away.

Usui trained in Zen practice for a number of years, trying to reach this state of An-shin Ritsu-mei, but it remained elusive, so in February of 1922, he climbed up Mt. Kurama and began to fast. "At midnight after three weeks, he felt a great shock in the center of the brain, as if being struck by lightning, and lost consciousness for some hours" (Ibid., 35). When he woke up, Usui felt "an extreme refreshment that he had never felt before…Reiki of the Universe had pierced his body and mind, and he resonated with Reiki in his body." In Usui's own words: "It is difficult to explain what it exactly is. I realized that I was granted the healing ability accidentally when I felt the sacred energy and got initiated by the mysterious way while fasting" (Ibid., 101).

In 1922, Usui condensed his teachings into a coherent system and founded the Usui Reiki Ryoho Gakkai, meaning the Usui Reiki Healing Method Learning Society. Teaching was divided into three levels: Shoden ("the entrance"), Level I; Okuden ("deep inside"), Level II; and Shinpiden ("the mystery" or "secret teachings"), Level III. They're such evocative names, aren't they?

At this point in Reiki's story, there's a lengthy segment regarding how Reiki was almost entirely forgotten in Japan, how it made its way to the West, primarily through a woman named Hawayo Takata, and how it returned once more to Japan, but I want to shift now from the

---

1 The concept of kokoro has nuanced meaning depending on the context, but here it can be interpreted as consciousness.

past to the present. If you want to learn more about the history of Reiki, two of the more accurate sources I have found thus far are *A Modern Reiki Method for Healing* (Doi) and *The Reiki Sourcebook* (Stiene).

What Is Reiki?

Let's take a closer look at this energy we call Reiki. For starters, we know that it's universal. This energy is in everything that exists, and Doi describes it as "the power that gave birth to the Great Universe, created the solar system, brought about all the creatures on the earth and maintains them in good order…This is the fine energy vibration…of Love radiating to the Universe from the highest consciousness with the purpose to carry out its will" (Ibid., 19).

In essence, if you are dealing with pure Reiki energy, this energy can do no harm, because by definition it moves whatever it interacts with in the direction of love and light. This is one of the many reasons I love using Reiki. I have found that, when used properly, Reiki is an effective healing method that prevents the transfer of energetic ick from one person to another. During energy work, it's possible for the practitioner or recipient to transfer energy to the other in a manner that is unhealthy for one or both parties. You may be familiar with massage therapists who "catch" their clients' aches and pains or intuitive readers who feel the emotions of their clients long after the session is over. These are examples of unhealthy energy transfers, and Reiki, in my experience, seems to have built-in safeguards that prevent this from happening (to an extent; we also have personal responsibility in maintaining healthy boundaries).

There are different forms of energy in the universe, Reiki being one of them (we'll talk more about different energy types in chapter 3), and these energies are often categorized by their frequency. Generally speaking, energies in a more physical form, like the energy forming your body or the chair you're sitting on, are considered to be vibrating at a lower frequency. Not lower as in "bad," just slower and different than the frequency at which other energies are vibrating. Reiki is said to vibrate at a very high frequency. Looking at this in the context of human health, our personal energy is often vibrating at a lower frequency than Reiki. Throughout life, many things affect our energy, from physical activities (or lack thereof), thoughts, emotions—you name it. Everything we experience, both externally and internally, affects our energy, and those effects can range from helpful to harmful. Reiki, vibrating at a very high frequency, is able to enter our energy field and clear away blocks and stagnations, balancing deficient or excessively energetic areas.

Imagine a glass of water with mud on the bottom, representing a person's energy field. During a Reiki treatment, clear, clean water— Reiki—is being poured from a pitcher into the glass. As the Reiki pours into the glass, it might temporarily stir up the mud on the bottom, causing the water to become cloudy, but after a certain point all of the muddy water has been flushed out and we are left with a glass of clean water. The energetic "mud" isn't inherently bad, it's merely a matter of context. On the forest floor, this mud is fertile soil for supporting life, but I don't necessarily want it in my water glass. In our own field, energy that may be causing harm in one context or location often needs to be released and redirected so it can serve a better purpose elsewhere, and Reiki is a powerful method for doing so. There is, however, one critical difference between Reiki and our analogy: Reiki is conscious. It's not just energy that happens to be vibrating at a high frequency; it is imbued with Divine consciousness and knows precisely what we need to return to a state of healing.

To extend the analogy a bit further, the stream of water is a one-way path: the water in the glass is not flowing upward, back into the pitcher. When you are giving someone a Reiki treatment, potentially stirring up their energetic mud as part of the healing process, you are not taking this cloudy water into your own energy field. This is one of the major safeguards built into Reiki that can help you, as a healer, stay healthy even while working with those who are suffering from various states of dis-ease.

Reiki and Self-Transformation

While helping others find healing is certainly an important facet of Reiki, I have found Reiki to be infinitely powerful when it is used first and foremost as a tool to affect change within oneself. When helping others becomes our sole focus we increase our chances of burnout and "compassion fatigue." Not to mention, neglecting our own self-work causes us to eventually reach a limit in our healing abilities, because we can only assist others in traveling paths that we ourselves have walked. When, instead, we continually tend to our own sacred fire, we never run out of Source energy and insightful information that we can then share with others. Therefore, in our journey with Reiki we will consider self-transformation as our primary goal, with helping others as a lovely bonus!

One Mind, One Thing

To access deeper levels of Reiki's self-transformative power, we'll look in an unlikely place: a creation story, as told from a Hermetic point of view. The story begins with an all-pervading consciousness, what some might call God, the Divine, the All, Infinite Consciousness—take your pick. This essence is conscious and it is everywhere. Nothing exists outside of the All. To help visualize this, let's imagine a room. This room represents the sum total of everything that has been, is, and ever will be. This room is the All. A light begins to fill the room: This light is called the One Mind. However, a paradox exists: The room (the All) and the light (One Mind) are one and the same, yet they can also appear to separate, and this separation allows them to interact with one another in interesting ways.

Something begins to move downward, precipitating from the Light of the One Mind. It's a dark, watery substance, and we will call it the One Thing: a chaotic, roiling ocean at the bottom of the room. So now we have the One Thing, the ocean, on the bottom and above is the Light of the One Mind, both contained in the room of the All. The One Mind yearns to interact with the One Thing, and it does so by sending penetrating rays of thought energy into the water. This thought energy has been called the Word of God or the Spirit of the Divine. The One Mind projects thought energy, or ideas, into the One Thing, and in doing so, the four elements are created: earth, fire, air, and water.

There's a distinction between these elements and what we know as elements in modern-day chemistry, things like hydrogen, helium, and copper. These four elements are archetypal energies, not physical substances. Archetypes are like the ultimate template, providing the prototype or pattern after which other things are modeled. For example, the Water archetype serves as a template for the category of Water energy, a category that includes, but is not limited to, literal, physical water. Christopher Penzcak describes the four archetypal elements as "represented by the associated physical phenomena, but they are beyond manifestation. They are archetypal forces influencing all of creation. They are generated from a mysterious fifth element, known as spirit…and they return to it" (Penzcak 2014, 58). Carl Jung believed that the archetypes of the four elements are so deeply ingrained in us that they generate a powerful urge to seek balance amongst these elements within ourselves, even if we're not consciously aware of this drive.

After the four elements are created from the interaction of the One Mind and the One Thing, the One Mind creates another mind, called Mind the Maker, and Mind the Maker is tasked with using these four archetypal elements to fashion everything else in existence. Mind the Maker is called the demiurge or the Creator in some traditions, and Mind the Maker goes about fashioning the entire universe, using the archetypal elements as its building blocks.

After creating Mind the Maker, the One Mind leaps out of the watery One Thing and returns to the Above. Remember that all of these events are taking place within the "room" of the All, and the One Mind, the One Thing, and the All, while temporarily separated (in a sense) are ultimately one and the same. This temporary "separateness" in order for the parts of a whole to interact before "recombining" is a theme in Hermetic teachings, and it will be a theme in our work as well. According to the Hermetic creation story, each of us is a copy of the universe. The axiom "As above, so below; as below, so above" speaks to this fundamental reality. Thus, if we come to know ourselves, we can know the universe and vice versa, and if we work to create change within ourselves, we can create change in the greater universe. How do we do this? Well, the story says that each of us contains a microcosmic version of the One Mind and the One Thing, thus we, too, possess great creative powers. We can use the very same pattern depicted in the creation story as a user's manual for our creative capabilities, learning how to effectively wield these internal powers to generate the life our soul yearns to lead. This user's manual is mapped out in a series of seven steps, which we'll cover next. Master these steps and you unlock the fullness of your creative power, including the power to create health and wellness.

The Seven Steps of Self-Transformation

1. Illumination is the process of shedding the light of awareness on egoic elements that are cluttering our consciousness, elements like defense mechanisms, projections, and other mental constructs that cloud our ability to see ourselves, and everything and everyone around us, as Divine. We can think of this as removing lampshades that are covering up the Light of our internal One Mind.

2. Submersion brings us into deeper self-awareness by wading into the waters of our unconscious, our internal One Thing, thereby opening the door for productive dialogue between the conscious and unconscious selves, which can be thought of as our internal One Mind and One Thing, respectively. Remember, it's the

interaction between these two that powers all of creation, so getting these forces into a productive dialogue within us is important if we want to create the life our soul desires.

3. Polarization is a process by which we heighten our awareness of inner duality—our One Mind and One Thing—and explore the paradox of their underlying oneness and ability to separate. Just as we saw in the creation story, these two internal forces can use their separateness to generate a polarity, like the charge of a battery, and this battery powers our creativity.

4. Merging is the initial union of these polar forces, which can also be thought of as our internal active and receptive natures, the conscious and the unconscious, the spirit and the soul. Here we begin to blend the best of both, giving birth to what Egyptian alchemists referred to as the Intelligence of the Heart, thereby supercharging our internal battery and our creative abilities.

5. Inspiration takes the creative potential generated by Merging and animates it with the Divine breath of life, introducing new elements that are beyond our ability to plan for or control. This element of surprise challenges the ego-self's delusion that it is in charge, so a component of Inspiration is allowing this self-delusion to die and fall away so we can be reborn into the Light of Truth. In other words, so we can remember our True Self.

6. Refinement takes the divinely inspired solution from the previous step and purifies it even further, removing any last traces of the ego that would otherwise cloud our ability to see our True Self. We raise our individual psyche to the highest level possible to unite with the One Mind, and as you'll learn shortly, Reiki is a wonderful tool for doing so.

7. Integration completes the process by uniting the distilled essence of our One Mind and One Thing, allowing us to experience on

a deep level their inherent Oneness. This can also be thought of as the union between spirit and matter, soul and body. Said more pragmatically, we take this state of enlightened consciousness and we weave it into the very fabric of our day-to-day lives; it's not something we experience only when we're on a meditation cushion or in a yoga class.

And then, like the ouroboros, the snake eating its own tail, we return once more to the beginning, but this time bringing our newly transformed perspective to bear. These, in a nutshell, are the seven steps of self-transformation, and now it's time to weave Reiki into the picture.

How Does Reiki Fit In?

Let's skip right to the punch line: Reiki can be thought of as the pure thought energy emanating from the One Mind. Say what, now? To make sense of this, recall the Hermetic creation story: The One Mind used thought energy to create the universe; it sent penetrating rays of this energy into the One Thing, and in doing so, the building blocks of creation were formed. Clearly, this thought energy is incredibly powerful, and it is my belief that Reiki as a healing system is a direct channel for this incredibly powerful energy. As we are microcosmic mirrors of the Universe, learning how to reconnect with our internal One Mind and One Thing allows us to use the universal building blocks to create the life we want. Usui himself said, "I am the Universe. The Universe is me," which parallels our Hermetic teachings (Doi 2014, 103), and we'll see deeper connections in chapter 5 when we explore the different types of energy.

The healing system of Reiki is a method for tapping into the energy of the One Mind without the contaminations of ego. Remember our water pitcher analogy? Reiki, when used properly, ensures that we are pouring from the pitcher of the Divine, therefore the energy we're pouring isn't contaminated (and bonus: we're not depleted in the process of channeling it). To understand this more fully, let's talk about this notion of contamination. Contamination isn't synonymous with "bad." In this context, I define contaminated as more specific or differentiated, as opposed to less specific and existing as pure potential. Take stem cells, for instance. They represent the cellular version of pure potential. They haven't yet differentiated into specific types of cells, like skin cells, or muscle cells, or brain cells; they still have the ability to be anything. In the same way, energy can exist as pure potential, or it can differentiate to form specific things, like a chair, or anger, or clouds. When you're facilitating healing for yourself or someone else, you don't want to introduce a chair, or anger, or clouds into their system when perhaps they need something else. From our limited human perspective, it seems hubristic to assume that we will always know exactly what people need, especially if our egoic mind steps in and tries to "figure it out." Far better to channel the energy of pure potential, especially in the form of divinely conscious pure potential, which will know exactly what the recipient needs, how much, where, and for what purpose: this is Reiki.

In the context of energy healing, the most common ways for contamination to occur is, one, by using our own personal energy to try and heal someone, or two, channeling a transpersonal source of energy (including Reiki) and imposing our ego on it. In the first case, we are using energy that is suitable for us (or not—our personal energy can be out of whack and causing us problems, too) but possibly not suitable for the recipient. This is like putting diesel fuel into a gasoline-powered car; it's not suitable for optimal functioning. In the second case, the energy we're channeling *is* suitable, but we start to impose our own stuff onto it, usually courtesy of the ego, rendering it no longer the energy of pure healing potential, and the results might not be suitable for the recipient.

When we use Reiki without trying to control or force the outcome—without imposing our ego—Reiki will naturally enter the energy field as Divine potential, the pure emanations of the One Mind, and from there, it will do precisely what is needed to return things to a state of balance and wholeness. I like to think of the emanations of the One Mind as a sort of divine template containing, among other things, our blueprint of original wholeness, our True Self. When this template is reintroduced to our system, we remember our original wholeness and our energy begins to repattern itself according to this divine blueprint.

You can think of the seven steps of self-transformation as a framework for making contact with this divine blueprint of original wholeness and integrating it into our daily lives, long after a Reiki session is over. In doing so, we activate our innate creative powers, which include the powers of self-healing and the ability to manifest what we need in life, and we grow in our capacity to help others do the same. In the next chapter, we begin our journey with the first step of self-transformation: Illumination.

−2−
ILLUMINATION

The first of our seven steps is Illumination, and we'll be working with the archetypal energy of Fire for this process, so let's look at how this energy can affect us by using physical fire as a metaphor. For starters, fire introduces light, so the energy of Fire can help us see things that would otherwise be hidden. When something is on fire, the process of burning changes its qualities—for example, transforming a log into a pile of ash—so the energy of Fire can help us change form and qualities. And finally, fire removes water. When we view archetypal Water as symbolic of our emotions and the unconscious, Fire energy allows us to temporarily remove those aspects—for example, by giving us some distance from intense emotions so we can view a situation in a different light.

Illumination and the Ego

In Illumination, we will be focusing the transformative power of Fire on the ego, and specifically, the stories our ego constructs to help us make sense of the world and our place in it. As we go about our daily lives, the ego takes our experiences and turns them into narratives starring us as the protagonist. By its very nature, the ego is self-focused. It makes everything about us, so when we over identify with our ego, we take everything personally. That irritated glance from the woman in the checkout line? That was personally directed at you. The disappointed vibe you sensed while talking to your mom? Also a personal attack. The ego turns life into a battle of you against the world, and it's exhausting. Here's the paradox, though, and it's one that can serve as a trap in our personal evolution if we don't grasp its deeper meaning: That irritated glance from the woman in the checkout line and the disappointed vibe from your mom—those might actually be directed at you. And yet…they're *still* not personal unless you choose to take them as such.

This takes equal parts effort and surrender to fully grasp, and here are some of the threads being woven together within this paradox:

- People's behavior is a reflection of *their* internal state. It is not an accurate appraisal of you or your self-worth. If someone is angry with us, we often wonder, "Have I done something wrong?" Or if that thought is uncomfortable for us, we project it back onto the other person and think, "They've done something wrong!" Another person's anger is just that— another person's anger; it's not a value judgment about you.

- While someone's actions may be triggered by or in response to something you do or say, and these actions and words are your responsibility, the way someone chooses to respond is entirely their responsibility. If they choose to respond in anger or in love, neither of those is a reflection on you; it's an internal choice this person has made. Thus, you cannot *make* someone angry or *make* someone love.

- Likewise, no one can make you feel any particular way. Our language contradicts this: "He made me so angry!" "She makes me feel like crap when she does that!" However, the truth remains: Your feelings are an internal experience. They are not the creation of another person, even if you are feeling a certain way in response to the actions of another. (Don't believe me? Let's say someone tells a joke. Person A finds it hilarious; Person B is offended. If emotions were created by the joke teller, each person would have the same emotional response, but the clear fact that they don't indicates that emotions are an inside job.)

While we might understand and even intellectually agree with these distinctions, in practice we often slip back into blaming others or blaming situations for how we feel, which leaves us stuck: Unless these external factors, which we cannot control, change, we "have" to feel a certain way. When we fully understand that no one can make us feel anything, we are liberated. And on the flipside, when we realize that we cannot make anyone feel, or do, or be anything (and when we sit with the fear that this lack of control might trigger) we are free: free from the self-appointed task of controlling other people, and free from the responsibility that others might try to unload on us of their feelings and internal states of being.

This does not absolve us of responsibility for our actions, however—quite the contrary. Instead of fixating on other people's actions and feelings, we center focus on ourselves. Too often, we adopt the habit of taking responsibility for the way other people feel and behave as a distraction from self-responsibility. Any parts of our experience that we don't want to own, we invariably project it "out there" and see it in others. We might tell ourselves, if only so-and-so would stop doing that annoying thing, we would no longer "have" to feel irritated, so we doggedly try to get them to change while ignoring our role in the situation. This cycle of projection keeps us stuck and, more to the point, distracted from our own experience and from our True Self, because the voice of the True Self gets drowned out by all of the chatter, drama, and external focus. How do we break free? By owning our stuff: the good, the bad, and everything in between. If we're feeling angry, we own our anger; we don't project it onto someone else and then engage in a self-constructed battle with this external "angry person." If we're feeling vulnerable, we sit with our vulnerability; we don't project it onto someone else and either rush to take care of them or act like a bully, punishing them for the vulnerability that's too uncomfortable for us to feel.

Your Internal Fire

This brings us back to Illumination and Fire's ability to temporarily give us some space from watery emotions. Being able to witness our emotions, as opposed to drowning in them, allows an important shift to occur. When we experience our emotions as overwhelming, we often develop dysfunctional habits for minimizing this overwhelm, and these habits typically take one of two forms: distracting ourselves from the troublesome emotions or locking the emotions down before they have a chance to get "out of control." There's a big difference between distracting ourselves from or suppressing emotions versus witnessing them. Witnessing our emotions requires that we let them arise without interference. We don't try to push them down, we don't use distractions like Facebook, eating, et cetera, to escape, and we don't try to control our emotions by intellectualizing or creating stories to explain them away.

These unhealthy habits serve to hide something from our conscious awareness. What's being hidden? Often, we fear that what lies beneath the emotional churnings is the makings of our undoing, so it feels safer to keep this undoing and its emotional harbingers from knocking on our door, but in truth, what's being hidden is our True Nature and *the undoing of our ego-led life.* For example, while superficially we might fear failure (and, indeed, our ego can churn out stories to this effect regularly), deep down we're often more afraid of succeeding—and not merely on a superficial level, but succeeding by embodying our soul's calling. The call of the soul is weighty stuff, and it can feel scary to fully step into the power that lies dormant within, because with that power comes responsibility, as well as an invitation to develop new skills and life strategies to meet these responsibilities, all of which challenge the ego's status quo. So instead, it can feel safer to stick with a small Tupperware container of power. Outwardly, we might complain that we aren't able to make lasting change in our life or have the impact we desire in the world, yet we have handicapped ourselves; we have sub-consciously blunted our power because we're afraid of what it can do and what it might ask of us.

It's time to own that power, to stop distracting ourselves from our full potential. We distract ourselves with codependent habits (e.g., tak-ing on other people's baggage, worrying about what other people might think at the expense of being in touch with our own inner life), by eating, by shopping, by working at jobs that suck us dry, by spending hours on Facebook, by complaining, by staying way too busy all the time…and the list goes on. If we want to ignite our healing abilities, it's time to burn away the distractions and come face to face with what lies beneath the commotion. It's time for Illumination.

Accepting versus Fixing

This is a good time to talk about acceptance, because many of us on the path of self-development get caught up in fixing ourselves. We perceive that we are lacking or broken in some way, and we go about trying to fix this by reading books, going to workshops, meditating, et cetera. And yet, in spite of our efforts, we can never completely shake the fear that we're not enough. We think, perhaps *one* more book or *one* more workshop, and then I'll feel whole. From this mindset, it's all too easy to jump to the conclusion that if only we could get rid of these broken things we'd be fixed. "If only I could stop the negative self-talk, then I'd feel okay about myself," "If only I could get rid of my shame around money, then I could enjoy abundance," "If only I could stop being afraid of expressing who I really am, then I'd be free," and so on it goes.

There's a reason, however, why many psychotherapists and spiritual teachers assert that acceptance is the prerequisite to change. Imagine, for a moment, that you are a perfectly round circle. By your very nature, you are already whole and complete; there's nothing missing from you, there's nothing broken. Many of us, though, only accept a part of ourselves. So, imagine now that the circle has been divided into pie-shaped wedges, and one of these is yellow. The yellow slice represents the things you're willing to accept about yourself: the "good" parts, the parts that ensure people keep liking you, that ensure *you* keep liking you. The problem is that now you see only one part of yourself—the yellow wedge–and forget that you're the perfectly whole circle, and this generates a pain that can be hard to put your finger on.

Somewhere, deep down, you remember that feeling of wholeness and you want to get it back, so you go about getting a prettier yellow paint for your wedge, and maybe you even add a little glitter, but you still can't shake the sense that you're not enough. We get stuck when we believe that this nagging insecurity is an indication that we truly aren't enough, when it's simply a sign that we've *forgotten* we're enough. The perfectly round circle is still there—it's been there the entire time—we're just not seeing it because we're too busy trying to perfect our yellow wedge.

Imagine, now, that you're willing to accept those parts of yourself that aren't so easy to be around: your judgmental side, those times when you're not feeling compassionate and you're feeling downright spiteful (we all have them), and any other part of you that you think might elicit shame, blame, or judgment. With each of these qualities you see and accept, you are widening your vision of who you are. You're no longer just the yellow wedge, you're the yellow wedge and that pie slice over here…and over here…and a little more over there. Before you know it, those shadow aspects you've been spending so much energy trying to disown or distract yourself from are the very means through which you are able to see the perfect circle: your innate wholeness. You couldn't have reached that state by cutting out and throwing away those wedges. Far from being an obstacle, the rejected wedges were *instrumental* to your remembrance of wholeness.

Through radical self-acceptance, we are continually given access to more and more of our True Self, not just the parts that meet the standards of our harsh inner critic or the external critics in our lives (whom we often internalize). We're not trying to throw away the parts of ourselves that we've deemed unacceptable. We're working to accept ourselves in *all* our parts, and in doing so, those very parts that we have struggled for so long to get rid of, they begin to transform of their own accord. But acceptance is the prerequisite. We can't skip it and move on to change. And when we struggle with accepting ourselves? Well, we accept that, too. And in doing so, our resistance to acceptance begins to soften and transform. In the same way, the Fire of Illumination is not creating change by getting rid of things we don't like. Instead of throwing the undesirables out with the trash, the light of Fire allows us to see those things for what they truly are—valuable treasures leading us to our True Self—and in doing so, it changes the nature of those imbalanced areas and our relationship to them.

On a global scale, the health of the world is suffering, in large part, from a belief that we can just throw away the things we don't like, when really, there is no "away"—these things end up in our oceans, in our soils, or in someone else's backyard. Nor is the solution to rid the world of the people whom we don't like. When we don't take responsibility for the parts within that we struggle to accept, we project these "undesirables" onto other people and situations, and we see our trash in the world around us. The anger we don't want to feel? We send it "away" and perceive the world as an angry place. The disempowerment we feel? We project it "away" and blame the world for our sense of victimhood, or we use scorn to distance ourselves from those we perceive as being victims, judging them as weak or even to blame for the abuses they suffer.

There is no "away." Our inner world becomes our outer world, and if we hope to change the latter we must begin with our internal landscape, lest we forever try to throw our "trash" into other people's backyards. The key to this change is radical self-acceptance, which is the focus of your first exercise. Most of the exercises in this book are done in a meditative state, so we'll begin with a process for bringing yourself into and out of this state before continuing with the exercise proper. Refer back to this process in future exercises, as indicated.

Entering and Exiting a Meditative State

Settle into a comfortable seated position.

Close your eyes, and take a few minutes to slow down your breath, becoming aware of your current state: how you feel emotionally, physically, and the quality of your mind (thoughts racing, calm, somewhere in between).

If you notice anything that feels "off," simply breathe into it and say to yourself, "I love and accept you." Give yourself at least one breath to really connect with the sensation of love and acceptance.

Take as many breaths as you need to prepare, and when you feel calm and centered, proceed with the exercise.

When it's time to come out of the meditation, bring your focus back to your breath, back to your body. Take in the sounds of the room around you as you gently wiggle your fingers and toes, fully returning to the present. When you're ready, open your eyes.

You can do any grounding practices as necessary, such as planting your palms on the ground and releasing any excess energy into the earth, taking a short walk outside, coming into child's pose, or eating a small snack.

Now that you're familiar with the process of entering a meditative state, let's proceed to the first exercise.

Exercise One: Radical Self-Acceptance

Before you begin, decide on a recent experience that triggered a strong emotion in you; you'll need to recall this situation to mind later in the exercise.

Bring yourself into a meditative state (page 26).

Call up the triggering experience. Without getting into the storyline of who's right and who's wrong, outline the experience in your mind, doing your best to stick to simple observations, to the best of your ability. Avoid analyzing why something happened. If you find yourself starting to rant or complain, return to a more centered place before proceeding.

Let your thoughts begin to take a backseat. You don't have to obsess over having no thoughts, just turn the volume down on them a bit. Get in touch with what you're *feeling* in response to the experience. Are there sensations in any particular location in your body, and if so, what do they feel like—tight, hot, tingly, fluttery, buzzy? Give yourself time to really explore what you're feeling in response to this experience, rather than getting overly caught up in what you think about it.

Now, ask yourself, "If there were no rules, what would I like to do or say in this situation?" No matter how irrational or out of control that response might seem, just let your fantasy response unfold without judgment. The key is to focus on how *you* would like to respond in this ideal scenario, not on how the other person would respond if you had your way. Over imagining the other person doing or saying what you want them to, imagine a scenario in which *you* have full permission to do or say what you want. This is a vital step in taking responsibility for your own experience.

Spend some time exploring your fantasy response by asking, "What is the deeper need or belief underlying this response?" An example of a need is, "I need to feel safe," while a belief might be, "If people don't act the way I expect them to, I am unsafe." While they're both dealing with the issue of safety, it's helpful to tease them apart, and you may recognize that you have both a need and a belief operating under the surface.

Now, accept that need or belief, no matter how irrational or irksome it might seem. It can be useful to understand the difference between accepting something versus believing it to be true or identifying with it. You can fully accept a belief and at the same time hold the awareness that it isn't accurate. It simply is, and you are accepting the reality that this belief exists in your psyche, not its veracity.

Once you have identified at least one need or belief, accept it wholeheartedly. Perhaps see the need personified, and welcome this person with a generous hug. Or repeat the mantra, "I love and accept you," while holding in your awareness the need or belief. When you feel this loving acceptance deep within you, thank the need or belief for teaching you.

Bring yourself out of the meditation (see pages 25–26).

Rejection as Stagnation

Another interesting facet to self-acceptance is its absence: self-rejection. Whenever we reject an aspect of ourselves, it gets frozen in time. You might be familiar with the psychological concept of arrested development occurring when we experience abuse or trauma. It's as if the clock stops ticking during the initial wounding and that traumatized part is forever six years old. When we are unable to accept an aspect of ourselves and instead banish it to our internal wasteland even as adults—a form of self-inflicted trauma—that part gets cut off from the natural flow of life energy. It gets shoved in a drawer and stagnates, frozen in time. Because of this, it can't change and grow, so if this rejected part of ourselves is a belief, such as, "If I can't control things, my self-worth is in jeopardy," there is no influx of new energy, no new ideas, nothing to challenge that belief, and it becomes set in its ways. It's no surprise that this part, when triggered, has a very predictable response; it's a one-trick pony. It only knows one belief, one way of seeing and reacting to the world.

When we invite these parts back into the fold, they are availed of the life energy of our entire being. They can now change and grow and update their limited skills and outmoded beliefs. The behaviors that once sprang from these rejected parts, the behaviors that once seemed impossible to change, are finally able to shift. And they don't change because we've figured out how to get rid of them once and for all; they change because we finally choose to accept them.

Just because you accept something doesn't necessarily mean you'll never have to deal with those issues again, but you will bring a new perspective and greater maturity to the table if they reappear. So please, do not be discouraged if things, once accepted, return in different forms. Your journey is a beautiful spiral, not a straight line, and you're not backsliding when you revisit topics from a new perspective. You're simply being given the gift of more of yourself to accept and welcome home, and in doing so, you get a little bigger, and a little bigger still. You expand, which is precisely what your soul is here to do.

The Healer Within

Everything we've talked about thus far in regards to accepting our stuff versus rejecting aspects of self is crucial to your development as a healer. Too often, people are drawn to learn the healing arts because (1) they want to "fix" themselves—another way of saying they want to throw away the "bad" and hold onto the "good"—and (2) because they want to shift the focus away from their personal work to "fixing" other people. When we approach healing from that place, consciously or subconsciously, we are merely perpetuating the self-rejection and distractions that are at the root of dis-ease.

This is why, as a Life Alchemy Reiki practitioner, you will put your personal growth first and foremost. Usui is purported to have said that you cannot heal others until you have healed yourself. Until you are willing to look deep within at the parts that have been banished to the shadows, you cannot tap into the full extent of your power, and you will find yourself attempting to use Reiki as a bandaid to dissolve shadow aspects so you don't have to face and accept them. When you work with others from this place, you will find yourself taking on their issues (and possibly even their physical ailments) fueled by the *subconscious* desire to use this as a distraction from your own work. How often have you encountered healing practitioners who are consumed with fixing their clients' issues, yet their own lives seem to be a bubbling cauldron of chaos yearning for attention?

Self-care and self-love is your paramount duty as a healer. When you take care of yourself, when you love and accept yourself in all your parts, you are able to bring your remembered fullness to your healing practice. You are able to weave your magic as a healer because you live with the awareness that you are already whole and your clients are, too. You are not fixing your "broken" clients, just as you are not fixing your own "brokenness." And this is why your personal growth is vital: If you yourself have forgotten your wholeness, how can you ever hope to remind others of theirs?

Journeying to Your Inner Forge

To deepen our experience of the first step, Illumination, we need a few tools. This step involves using archetypal Fire to transform our ego constructs, which means that we need, one, access to this Fire, two, a way of identifying the ego constructs that we'll be transforming, and three, a container in which to carry out the burning process, lest it run wild and burn things we didn't intend to burn. To obtain the ingredients for our spiritual recipe, we'll break it down into three "shopping trips" or exercises.

Exercise Two: Attuning with Fire

For this exercise, you will need a candle and a comfortable place to sit where the candle can burn in front of you.

With the candle unlit, use the process on page 26 to enter a meditative state.

Flicker your eyes open and say to yourself, "I seek to attune with the element of Fire in a way that is correct and good for me." Light the candle.

With a soft gaze, look at the candle flame. Notice the different colors, watch it sway and flicker, all the while holding your intention to attune with the element of Fire. Do this for a few minutes, then close your eyes.

Picture the candle flame in your mind's eye. Try to conjure the image in your mind, gradually layering in more and more details, from the color, the movement, the heat and the sound. Don't force or strain, just explore how your mind is able to create this image and have fun with it. If the image comes in and out of focus, that's okay. If it fades, simply renew the image once more.

Release the image of the candle and use your feeling sense to locate where within you this sacred fire is already burning. Perhaps a certain area of your body comes to mind or you feel a slight increase of heat in your belly or chest. Remain curious while you hold the intention to connect with the sacred fire within you. Remember to breathe, as fire needs oxygen to burn.

When you have homed in on a specific area where you feel most connected to your inner fire, increase your presence in this area. Really move your conscious awareness there and notice if anything arises: any thoughts, any feelings, any physical sensations, memories, smells, sounds, et cetera.

Ask your inner fire what message it has for you right now. Then, sit in silence and listen. If you feel your mind starting to wander, say to yourself, "I am listening," and rein in your focus once more. Repeat as often as necessary to bring your presence back to this receptive state where you are open to a message from your inner fire.

Once you have received your message, which may come in the form of images, thoughts, feelings, or any other medium, say to yourself, "I thank the element of Fire for its presence and guidance."

Bring yourself out of the meditative state (see pages 26–27).

Jot down any messages or impressions from this experience in your journal. And—this is important—take some time to process what these messages or impressions mean to you. Throughout our entire journey, I want you to build the habit of internalizing and what I call "activating" the guidance you receive. Rather than simply writing in your journal, "Fire showed me a crow," use this image to go deeper. Before you reach for a book or Google "crow symbolism," take some time to think about what crow means to you personally. Do you have any memories of crows from childhood, daily life, books or movies, etc? What do you think or feel when you envision crows? What do you know about crows, about how they live and communicate, what they eat, when they're most active? Does any of this resonate with your life?

To take the process even deeper, go into meditation and ask Crow to help you understand why it appeared to you: "Crow, what is most important for me to know about you right now? What messages do you bring?" This doesn't have to be a lengthy, epic meditation—even five to ten minutes can yield rich insights. As before, jot down any impressions or messages you receive. And then, if you want to add another layer, look up crow in external resources. I like to look at spiritual and mythological symbolism of animals (or plants, crystals, et cetera), as well as information on their biology, behavior, et cetera. While doing this research, pay close attention to any details that resonate with you. For example, if you read in a field guide that cardinals are "accomplished songsters," meditating on this phrase could reveal a desire to sing, speak, teach, and so forth. Use the symbols and messages as an invitation to go deeper and to explore what that resonance is urging you to do, be, or experience in your daily life.

Let's move on to the second ingredient on our spiritual shopping list: identifying the ego constructs that prevent us from seeing ourselves, and the world around us, as Divine. It's impossible to identify all of our ego constructs in one sitting; this is a process that will continue to unfold throughout your lifetime(s), so to be clear, you are seeking to identify the ego construct or constructs that are most important for you to be aware of right now, and you've already gotten a taste of this work in Exercise One: Radical Self-Acceptance.

What Are Ego Constructs?

Simply put, an ego construct is a belief created and employed by the ego to make sense of the world and your place within it. These beliefs are shaped by your life experiences, and once they're established, they continue to color your experiences long after their initial creation. Ego constructs aren't just any ol' beliefs, though—they are concerned with constructing and preserving your self-image, thus when you start to work with or challenge these constructs, this can trigger a whole host of feelings, including fear and anxiety, and shame, so let's discuss the value of undergoing this process and how to stay grounded and feel safe even when the ego is going haywire.

For starters, your identity is not as fixed as you think, and to understand this let's take a cue from Internal Family Systems (IFS) Therapy, a framework that I have found to be profoundly transformative. According to IFS, our psyche is populated by a colorful cast of characters that fall into one of two categories: protectors or exiles. Who you think you are in any given moment depends on which of these characters is dominating your internal stage. If a Judge Judy part (a protector) is on stage, you will see the world and yourself through her eyes. While she's in charge, you won't discern a difference between Judge Judy and your identity—in other words, you will identify with Judge Judy and think and act accordingly. But if a Worrywart part climbs on stage, you'll switch to identifying with this part, and your thoughts and actions will stem from this part's worried worldview.

Through Illumination, we aren't seeking to rid ourselves of these parts—quite the contrary. We are seeking to transform our relationship to them, starting with awareness and acceptance. In order to accept these parts, we must be able to witness them, and this brings us back full circle to our original discussion of Fire as a tool for shedding light on hidden aspects, such as these internal parts, and as a tool to give us some space from emotional flooding (recall Fire's ability to temporarily "dry out" the waters of emotion), making it easier to remain in a more neutral witness stance.

Life gives us ample opportunity to witness these internal parts in action: when someone's comment on our Facebook post gets us riled, when life isn't going the way we'd planned, when we reach out and someone rejects us, when we have an argument and really want to be right. There are never-ending opportunities for awareness, and what makes this so liberating is this: When we use the energy of Fire to bring awareness to and give us space from these constructs, their power over us begins to lessen. Why? In part, because whereas before we were unconsciously identifying with these parts, seeing the world through their limited lens whenever they stepped on stage, when we become aware, the simple act of awareness brings us into the role of witness. Instead of identifying with Judge Judy, you are now the witness who is aware of Judge Judy.

How does this witness awareness have such an enormous impact on our lives? Well, prior to awareness, if someone says something rude on social media, for example, an unconscious part gets activated, and this part might be convinced that we "have" to take the rude comment personally and defend against a perceived attack on our self-worth. When we identify with this part, we accept its reasoning hook, line, and sinker, and while this part is activated we can't imagine approaching things any other way. The internal witness, however—what we will come to recognize as our True Self—is able to offer a different response. The witness can heal those internal parts that are being triggered simply by being aware of and accepting them, and in doing so, it frees us from their rigid rules of thought and conduct. And viewing this from another angle, *it frees those parts* from their rigid rules of thought and conduct. While we might think that Judge Judy's only role is to make us miserable, Judy is performing the role of judge because she believes, from her limited point of view, that she's protecting us with her judgment. When Judy meets the witness, the True Self, and is held and accepted by that Self, she is no longer locked into her judgmental role, because she has learned that there is a larger Self that can handle the vicissitudes of life without her judgmental "helping." She can choose a new role in your psyche, one that is more in service of your health and happiness, and this means that energy that was once trapped in a cycle of judgment has now been freed for more soul-aligned purposes. It truly is a win-win.

In order to introduce these internal parts and the ego constructs they're carrying to the True Self, we must first become aware of them, which is the focus of your next exercise.

Exercise Three: Illuminating Ego Constructs

Enter a meditative state (page 26).

When you feel ready, call to mind a recent situation that left you feeling triggered. It could be something as fleeting as someone cutting you off in traffic or something more chronic, like an ongoing situation at work. If the latter, narrow it down to one specific incident.

You're going to practice creating some separation between you and this situation. Construct a stage in your mind's eye, complete with curtains, spotlights, and rows of seating, and then see yourself taking a seat in the audience, perhaps a few rows back to create additional space. Take as much time as you need to imagine the stage and to picture yourself sitting in the audience. Feel the separation between where you are and the action on the stage.

Look down and see that you are holding a remote control. It has large, easy-to-read buttons: play and stop.

Still feeling yourself sitting in the audience, create the triggering situation on the stage. Fill in the actors, one of which is you, because "real you" is sitting in the audience watching. As much as feels necessary, fill in the surrounding details to help capture the feel of the event.

Press play on the remote. Let the situation unfold as you watch from the audience. What does actor you say or do? What do the other people say or do?

Press stop. Take a breath or two, perhaps re-establish the awareness that you're sitting in the audience and you're not on stage.

Ask for guidance from your Higher Self and the Divine in meeting any internal parts that are relevant to this situation.

Press play again. The scene will run again from the beginning, and as you watch, look to see if any new characters appear, either on the stage or elsewhere in the theater. Press stop.

If more than one character has appeared, focus on the one that feels most interesting to you right now—we'll refer to this character as the Focus Part. Check in to see how you are feeling about this part. You will know you are centered in your True Self and serving as a healing Witness if you feel some combination of curiosity, openness, or compassion. If another feeling arises, perhaps worry or judgment or anger, recognize that this is another character, and even if you can't visualize it, ask this character if it will step aside so you can get to know the Focus Part. If it isn't willing to step aside, you can explain the value of allowing you to proceed. For example, if an angry part appears, you might explain that if it allows you to get to know the Focus Part, you might be able to resolve the issue that it's feeling so angry about. If it still isn't willing to step aside, make this part the Focus Part. (Repeat this process of asking parts to step aside whenever you feel another part appearing, taking you out of the role of the compassionate Witness.)

With your attention back on the Focus Part, begin to get to know it. You can start by asking it what it's feeling. If it's concerned or angry, et cetera, ask it what it's concerned or angry about. Then, ask this part what is its role. This is important— you are exploring what role this part plays in your psyche and your life. If you need more clarity, you can ask the part how it performs this role or to show you an example of it performing this role in your life. It might show you an early memory or a scene that is more symbolic than literal.

Check in with how you're feeling toward this part. Are you still centered in the True Self? Remember, if you're feeling open, curious, and/or compassionate toward the Focus Part, you are in Self. If you notice that you're taking on the emotions of the Focus Part, ask it to separate from you so you can get to know it better. And if you see other parts appearing and trying to take over, repeat the stepping-aside process from earlier.

Finally, ask the part what it's afraid would happen if it didn't perform this role. Ask any clarifying questions as needed.

When this process feels complete, thank the Focus Part for sharing with you, and thank it for the work it has done in performing its role. Remember, even if the role has caused problems, the part is simply trying to do what it thinks is best for you. Thank it for all its hard work.

When you feel ready, set the remote down in the seat next to you, then watch as the entire auditorium fades.

Bring yourself out of the meditative state (pages 26–27).

Take some time to journal about the experience. Write down a description and/or name of any parts you met, and flesh out details for the Focus Part: what its role is, how it performs this role, its fears if it were to stop performing this role, and anything else that feels relevant. This material is your second ingredient, the ego construct you will be transforming in sacred fire at a later stage. For now, let's move on to the third ingredient on our list.

The Sacred Vessel

I'm going to skip to the punch line on this one. Your sacred container? It's you. It's your body and your energy field. If our container is lacking strength or is damaged we're not able to control incoming and outgoing energy very effectively. To illustrate this, imagine a group of people eating dinner together. As you look closer, you see that each person has holes in different areas of their body, and as they eat, speak, think, and so forth, their energy escapes via the holes. Perhaps another person says something rude, and their word energy travels from their mouth into a hole in someone else's body, and the recipient turns red with anger. Without a healthy container, our energy is easily dissipated and triggered.

We often expend a lot of effort working to control the energetic flow of life experiences by trying to manage external factors. For example, we don't like when someone's critical energy enters our field, but too often, instead of plugging up the holes in our own container, we try to control the situation and the other person in the hopes of preventing them from being critical. This is a lot of work, and our energy would be more productively spent working on bolstering the strength and integrity of our container. The energetic flows around us are very complex and far reaching. The critical person above is likely responding to forces that extend far beyond their present interaction with you, a tangled up ball of everything from their childhood to their morning commute, and trying to control these complex energy flows is fruitless. However, when we tend to the integrity of our container, our experience of these energetic flows will be very different, all without us wasting massive amounts of energy trying in vain to micromanage the world.

Not only does the quality of our container determine whether energy can enter or exit, it also colors our experiences. For example, because of my family history with money, when the energy of money entered my container, it would activate qualities like lack and feeling manipulated. When I made money, it was a challenge not to get rid of it right away so I didn't have to feel those uncomfortable associations. I spent many years trying to control the overall energy of money, but that wasn't the issue—money itself is neutral. My interpretation of it, due to the quality of my container, was not, but luckily my container was something I could affect and transform, and in doing so, I transformed my relationship with money.

As healers, this integrity of our container takes on even greater import, for as you work with Reiki you will be acting as a container for this energy. The energy will pass from the Universal Source, through you, and into your client. While one of the (many) wonderful qualities of Reiki is that it can be remarkably effective even under the most challenging of conditions, you can nonetheless enhance your healing capabilities by boosting the strength and integrity of your container. The energy of Reiki itself does not change, regardless of our container, but our experience of Reiki and our ability to effectively channel it when healing others can be altered. We're not aiming for perfection, simply an active engagement with the process of "vessel strengthening." You will never have a perfect container, nor do you need to, but you can expand your capacity for self-healing and helping others heal by adopting a lifelong practice of tending to your sacred container.

So for our third and final ingredient you will get in touch with your container and really feel into the sensation of taking energy in, containing it, and releasing it.

Exercise Four: Your Sacred Container

Bring yourself into a meditative state (page 26).

Bring your awareness to where your breath enters your nostrils. Really focus your attention and see if you notice more breath entering one nostril over the other. Notice if it's easier to perceive the breath as it's entering or exiting your nostrils, or if it's hard to discern any air movement at all.

Bring your attention to your body as a whole. Run your awareness along the surface of your body, starting at the top of your head, moving over your face, the front of your neck and throat. Travel down one shoulder, all the way down the length of your arm to the tips of your fingers, and return to your throat. Repeat on the other side.

Continue this process of bringing your awareness to every surface of your body, front, back, and sides, then return to the crown of your head.

Feel the surface of your body as a continuous whole, as a structure that, quite literally, contains your insides. Really focus your attention on your body's ability to hold and contain, to act as a selective barrier between what's inside and everything else.

Shift your focus to your internal body, and feel how this space is contained by your skin. If you're visual, perhaps imagine yourself in the center of your body, looking outward at the protective barrier of your skin.

Expand your focus to include your breath. As you inhale, imagine your internal space filling with air, filling with life force. On the exhale, see this space once again returning to emptiness. Continue this for a few more rounds of breath.

Begin to notice if there are any areas that seem resistant to the influx of new air on the inhale, or areas that seem to hang onto or trap air on the exhale.

Say to yourself three times, "My sacred container is healthy and balanced on all levels."

Now, bring to mind the feeling of love, perhaps picturing a person or animal you love and using that image to generate the felt sense of love. On the inhale, breathe that feeling into your internal space. You can imagine the energy as a particular color and see the color entering your body and filling the space. On the exhale, see the color leaving your body. Do this for a few rounds of breath until you have a clear sense of the energy entering and leaving your body.

Try it again with another energy of your choice: perhaps awe, peace, beauty, et cetera. Does it feel different to contain this energy? Notice any sensations that arise.

When the experience feels complete release the energy and bring yourself out of the meditative state (pages 26–27).

Journal about your experience, noting if there were certain aspects that felt easier or more difficult for you, or any thoughts, memories, or sensations that feel important to remember.

Putting the Ingredients Together

Now that we have our three ingredients it's time to go deeper with our understanding of Illumination before using these ingredients in the Illumination meditation. In the Attuning With Fire Exercise, you made contact with your inner fire, which you can imagine like an internal campfire that you carry within you at all times. When you're sitting near the campfire—when you're centered in Self—you can see by its light. When you stray away from the campfire, it becomes harder and harder to make your way, and before too long, you find yourself lost in the darkness. This campfire represents your inner truth. When you're near the campfire, you are in touch with this truth, you are in touch with what lights you up, what you feel passionate about. When you stray away from the fire, you start to lose contact with that knowledge, and you are more easily swayed by external influences.

Let's imagine that you're having conflict with a coworker. For many of us, it's easy to get caught up in analyzing why our coworker is acting in this undesirable way. We try to crawl into her head and figure out what's driving her to be such a turd, and we sometimes get stuck in thinking, "If only I could figure out why she's doing this, then I'll know how to respond to make her stop." Nine times out of ten, when we're choosing our behavior based on how we think another person will react, we're engaging in codependence, a type of relating that is characterized by relying on how other people are responding to us to determine our sense of self. A common pattern with codependence is trying to control how other people act and what they think about you by people pleasing. If your efforts don't result in them acting the way you'd hoped or in them having a favorable opinion of you, anxiety and resentment often result, because under the surface there's an unconscious bargain being offered: If I try to please you by being nice or acquiescing to your requests even though I might not want to, you have to reciprocate by acting the way I expect you to act. If you don't, I feel like I've been used.

To bring this back to the campfire metaphor, in order to engage in codependency, we have to walk away from our campfire as we seek to figure out what's going on in the other person's head. You can see this as your ego constructs luring you away from the light of your campfire and into the dark. The subconscious "reasoning" is, if I can figure out what they want and give it to them, then they will respond by giving me what I want, by acting the way I want them to, or by not rejecting me. The line of thought we're often more *conscious* of is, "This person is being such a jerk. If they would just stop doing/acting/thinking this way, this wouldn't be an issue." These two lines of thought might not seem, on the surface, to be related, so let's go deeper to find the connection.

When we struggle with codependency, experiencing conflict with another person can be deeply upsetting and anxiety producing, not simply because conflict is difficult but because we feel a loss of control. We rely on control to ensure that other people act in ways that feel safe to us and that they don't do anything that feels like rejection. When our control doesn't seem to be working—when we're trying our hardest to please and/or control them and they're *still* not doing what we want—it can feel really, really scary. In those moments, we're no longer sure how to keep people from rejecting us. Our tools aren't working, and the outcome is unsure.

Rejection doesn't simply take the form of, for example, being dumped by a partner. Feelings of rejection can arise as the result of someone not taking your advice, not valuing your contribution, misunderstanding what you're saying, talking about you behind your back, telling you you're overreacting or being "too sensitive," continuing to act in a way that you don't like, et cetera. And codependency links our (imagined) ability to control these things with our sense of self-worth. If we can't control the outcome, it must mean there's something wrong with us, so when someone doesn't take your advice, doesn't value your contribution, misunderstands what you're saying, and so on, it feels like so much more than that; it feels like they're calling your self-worth into question. In response, codependency urges us to crawl into the other person's head and figure out the "right way" to act in order to get them to start responding in a way that affirms our self-worth. If they don't, we feel lost and anxious, and if those feelings are too difficult to bear, we might retreat to feeling angry and resentful at the other person who is the "cause" of our painful feelings.

In short, when we're engaged in codependent interactions, we leave our own campfire, we abandon our inner truth, and we spend our time trying to "fix" other people. Over time, we forget how to get back to our campfire. We're so focused on what other people want that we forget what *we* want. We lose contact with our inner truth, and we feel easily swayed by what other people think of us, thus fueling the cycle to try and please them so they'll think nicely of us. The more we stay centered around our own campfire, the more we stay tethered to our own sense of truth. Over time, we become less concerned about what other people think. We're able to forge healthy connections in which we can enjoy true intimacy while remaining autonomous. We can experience love without controlling, or being controlled by, another person. We can be authentic and know that we are innately worthy, even if someone is upset with us or not responding in the way we'd like. And when we do experience conflict, we can bring our full Self to the situation as we creatively problem solve, rather than trying to figure out which parts of ourselves we need to reject in order to please the other person and make the conflict go away.

This practice begins, as always, with awareness, with recognizing when we are starting to stray from our inner campfire. Are we:

- Replaying in our mind what the other person said or did?

- Trying to figure out why the other person is acting a certain way without directly asking them?

- Trying to figure out what the other person is thinking or feeling without directly asking them?

- Unable or unwilling to explore how we are contributing to the situation?

- Feeling resentful that the other person isn't acting the way we want them to?

- Feeling anxious that the other person doesn't like us (even if we don't like them)?

- Saying yes when we want to say no?

- Feeling like we have no choice but to do what the other person wants?

As a healer, it's especially important to be aware of these red flags, because many of us are in the healing arts because of a codependent desire to "fix" other people in order to feel needed and loved. It is our work to transform the codependent need to fix into the true practice of healing, which requires us to be firmly attuned to our inner campfire. As healers, we help others rekindle their inner flame, to remember that they are already whole and have the answers within, but if we've lost the way to our inner fire, how can we hope to lead others back to theirs? For this reason, I consider *Codependent No More* by Melody Beattie required reading for all healers. View it as a tool to help you feel more empowered, more liberated in your personal and professional relationships, and more attuned with your natural healing abilities.

You cannot neglect your personal growth because you want to focus on "serving" your clients. If you think of your healing practice as a door through which healing and wisdom can pass, doing self-work opens that door for both you and your clients. Neglecting self-work closes the door, and neither you nor the people you want to help will be able to benefit fully from your healing work. Particularly for women, it can feel like we're being selfish when we're taking care of ourselves, but know that you cannot truly offer another the gift of healing, love, or any other transformative experience if you are withholding that gift from yourself. The way we learn to give these gifts to other people is by giving them to ourselves. From a deep, self-initiated relationship with these gifts, we then understand more deeply how to receive, contain, and release them. Without this, we can only understand healing, love, and other energies on a superficial level. You must allow yourself to experience the wonderful things you wish to give to others.

We've begun our journey of self-transformation in a powerful way, working with the archetype of Fire and connecting with our inner fire, and now we're going to allow Reiki to take this process even further. Reiki is Divine intelligence, and it has a much more expansive view of our situation and how our personal experiences relate to the greater, cosmic whole, so it can guide us in ways that we cannot imagine with the approach of the finite mind. In this next stage of your journey, you will prepare to receive your first Reiki attunement, and then, once the attunement is complete you will return to your inner fire and meet with your Focus Part and its ego construct once more to see how this interaction changes with the presence of Reiki.

—3—
BEGINNING YOUR REIKI JOURNEY

To be a Reiki practitioner, you must receive an attunement, right? Well, to understand this question (and to help you develop your own take on the matter), it's useful to define what an attunement is. On a basic level, an attunement is a ritual in which a Reiki Master completes a series of movements around a seated student using energy and focused intent. In most modern teachings, the purpose given for the attunement is to open the student up to the channel of Reiki. Opinions vary as to whether or not the student was already capable of channeling this energy before the attunement, but in my experience we are all born with the ability to channel Reiki; the attunement simply allows for a much greater and clearer flow of this energy.

I will admit that prior to my first attunement, I was skeptical and assumed that the attunement was simply a means of creating an exclusive group. Whether or not some people use attunements in this manner, I can't deny that the feel and quality of the energy I experienced before and after the attunement was markedly different, as is the experience of receiving energy work from those who have been attuned versus those who have not. This is not to say that those without an attunement aren't practicing legitimate healing and energy work—many of them are. It simply feels different, so clearly, some kind of shift is occurring as a result of the attunement.

To deepen our understanding of what might be taking place, I find this analogy from the International House of Reiki useful. Here, the authors refer to any Reiki treatment, but I see the following process happening in a more lasting way as a result of an attunement:

> If we already have energy or ki, why do we need the practice of Reiki? To help understand, imagine a free flowing river. This beautiful river is like energy flowing easily down through the body. Occasionally a pebble or even a rock will fall into the river, making the flow of the water a little more difficult. These pebbles are human worries, fear, and anger, and each pebble builds on top of the other. Soon there is only a trickle of water running in that once beautiful free-flowing river. And so it is with the energy of the human body. Energy flow can be obstructed so much that physical pain may be experienced at this point. During a Reiki treatment, the pure flow of energy is realigned with the body. It washes down, clearing obstructions and strengthening the flow of energy (International House of Reiki 2010, Shoden Level 1 Participant Manual, 2).

In response to the question "Is an attunement all that's needed to practice Reiki?" the above authors reply:

> No, you must work with the other elements of the system of Reiki and also practice. Remember that this system is about self-

empowerment. The more work you do on yourself, the clearer your energy channels will become and the healthier and calmer your life will be (Ibid., 11).

The insinuation here is that attunement produces a powerful shift in your ability to receive and channel Reiki, but there is also the aspect of practice to maintain these strong channels of energy flow. Frans Stiene prefers to use the word "initiation" over attunement, as that "indicates an 'initial' experience" (Stiene 2015, 118). In other words, the initiation is just the beginning, an opening of the door that you must walk through of your own accord. Furthermore, hanging out just beyond the threshold is not the point; we continue to journey beyond that initial opening through our daily practice. Thus, it is important to remember that an attunement is not like checking an item off our to-do list where we might think "A-ha, now I'm attuned! Glad that's taken care of!" It is merely the beginning.

Attuning to the True Self

An attunement gives us a powerful glimpse of our True Self to remind us of who we really are, but it is our responsibility to remain true to this nature after the attunement is over. This is why we don't see all Reiki Masters automatically living harmonious, balanced lives simply because they've received a Master Attunement. The choices they make following the attunement determine whether they live with remembrance of their True Self or slip into a place of forgetfulness.

Stiene writes that during a *reiju* (the word Usui used for an attunement), both teacher and student will receive the most benefit if their energy is "like a calm lake," which is a state that takes dedication to cultivate, particularly in today's world. Stiene explains:

"A calm lake is a mirror and a mirror can reflect everything. However, a mirror doesn't judge or label, it just reflects. Therefore we can also see the reiju as the teacher holding up a perfectly clear mirror so that the student can see his own True Self....If reiju allows us to glimpse our True Self, then we can remember it again and again in our daily life. The more we remember it, the more we will embody our True Self" (Stiene, 120).

Seven Types of Energy

To further understand how an attunement might work (and I say "might" because I don't think we can know what is occurring with 100 percent certainty), I'll flesh out my own interpretation, which draws heavily on material from *The Spirit of Reiki*, in which co-author Walter Lübeck outlines seven different types of life energy categorized based on their primary function, which, in turn, is related to how well each type of energy is able to organize (Lübeck 2001, 54–60). The first type of energy, Kekki, has the least ability to organize, while the seventh type, Reiki, has the greatest ability to organize. We'll start with Kekki and move our way through the seven energy qualities until we reach Reiki; throughout, we'll construct one way of understanding attunements.

Kekki is associated with the root chakra and the descriptor "Ki of the blood" or "energy of the blood." One of the primary functions of blood is delivering nourishment throughout the body, and this parallels the main function of Kekki, which provides . Because Kekki is also the least organized or least differentiated type of energy, "it is therefore the easiest energy for the higher organizing forces to use in nourishing specific structures" (Ibid., 54). It's interesting to tie this in with the Hermetic creation story and the concept of the One Thing, which has an undifferentiated, non-specific quality that then allows it to become, and to nourish, anything, similar to Kekki.

If Kekki nourishes and acts as a basic building block, then there must be something that requires this nourishment and foundation; for this, we look to the second type of energy, Shioke. "This is the form of Ki that gives the body the structure in which the vitality (Kekki) can gather and have an effect" (Ibid., 54). This form or structure may last for the life of a cell, the life of an entire organism, or the life of a galaxy. Lübeck also says this of Shioke, which I find very interesting: "Something that does not want to fulfill a purpose doesn't need a structure that is suitable for fulfilling a purpose" (Lübeck, 55). In other words, Shioke, the energy of structure, would not need to exist if life simply required the basic building blocks of Kekki to sit around doing nothing. The fact that structure arises suggests the existence of an underlying purpose that this structure serves to fulfill. For example, without the need to eat, we wouldn't have the structures of our digestive tract. Evolution would not have given rise to them "just because."

If you recall, the Hermetic creation story shows that we are microcosmic versions of the larger cosmos, making our structure a reflection of the cosmic structure…so could it be possible that our individual purpose is also a reflection of greater cosmic purpose? I believe so. And what is this common purpose that we conceivably share with the cosmos? I would offer that it is a desire to know oneself, and this desire led to the evolution of human consciousness in the same way that the All differentiated into the One Mind and the One Thing in order to know itself more fully. It's as if all of existence is seeking to differentiate a part of itself from the whole and so one part stand somewhere called "over there" looking back at and interacting with itself in new ways, thereby enriching its self-awareness.

"What is now occurring within individual human consciousness through the personal transformations many people are experiencing is not an arbitrary process disconnected from what happens in the cosmos or from evolutionary changes that have gone before; rather, evolutionary cosmology helps us to see that these personal transformations are a continuation of evolution and that they are intimately connected to the cosmological context in which they take place" (Le Grice 2011, 231). If it seems difficult to imagine that our individual development could have that much of an impact on the development of the whole, think of how evolution plays out in the unfolding of a family and its ancestral line. In certain forms of shamanism, the dreams we experience between midnight and two in the morning are said to be messages from our ancestors who are hoping we will be the ones to heal family wounds and break free of harmful chains, thereby freeing our entire ancestral line. Whether or not you believe this to be true, imagine if each and every one of us took it as our sacred duty to heal our ancestral wounds and multiplied that desire across all families—we'd change the world.

Teilhard de Chardin, a Jesuit priest and paleontologist believed that if we came to recognize the inextricable link between our personal evolution and the evolution of the entire cosmos, this realization would align "individual human consciousness, with its own will, intentions, purposes, and desires [with] cosmic will…" But in order for this to happen, we must experience an activation of energy, an "awakening of those potent primordial drives ordinarily excluded from human experience. Once activated, those impulses for freedom and excitement that the individual was never able to act on burst to the surface with all the urgency that comes with their sudden release…all the powerful drives for intense pleasure and depth of experience that could not previously be expressed seize their chance for gratification." (Le Grice, 234)

Could this parallel the energy activation of a Reiki attunement or even "just" a Reiki treatment? Particularly with an attunement, many people experience an "awakening of those potent primordial drives" in the form of greater awareness of non-physical reality and latent desires bubbling to the surface, yearning to be realized, and so forth. (Ibid., 234) Taken together, these threads suggest that one of the driving forces of the universe is to know itself and this same force resides within us. This force is propelling evolution forward, and our active participation is required, not only for our evolution as individuals but to further the greater evolution of the cosmos. We must seek to know ourselves as individuals in order to play our part in the big-picture unfolding of cosmic self-awareness, and I see Reiki as a potent ally on this path. Every level of existence is seeking to know itself; fulfilling that purpose requires structure in the form of Shioke.

The structural and organizing force known as Shioke requires relationships and interaction with other forces because it's impossible to know oneself in a vacuum. This observation again parallels the All separating into the One Mind and the One Thing in order to know itself more fully. By creating duality, relationship became possible. For this relationship, we look to the third type of energy, Mizuke. Mizuke awakens in us a desire to know "the other," to merge and dissolve the sensation of separateness Shioke's structure created. This is the paradox: we create separation only to yearn for the underlying unity. This unity does not permanently destroy the structure or separation in the same way that we can experience deep intimacy with another without completely sacrificing our sense of autonomy and healthy boundaries. In fact, it is the awareness of boundaries and structure that makes it more potent when we choose to merge with another for a time. This ever-changing experience of dissolving and reforming, merging and separating, captures the essence of Mizuke, "the force that brings together the Kekki bound within the various Shioke forms…Without Mizuke, the Shioke forms would remain isolated…rigid and sluggish without any genuine movement." (Lübeck, 56)

In order to engage in this dance of merging and separation, forging healthy relationships without losing ourselves entirely, we require the fourth type of energy, known as Kuki. "Kuki imparts the motivations for us to want to take our own path and experience who we are. Kuki also makes sure that we do not let ourselves become diverted from our own appropriate course under the influence of other people." (Ibid., 57) In the West, where individualism is prized, I think it's interesting to contemplate different ways of understanding what Lübeck is saying here. Many Westerners are familiar with the idea of being our own person (even if it's sometimes hard to live by), thumbing our nose at "the Man," and going our own way. I believe it's far more difficult to learn how to go our own way without simply turning our way into a rebellion against the status quo. Some of us become so focused on being unique and not being held down that we can divert *ourselves* from our appropriate course. Our choices become defined just as much by what we genuinely want to do as they are by doing the opposite of what we think is expected of us by society, our parents, and so on. Neither extreme—a mindless sheep and a rebel without a cause—serves to connect us with our purpose; both are distractions that keeps us from remembering our true nature. The deeper change comes with the appropriate use of Kuki, the energy of growth, self-fulfillment, and self-awareness, and works best in conjunction with the fifth energy type, Denki.

Denki integrates our desire for self-fulfillment with the ability to remain in relationship with others. It is what Lübeck describes as "the urge to grow in a way considerate of others." (Lübeck, 57) Joseph Campbell captures this dance between the individual and the collective imperative beautifully in the culmination of the Hero's/Heroine's Journey, his way of describing the journey we undertake in our quest to realize our True Self. (Campbell 2004, 10) After the heroine follows the call to adventure and travels to strange, new (inner) worlds to confront and transform beasts and monsters, another challenge awaits her: reintegrating with the world she left behind. She has changed dramatically on her journey, but can she bring that change back to the world and become an agent of change herself? In other words, can we take our individual growth and development and share it in a world that might not always understand or accept the gifts we have to offer, or do we shut down and adopt an attitude of resentment or victimization?

The whole idea is that you've got to bring out again that which you went to recover, the unrealized, unutilized potential in yourself. The whole point of this journey is the reintroduction of this potential into the world; that is to say, to you living in the world. You are to bring this treasure of understanding back and integrate it into a rational life. (Campbell 2004, 119)

Earlier I said that we must give to ourselves that which we wish to give to others. If we are withholding love from ourselves, it is hard to extend love to others. If we are misusing our bodies, it is hard to support physical healing in others. In this sense, our personal journey of seeking out and welcoming home those previously rejected parts of ourselves allows us to help others feel safe seeking out and welcoming home their rejected parts. To facilitate this, we must first do the work of descending into our own depths and then return and share the fullness of that self we journeyed to retrieve. If we come back and continue to hide those parts we worked so hard to retrieve out of fear of rejection, we're missing a vital piece of the puzzle. How can we show others that their hidden parts are safe and valuable to reveal if we are living in fear of revealing our own?

The energy of Denki supports us in connecting with our self-realization in the context of community and the self-realization of *all* beings. And to support our quest for self-realization Denki partners with the sixth energy type, Jiku. Lübeck describes Jiku as the force that drives us to look at our shadow aspects, including latent talents, with the purpose of aligning our will with Divine Will. (Lübeck, 58) Jiku becomes available when we accept and view as meaningful the challenges of life and use them to deepen our understanding of ourselves. Jiku also helps us forge deeper, more authentic relationships with others, springing from a deeper, more authentic relationship with our self.

As mentioned in an earlier chapter, seeing how truly effective we can be in the world gives us a sense of responsibility, which is why many people believe it's safer to stick with a small Tupperware of power instead. Jiku helps us connect with the full extent of our power by confronting our shadow and integrating the energy and gifts it contains, allowing us to fully express the unique purpose we came into this life to embody.

We finally arrive at the seventh energy: Reiki. Reiki brings together and organizes the interactions between all of the other six energy types, which underscores the similarity for me between Reiki and the pure emanations of the One Mind, which possess a template of Divine organization. Lübeck describes another type of divine energy called Shinki that underlies and gives rise to all seven energies, from Kekki to Reiki. He says: "Shinki works outside the material world, through Reiki…Reiki is close enough to the principle of unity, as well as the principles of separation, to form an interface for contact between the two." (Lübeck, 60) This description sounds strikingly similar to the idea of the One Mind arising from the All, like Reiki arising from the unity of Shinki and the One Mind, then acting as an organizing, intelligent intermediary between the All and the One Thing.

There is one more concept that can help us understand what might be occurring in an attunement. Reiki has immense healing power but cannot override our free will, as this will is a gift of the Divine force, a built-in feature of our existence. An attunement could therefore be considered an invitation to the Divine, an act of giving the Divine permission to work in and through us. While Reiki is everywhere and available to all, perhaps the attunement is a ritualized way of granting Reiki permission to co-create with us, of initiating the coupling of our free will with the will of the Divine. Take some time to really sit with the implications of this, with what it might mean to say to the Divine, "Yes, I want to be partners in co-steering the ship of my life." Notice you are not absolving yourself of responsibility, nor are you refusing to surrender in order to maintain complete control. You are actively choosing an interplay of both. You are surrendering the plans of your ego and allowing the Divine to guide you toward different choices, choices that *you* must actively live out. It is a dance of surrender and responsibility. How do you feel about stepping onto the dance floor?

Preparing for Your Attunement

In mainstream culture, there remain very few initiatory experiences. When transitions in life aren't fully honored, we often feel unprepared for the next stage, and following the experience, the effects might be relatively fleeting because they haven't been fully integrated into our life. If we are given a glimpse (or even a powerful vision) of our True Self yet don't have a way to integrate the new awareness of who we are into our life, we feel a disconnect, which we might try to blot out with any number of potentially unhealthy distractions.

Instead, let's take a different approach with your Life Alchemy Reiki attunement. Here we'll prepare for the shift and adopt some tools and strategies for meeting the experiences that may unfold after the attunement with more fullness of self. We're going to use a framework based on an ancient Celtic practice called the Tara tests, which were performed on the Hill of Tara in modern-day Ireland, where today there still stands an impressive stone thought to be the *Lia Fáil*, or Stone of Destiny at which the High Kings of Ireland were crowned. The tests as presented here build on an interpretation by psychologist Silvia Brinton Perera.

The Tara tests were a set of magical challenges a potential king was required to meet in order to assume kingship, but rather than thinking of them as questions with right-or-wrong answers, think of them as a way of igniting potentially dormant qualities within you that are necessary to step into your power and become the sovereign of your life. In order to co-create with the Divine, you must be a benevolent ruler of the many parts that comprise your internal system, not a tyrant who cannot bear to share control nor a servant who cannot take action without orders. Keep a journal of your experience throughout the four challenges, and proceed with open eyes and an open heart as you seek to know yourself more fully.

Challenge One

The significance of the first challenge is to explore whether your life supports your current path, in this case, your choice to become attuned to Reiki. In the Celtic version of the test, "the regal aspirant passed the first test if his chariot did not fly up and throw him, and his horses did not attack him." (Perera 2001, 91) I'm not going to ask you to take to the streets in a horse-led chariot; instead we're going to look to the tarot for a modern adaptation of this challenge. In the tarot, the Chariot is one of the major arcana cards; a helpful way of viewing this card is as the culmination of a series of cards dubbed the "Worldly Sequence" by tarot author Rachel Pollack. (Pollack 1997, 43)

The Worldly Sequence depicts our developing maturity in relation to the demands of outer life. Moving through this sequence, we are steeped in the duality of the physical world and must learn how to relate to the polarities of, among other things, freedom and structure, pleasure and pain, autonomy and community, giving and receiving. Through all of this, we are developing an ability to balance the seemingly opposing aspects of our nature. We balance animal instincts with moral reasoning, personal desires with the common good, and so forth. This balance is illustrated in the charioteer's bringing together of the beasts pulling the Chariot, beasts which are usually depicted as black and white.

Some of us stop questing when we reach the Chariot. When we've reached a level of outward success, that of "having it all under control," we feel we've done all that we're supposed to do, because according to mainstream culture, we have. But there are others—and if you're reading this book, I'd count you as one of them—who sense there's something more...something more to life than landing the job, the partner, and the house with the white picket fence. But here's the paradox: It can be difficult to pursue that "something more" if we haven't reached a basic level of security in the physical world. If we're worried about whether we can pay rent this month, it's hard to bliss out on the meditation cushion. If our physical health is in shambles, it's hard to devote energy to anything beyond the bare bones of getting through the day. If we're not sure if we'll have money for groceries, it's hard to drum up courage and a sense of safety to explore our inner demons. In short, if we're stuck in survival mentality, it's hard to thrive. Reaching the stage of the Chariot is an important foundation for the deeper work of self-transformation, regardless of whether the paths that led us there are markedly different from the status quo.

Once we reach the Chariot, however, we find that the end is just the beginning—in this case, the beginning of going beyond the ego we've worked so hard to create. To the ego, this makes about as much sense as spending years building a house and then sleeping outside under the stars instead, but the continual process of letting go of structures once they're no longer useful is one we must be willing to undergo if we don't want to get trapped in a shell we've outgrown. In this human life, an ego helps us function in waking consciousness but becomes detrimental when the structures of the ego no longer fit, and we are unwilling to cast off the shell because we're overidentified with it. Like the hermit crab who knows she still exists even when she's in between shells, we must learn to expand our ability to dis-identify with ego structures. This enables us to use them in contexts where they're helpful without being bound by them.

In a parallel fashion, the journey leading to the Chariot ideally equips us with the unique skills we need to create stability in our outer world (find a nice crab shell), yet at the same time, we do not become so overidentified with these forms of outer stability that we think they're all there is to life. It's all about balance, baby. Can you hold down a meaningful job *and* know that you're worthy even if the job is no more, or do you gravitate toward one of the extremes: becoming unable to support yourself in the belief that meaningful work and well-paid work are mutually exclusive, or becoming so enmeshed with your job that it becomes synonymous with your self-worth?

Integrating the True Self glimpsed during the Reiki attunement into our daily life requires us to find ways to embody the duality of human existence, and we do this not by trying to remove ourselves from the messiness of life but by using that messiness to show us where we need to expand. If we get curious when our shell feels too small, we are given glimpses of the grander totality we are striving to embody—and remember, this grander totality *is* our True Self. For example, when we suddenly feel that our old way of people pleasing in order to feel loved is a too-small shell, in confronting this pattern we catch a glimpse of our True Self, which exists in a state of inviolable oneness with Love. Nothing can separate you from Love. While you're inside the too-small shell, you might *think* you're separate from Love, but this is an illusion. It just takes shedding shells, again and again, to remember more deeply with each successive shedding that you *are* Love. In this human life, if we explore the areas where we feel constricted, they point to the very ways in which our soul yearns to expand, so those too-small shells are clues to lead us back to wholeness in a very real sense *if we treat them as such* and not simply as pesky barriers to happiness we can't wait to be rid of.

Thus, returning to the first challenge, "the regal aspirant passed the first test if his chariot did not fly up and throw him, and his horses did not attack him." We can consider this challenge an invitation to look at whether we have cultivated a sense of stability in our physical existence such that our chariot does not "fly up and throw us," while at the same time retaining awareness of our True Self. When we can live in this world and enjoy a measure of stability and success however we define it (our chariots do not fly up and throw us) without losing touch with those parts of ourself that are not domesticated and defined by the laws of society (our "horses do not attack us"), we have passed the first test.

The first challenge calls for compassionate self-inventory. If our physical existence is in shambles, the lessons of the worldly sequence are calling for our attention. Trying to bypass the lessons of the physical realm by retreating to spiritual work is not the solution. Doing an inventory of this area is not meant to be an opportunity for harsh self-criticism; it is meant to lead you to areas where your soul is asking you to expand. Are you stuck in what feels like a dead-end job? Your soul is asking you to expand by exploring what meaningful work feels like to you and the beliefs you might be harboring that make meaningful work seem unattainable or mutually exclusive with well-paying work. Is your health detracting from your ability to participate fully in life? Your soul is asking you to expand by exploring what is underlying the symptoms, the physical manifestations of dis-ease, and what needs are getting met by being sick such as feeling deserving of care and attention, that could be better met in other ways.

If our outer life isn't where we want it to be, are we unfit to move forward with the attunement? Not necessarily. Again, think of these challenges as opportunities to explore parts of yourself that might be yearning for attention, not as something you have to get right in order to proceed. Only you can decide if receiving an attunement feels in alignment with your journey right now. Asking the following question can help you feel your way to a decision: "Do I believe getting this attunement will fix the problems I experience in life?" Really think about the answer. Perhaps you're envisioning becoming a Reiki practitioner and ditching your crappy day job to become a full-time healer. Or maybe you want Reiki to create perfect physical health or mend your relationship with your partner. Maybe you feel it will make you more confident and less worried about what other people think, giving you the freedom to express your authentic self. Here's the thing: Reiki *can* help with all of those things, and a desire to experience change in those areas is nothing to be ashamed of. Where we sometimes get stuck is in thinking that Reiki is the hot new thing that we must have in order to *finally* be who we want to be. Remember, an attunement is a declaration of *partnering* with the Divine, of casting off the role of victim and taking ownership of your personal evolution. Reiki will not do these things *for* you, but it will help you access dormant parts of yourself that contain the power to create the life your soul is here to lead.

If you are ready to step into your full power, even if you don't know quite what that looks like yet, this is a good indication that you're ready for your attunement. If you're prepared to look honestly and compassionately at how you are helping create every situation in your life, Reiki will support you on your journey. If, however, your dominant need is one of "fixing" yourself and others to forego the challenge of *accepting* yourself and others and bypassing the development of skills to approach people and situations without fixing, it might be prudent to work on building a practice of self-love and radical self-acceptance, while also exposing yourself to alternative relationship tools and strategies that do not involve rescuing and fixing. *Codependent No More* and *Non-Violent Communication: A Language of Life* are excellent resources.

And yet, I cannot give you hard and fast rules here. We are all human; there is no perfect end goal that must be reached before attunement is "allowed" or advisable. And Reiki can help a great deal with dissolving the aforementioned codependent fixing and rescuing, so again, these are not linear metrics where A *must* occur before B. The purpose of all of this questioning is in large part to clearly mark this attunement as an initiation. It is not something to be taken lightly and forgotten a month later when you take another workshop. An attunement will fundamentally change you, so we must enter this stage of initiation with awareness to reap the full benefits of these divinely guided changes. The inventory, then, seeks to prepare you to enter with eyes and heart wide open, not instill fear that if you're not perfect, you shouldn't get the attunement. Not to conjure up shame if you feel your life is "out of control." We want to give ourselves the time and space to feel the fullness of our decision to be attuned, to honor the initiation we are about to undergo, to mark the transition from one phase of life to the next. We need not do this perfectly, simply with an open heart. This is the task of the first challenge, so give yourself time to really sit with the questions and concepts presented here. As much as possible, release the need to approach these questions as a way to prove to yourself or others that you're worthy of the attunement. And if you're asking yourself, I'll save you the trouble: You're already worthy. Journal on these questions, spend some time meditating on them. Pay attention to your dreams. Pay attention to your physical body—to your health or any sensations that arise. Open to receive a multidimensional awareness of your response to these questions that is not just mental but emotional, physical, and spiritual as well. When your internal cues give you the green light, move on to the next challenge.

Challenge Two

While in the first challenge, our inner sovereign was tasked with steering the chariot of life in a meaningful and effective manner, the second challenge asks whether the cloak of kingship fits. In order to be the sovereign of our life, we are required to have a balance of honoring our gifts and stepping fully into our inner authority while simultaneously avoiding the trap of grandiosity. It's easy to resort to false humility when we don't want to appear too big for our britches, but there's a big difference between useful humility and trying to *appear* humble. There is no religious undertone to this humility; I call it useful humility for a reason. The form of humility we're after is the form that is *useful* in our daily lives, in the sense that it helps us carry on with pursuing our soul's work without getting in our own way.

We often trip ourselves up when we have an overblown ideal of what we're being called to do. When I experience writer's block, it is often because I am setting out to write not just a very good book about

Reiki but the end-all-be-all-mother-of-Reiki books. It takes humility to accept that, as a human, I cannot write the perfect Reiki book, and *useful* humility helps me to keep writing in spite of my imperfections. Perfectionism and narcissism often lead to chronic procrastination, because if we cannot do it perfectly and/or we cannot bear to see ourselves as someone who cannot do it perfectly, we believe it's better to not do it at all.

If we are consumed with a sense of unworthiness, we cannot step into full sovereignty—the cloak will be too big on our shoulders. Likewise, if we're too full of ourselves, the cloak will be too tight, and not because some power from on high is punishing us for our arrogance but because our self-inflation gets in our own way. Sylvia Brinton Perera shares the experience of one of her patients, who had postponed writing for decades "out of fear of her own incapacity to carry her sense of a writer's necessary greatness" and healing came when she recognized it "was not the mammoth undertaking that her idealization had made it seem. It was, as she put it, 'a vast relief to be finally doing it, but also no big deal—just daily hard work.'" (Perera 2001, 92)

We aim to cultivate a healthy sense of self and a more or less accurate sense of our skills, talents, and desires, and we must also cultivate useful humility so that grandiose, idealized visions of ourselves don't get in the way of doing the work. When we are able to strike this balance imperfectly and with an open heart, compassionate of our foibles and self-encouraging to keep practicing in spite of them, we don the regal cloak of inner sovereignty. So for this challenge, explore your relationship to both aspects: your ability to own your authority and skills and your ability to cultivate useful humility. Journal, meditate, pay attention to your dreams. Perhaps use the following questions to spark inner dialogue:

- How does perfectionism play out in my life? Do I sometimes postpone or avoid doing things out of fear that I won't
  do them perfectly?

- Do I judge others for not doing things up to my exacting
  standards? Do I often feel that I have to do things myself
  because others can't be counted on to do them well?

- Am I competitive? How does this play out in my relationships? How does this play out in how I treat myself?

- How well can I take a compliment? Do I deflect it or can
  I simply say, "thank you" and enjoy it?

- How well can I give compliments? What does it feel like
  when I give a compliment?

- Do I find myself telling stories where other people are
  voicing the affirmations and compliments that I want to
  hear, even if the conversations didn't really go that way?
  For example, playing up how complimentary your boss
  was about your performance during your review because
  you really want to be recognized for your work.

Give yourself time to explore your relationship to inner power without judgment—where it feels scary to own it and where it feels scary to
relinquish it. These are potent clues leading you to areas where your soul
wants to expand, and the road to expansion lies in seeing these aspects
more clearly rather than trying to paint them in more flattering or more
unbecoming colors, and accepting them fully instead of rejecting them
as strikes against your idealized self.

Challenge Three

In the third Tara test of the Celtic High Kings it was said that "the test stones will open to let the chariot through if the aspirant is destined to rule…This implies that the transpersonal path is opened. No longer impenetrable, the way feels right and clear" (Perera 2001, 92). Your next challenge, then, lies in discerning the difference between what author Danielle LaPorte calls "cheap easy" versus "quality easy," because being comfortable operating from a place of quality easy is a sign that "the transpersonal path is open" (LaPorte 2016). So what is cheap easy and how does it differ from quality easy? Cheap easy is what we typically mean by the phrase "taking the easy way out." It's a compromise, skirting around the real work your soul is calling you to do. In our modern go-go-go culture, easy is often a catchall label for anything that doesn't involve constant "forward" movement. From this limited viewpoint, it doesn't matter if the forward movement is aligned with your soul or if it's simply a means to get ahead, but your inner sovereign knows that the distinction is vital. As LaPorte writes, "cheap easy is a sucker for a discount. Cheap easy can't see that some losses are gains. Cheap easy stays in a stifling relationship because it seems easier than facing the heartbreak and dividing up the furniture. Cheap easy is frequently in a rush, a smidge desperate, and usually scrambling for options. Cheap easy tells little white lies to get things done" (Ibid.).

We must learn to feel into our decisions and discern when we're opting for cheap easy, when we're choosing chronic pain over conscious change. When we're living a smaller, quieter, duller life than our soul is craving out of fear of failure, resentment, perfectionism, or any other obstacles that can tempt us toward the path of cheap easy. When we choose cheap easy, we feel a hollowness where authenticity usually resides. Deep down—and at times, right on the surface—is an awareness that this choice is at odds with what we truly need to grow and change. Indeed, cheap easy often feels easier than speaking our truth, walking away, or staying even when we want to walk away. In other words, doing what it takes to step out of our comfort zone and into what Dr. Gay Hendricks calls our "zone of genius" (Hendricks 2009, 113).

And then we have quality easy. "Quality easy has fewer things on the to-do list and is a brilliant delegator. Quality easy trusts the timing of things. He knows it's better to hold out for what's right than to deal with the mess of extracting himself from a bad compromise. The minute resentment and irritation set in to a task, Quality easy goes on red alert…Over time, Quality easy gets comfortable saying no, thank you, to things that are just too complicated and too distant from what she really wants. She is willing to let it go, get over it, and walk away—because she has better things to do with her life energy" (LaPorte 2016).

Quality easy is a practice that aligns us with the flow of the Divine, choice by choice. It keeps us on course and vibrating with our soul's purpose, not chasing markers of success that don't really do it for us deep down. When we're choosing quality easy, there's a certain feeling of ease and flow, of "Yep, this is what I'm supposed to be doing right now." The challenge lies in being able to home in on that feeling of quality easy, which won't always *look* easy on the surface; sometimes it inspires you to burn the midnight oil writing your book; get up at sunrise, slip on your muddy running shoes, and hit the trail; or commit to meditating today, even when Netflix is waiting. But here's the thing: Quality easy never takes more than it gives, and it gives in the form of ever renewable passion, inspiration, creativity, ideas, and energy. Cheap easy, on the other hand, is a slow drain that leaves you depleted and aimless.

As inner sovereign, your duty is to learn what these forms of easy feel like for you, because when you are co-creating with the Divine, quality easy will become your M.O. Does this mean you will never experience suffering? Of course not, but you will feel connected to a source that offers ever-renewable nourishment, even amid your suffering. When you are co-creating with the Divine, you will feel a subtle (sometimes not-so-subtle) energy, like a wind in your sails or a current carrying you forward. "Quality easy brings a sense of expansion to things. Quality easy is compelling—because when you say yes to grace, you're saying yes to the natural flow of life" (LaPorte 2016).

For this challenge, make a list of decisions you've made in the past that felt like you chose cheap easy. Really get into each moment and look at everything from all angles; notice sensations in your body, perhaps familiar-sounding thoughts that arise, or memories of an earlier event that might not seem related at first glance. Explore the shape and feel of cheap easy until you *know* it. Make note of the markers you feel in your body when you're courting cheap easy. Is it a chill in your gut? A sort of desperate flutter in your heart, a fear that this might be your only option so take it now? Learn what your cheap easy tells are and write them down.

For example:

Moment: When I told Chris that I'd meet him for dinner because it felt awkward to say no, even though I'm really not interested in spending time with him.

Feelings: Like rabid woodchucks in my solar plexus and belly. I feel like my intuition is firing on all cylinders, and I'm actively working to suppress it. It's super uncomfortable. I also get a tight ache in the back of my throat up to the roof of my mouth, possibly connected to "biting back" my truth.

Now, do the same for quality easy. Make a list of times where you feel you chose quality easy. Again, get into each moment; really feel it from all angles, and describe your personal markers of a quality-easy choice.

For example:

Moment: When I penciled in writing time every weekday this month and followed through.

Feelings: Like I was finally allowing energy that had been dammed up to flow. Exhilaration in my heart and throat region—an expansive, sparkly sensation. An interesting blend of calm mind with a steady flow of ideas.

Moving forward, use this embodied understanding to discern the difference between cheap easy and quality easy to support yourself in empowered decision making and to stay in alignment with your True Self.

Challenge Four

The royal aspirant passed the final challenge if the *Lia Fáil* (Stone of Destiny), shrieked when the rightful king stood upon it, and this act "conveys the deep sense of entitlement and charisma that others intuit and cooperate to support" (Perera 2001, 93). Today, the word "entitlement" is a loaded one, so let's define it in this context. If we are to become channels of Divine energy, we must get comfortable with our birthright as beings who are by our very nature, channels of Divine energy. This doesn't make us superior to others—the simple truth is that everyone is born with this ability. We therefore need to own it and accept as fact that we have the right to channel this energy. If we are trapped in a web of self-effacing fears that we're being too full of ourselves, well, it's going to be hard to step up and be sovereign. Recall the second challenge in which the king is asked to demonstrate an ability to be in full possession of inner power without getting in his own way through grandiose or narcissistic tendencies. We are asked to fully own our powers so we can be able partners in co-creating with the Divine. At the same time, we are asked to practice useful humility to avoid the trap of making our work feel so big and important that we as mere mortals couldn't possibly carry it out, resulting in procrastination and disconnection from our sacred service. Here, too, we must fully own our role as channels of Divine energy without becoming overly inflated by this role and tripping ourselves up.

For this challenge, I want you to meditate on the mantra, "I have a right to be a channel for Divine energy." Really open up to any thoughts, sensations, or memories that arise. Does it feel uncomfortable to say this? If yes, why? Do you feel like you might get struck down (or otherwise brought back "down to size") by the powers that be or other people? If the latter, by whom in particular? When you imagine them putting you in your place, what does that look like, what words do they say, and how do you feel? When you use this mantra, do you feel embarrassed? Afraid of the responsibility? Or perhaps a rush of excitement? Really explore this. Do any images come up, any memories? Are there any grandiose fantasies?

The key is to explore with open eyes and an open heart. Judgment will only cause the parts of yourself that are likely to manifest later as obstacles to run and hide in secret places where they become potholes on your path. If you can maintain an attitude of curiosity and self-compassion, your inner sight will be better able to identify those aspects that yearn to be accepted and transformed. For example, perhaps you seen an image of yourself healing a client and feeling needed and powerful. If you follow this with shame and self-judgment, that image will likely get pushed down, free to influence you from the basement of your subconscious. The first step is acceptance. Seek to understand, not to shame. Explore the image; ask what you're getting out of this desire. A sense of self-worth and a feeling of being loved and needed? These aren't shameful things. By accepting your desire to feel worthy, loved, and needed, you can make conscious choices about how you get those needs met. When we suppress them, the desires are still there but their fulfillment is now being orchestrated by the unconscious. We might find ourselves engaging in relationships or making choices that don't feel good to us, yet we feel powerless to stop because the drive to meet the unconscious need is still present. The more you accept yourself in all your parts and can live consciously and mindfully, the less you are driven by desires and thought patterns hidden from conscious view.

The Final Preparation

Congratulations on working through the four challenges. Your explorations have cleared the way for a deeper relationship with your Self, a relationship that will be further enriched by your attunement. The night before your attunement, go over your journal entries from the four challenges. Do you notice any themes or words that pop up repeatedly? Meditate on their significance for you. Plumb your inner depths for any messages that wish to be heard. Continue journaling on any new insights that arise.

The next exercise can be done the evening before your attunement or the morning of—whichever feels best for you—and it's designed to give you one final check in with higher guidance prior to your initiation. Whether or not you receive new insights during the exercise, you are still connecting with your True Self, and if you recall Stiene's recommendation from earlier in the chapter: both teacher and student will receive the most benefit if their energy is like a calm lake. This exercise will help you enter that state of calm and oneness with your True Self, paving the way for a powerful attunement.

Exercise Six: Secret Garden Meditation

It's nice to mark this meditation as different than the meditations you've done thus far. You could light a candle or some incense or dab an essential oil blend on your pulse points (make sure to dilute it appropriately before applying it to your skin). Choose whatever feels good to mark this special occasion.

Bring yourself into a meditative state (page 26).

Bring your awareness to your heart. Feel your heart beating. Then, expand your heart awareness to encompass your soul. Feel your heart and soul beating as one. Notice if your heart rate feels rapid. Breathe slowly and deeply into your heart and soul as you say, "I love and accept you."

With your attention still on your heart, imagine a secret walled garden at your heart center. As it comes into view, notice whether you are on the outside of the garden wall or if you are in the garden itself. If you're outside, what is the wall made of? Is it covered with plants? Take in the details, noticing the season, any particular flowers or plants or animals that appear. If you're outside, look now for an entrance. Is there a door or is it simply an opening? Is the door locked or are there any obstructions? Ask now to enter the secret garden of your heart. Make your way inside.

Once in the garden, take some time to look around. Make note of any plants or animals, the season and time of day, and any other details that appear. When you feel ready, ask to meet with your Higher Self here in the secret garden. Breathe and wait until you feel a connection with your Higher Self. Do they appear in a particular form? What does it feel like when you're connected? Take your time and notice whatever is coming up for you right now.

Tell your Higher Self about your upcoming attunement. Share any thoughts or feelings you're experiencing (excitement, trepidation, eagerness, peace, et cetera), and ask any questions you might have. Remain open to receiving communication from your Higher Self in multiple forms—sounds, sensations, sights, smells. If something is unclear to you, ask to be given the information in a way you can understand. Ask any further questions you have of your Higher Self.

When the experience feels complete, thank your Higher Self in whatever way feels meaningful to you. Prepare to leave the garden, then allow the image to fade from view as you bring your awareness back to the room.

Bring yourself out of the meditative state (pages 26–27).

Journal about your experience. If you did this exercise the night before your attunement, you might choose to spend some time the following morning reviewing your journal entry, connecting with the feeling sense of communing with your Higher Self in the garden, and/or reviewing your dreams from the night before. On a practical note, be sure to drink plenty of water before and after your attunement. I've found energy work to be much more powerful (and less likely to induce uncomfortable reactions) when properly hydrated. When the attunement is ready to begin, set the intention to receive whatever you need in this moment and surrender to the experience. Don't worry about feeling the "right" thing; be curious and allow the attunement to unfold. Remember that Reiki knows precisely what we need. The less we try to manage the experience with the ego, the more transformative it will be. Enjoy your attunement!

Integrating the Attunement

Now that you've received your attunement, it's time to return to your inner campfire, where you will once again meet with the Focus Part you encountered in exercise three, this time with Reiki's support.

Exercise Seven: Returning to the Fire

Enter into a meditative state (page 26).

Bring your awareness to the container of your body and energy field. Feel how your body contains you, how it provides the space in which you live. Run your awareness over the entire surface of your body, from crown to feet on all sides.

Become aware of the integrity of your container, the strength of your container. Say to yourself three times: "My sacred container is healthy and balanced on all levels." Breathe into your body, feeling the contained space expand to hold more air, then release, noticing the changes in your container as you exhale all of the air out. Repeat for a few breaths.

Bring your attention to your inner fire. Locate where in your body you feel the fire most intensely, and see your inner campfire burning here. If it helps you to connect, place your hands over this part of your body while you deepen the image of the sacred campfire.

See yourself sitting down next to your inner fire. Give yourself time to attune to your inner fire, breathing as you gaze into the flames, feeling your deep, unbreakable connection to this sacred flame.

Now bring to mind the Focus Part and invite it to join you near the fire. You might call it by name, visualize it, envision the meditation in which you first met, or use whatever method allows you to reconnect.

Maintain the image of the fire and you sitting beside it and wait for the Focus Part to appear.

When you feel or see or otherwise sense the presence of this part joining you by the fire, allow it to sit with you for a while. Simply breathe, acknowledge it with a nod and a smile, and maintain your open awareness and curiosity.

Place your hands over your solar plexus and welcome Reiki to the campfire. Breathe as you give yourself time to feel the flow of Reiki, perhaps as heat or tingling in your hands. Set the intention to transform your relationship to this part in a way that is correct and good for all involved. Ask Reiki to guide the process and allow the experience to unfold.

If you need more direction, ask the part "What messages do you have for me?" Give yourself as much time as you need to sit with the Focus Part, asking and learning. Remember to give the part all the understanding and compassion you would a dear friend because it is trying to keep you safe and wants to help you.

When this process feels complete, thank the part for all of the hard work it's been doing for you. Thank Reiki and your Higher Self. Thank your body for providing a strong container in which to do this healing work.

Gradually let the image of the campfire fade until the screen of your mind is empty. Return your awareness to your breath. Take in a few deep and nourishing inhales; let out long and cleansing exhales. Let go of anything from your journey that doesn't serve you in this moment with every exhale. Open to receiving what you need with every inhale.

Bring yourself out of the meditative state (pages 26–27).

Journal about your experience, making note of any changes you experienced by introducing Reiki. How do you feel about the Focus Part? Have those feelings shifted since your first encounter? Remember that healing these internal parts requires that we witness and relate to them from the True Self. Reiki helps us reconnect with this self and therefore has the ability to supercharge our internal healing. Throughout our journey, we'll continue to build on this concept of using Reiki to return to a calm, compassionate center with the knowledge that any thoughts and actions arising from this state carry the potential for profound healing. In the next chapter, we'll go deeper into Reiki's teachings and expand the ways in which you can use this powerful energy.

—4—
THE REIKI PRACTICES

Usui's teachings included the following four components of Reiki practice: *gassho*, a ritual gesture in which the hands come together in prayer position; *reiju*, a practice in which you connect with your spiritual intuitive faculties; *chiryo*, or healing treatments; and the Five Reiki Precepts or Principles. In this chapter, we'll explore the first three components, and in a later chapter we'll look at the Five Precepts. More than simply going through the motions outlined for the different techniques you're about to learn, it's very useful to also build the habit of paying attention to what you feel while doing each exercise. At times, you might not feel much; here, a certain amount of "fake it 'til you make it" can be useful. By doing these exercises, you heighten your awareness of the energy, what it feels like when you breathe it in, when you send it to different parts of your body, when you breathe it out through your fingertips, and so forth. These practices will sharpen your skills as a healer if you move through the exercises with intention, even during those times when you're not feeling energetic bells and whistles. Trust that when done mindfully, these exercises are changing your ability to perceive and work with energy.

Exercise Eight: Gassho

Gassho means "two hands coming together," and to engage gassho as part of your Reiki practice, you can use this very simple meditation.

Come into a comfortable seated position with a straight spine (support your back as needed) and bring your hands together in prayer position, palms touching, each finger matched up with its partner on the other hand from base to fingertip.

Your chin is slightly tucked into your chest to lengthen the back of the neck, which serves to open an important energy point called the Wind Palace in Traditional Chinese Medicine.

Raise your hands to heart level; you should be able to feel the wind of your breath on your fingertips.

If it's comfortable, breathe in through your nose and out through your mouth. You can also lightly touch the tip of your tongue to the roof of your mouth as you inhale through your nose, then let the tongue relax as you exhale through the mouth. Continue this pattern for successive inhales and exhales.

Throughout the entire meditation, train your awareness to the meeting of your two middle fingertips. Whenever your mind starts to wander, gently return soft focus to this spot, perhaps lightly pressing the two middle finger pads together for a moment to direct your concentration. If your arms get tired, you can lower your prayer hands into your lap, still focusing on the meeting of your middle fingertips.

Frank Arjava Petter outlines the esoteric Buddhist symbolism of the hands and fingers, and they're quite apt for our self-transformative work with the elements (Petter 2001, 148). The left hand is related to the moon, while the right hand is connected to the sun.

Thumbs symbolize the Void

Index fingers symbolize Air

Middle fingers symbolize Fire

Ring fingers symbolize Water

Pinky fingers symbolize Earth

When we bring our hands together in gassho, the sun and moon and all the elements come together. "Focusing our attention on the middle finger emphasizes the fire aspect of meditation—awareness burning the unconscious elements," which sounds very much like the process of Illumination, doesn't it? Gassho meditation is a great way to prepare for Reiki self-healing or a client session. It helps you become centered and connected to your heart, and it's great to use in daily life. If you're feeling overwhelmed by racing thoughts or intense emotions, try the gassho meditation.

The second component of Usui's teachings is *reiju*, the word Usui used for a Reiki attunement that translates as "spiritual blessing" or "spiritual offering." Doi writes that reiju was given regularly at study meetings of the Usui Reiki Ryoho Gakkai, where students were encouraged to attend as many meetings as possible to benefit from repeated reiju, and this makes sense if we view an attunement, reiju, or initiation—whichever term we prefer—as a means of reminding us of our True Self. The more reminders we see, the more likely we are to stay in this state of remembrance.

The concept of reiju sometimes causes confusion in modern Reiki circles, because some practitioners use it to refer to an attunement received upon completion of a level of study, which then gives the person the ability to channel Reiki for hands-on healing, while others use it to indicate a blessing that can be performed more often that may or may not give the ability to do hands-on healing. In my view, the point is moot because you already have the ability to channel Reiki, whether or not you get an attunement or reiju. Usui used this process to give his students an experience of their True Self, and he coupled it with other practices and principles such as the Reiki Precepts to help his students remember their True Self following the attunement or reiju.

The third component of Usui's teachings is *chiryo*, or treatments. The following is a selection of practices I have found to be both incredibly helpful in my self-healing work and simple to implement on a regular basis, thereby increasing the chances that I'll actually use them.

Exercise Nine: Kenyoku or Dry Bathing

Kenyoku is a great technique to have in your repertoire; as the name suggests, it has a cleansing purpose that's useful in between sessions with clients or whenever you need to wipe the energetic slate clean. If you find yourself ruminating on a situation long after it's over or otherwise caught in a loop, try using Kenyoku to make a clean break. The following is said to be the method as Usui originally taught it, although there are other variations that can work just as well.

While seated or standing, place your right palm near your left shoulder, just over the outer edge of the collarbone (clavicle). Brush this hand over your skin, diagonally across your chest to your right hip.

Repeat on the opposite side, placing your left palm on right collarbone, swiping it diagonally to your left hip.

Repeat steps one and two.

Use your right hand to stroke your left wrist, over your open left palm and off the ends of your fingertips.

Use your left hand to stroke your right wrist, over your open right palm and off the ends of your fingertips.

If desired repeat steps four and five.

The following technique, *Joshin Kokyuu-Ho*, means "breathing exercise to purify the spirit." To understand what it entails, we need to talk about the tanden. The tanden is an energy center in the lower abdomen, often described as 1 to 2 inches below the navel, closer to your spine than your navel in terms of depth. This center corresponds to the Lower Dantian (sometimes spelled tantien or tan tien) in Traditional Chinese Medicine. The tanden is your energetic center, a crucial energy point that when developed, can balance out the Western esoteric and mystical practice tendency to emphasize development of the third eye and crown centers which can lead to a state of energetic top heaviness.

Taoist Master Mantak Chia writes: The importance of the navel center cannot be overemphasized. It is the center of physical gravity. The body moves around this center when sitting, standing, or practicing Tai Chi. The navel center also transforms [many forms of energy] into life-force energy that is useful to the body, in a process similar to our physical digestion of food…The lower tan tien is also the storage site of Original Chi, the mother of the body's energies, which can heal the human body and restore it to its original wholeness [like your] 'battery' or 'power pack.' It needs to be clear of congestion and tension so that the energy can easily flow in and out…The importance of the lower tan tien stems in part from its role in the development of the embryo. Not only is the fetus nourished by navel energy, but waste is eliminated through the navel. After birth, and the child's body grows, the body continues to eliminate toxins into the navel area…The navel center is the doorway between the physical body and the energy body (Chia 2007, 26–27).

In the following exercises you'll learn how to get a feel for where the tanden is and then breathe into the tanden with *joshin kokyuu-ho*, the "breathing exercise to purify the spirit." Petter writes that this technique "magnifies your Reiki energy and helps you feel like a piece of hollow bamboo—a clear channel for energy" (Petter 2001, 158). It's a great preparation for Reiki treatments or anytime that you wish to connect with your center.

Exercise Ten: Finding the Tanden

To find your tanden, stand with your feet shoulder-width apart and take a few deep, cleansing breaths. Think of something pleasant while you move your awareness throughout your body, breathing into any areas of tension that you find, sending them love and acceptance.

Breathe in through your nose, optionally placing the tip of your tongue lightly on the roof of your mouth. Breathe out through the mouth, letting the tongue relax.

Begin bending your knees very, very slowly, keeping your knees tracking straight forward, not letting them bow out to the sides or inward. As you bend your knees, focus your attention on your lower abdomen until you feel heightened awareness at a spot usually an inch or two below your belly button. You don't need to bend your knees very far—you're definitely not doing a squat—just a few inches is usually sufficient for heightened awareness to kick in.

The sensation can be very subtle, so don't be discouraged if you're not feeling anything dramatic. While your experience might be different, here are some pointers: For me, it helps to lightly tuck my tailbone under. If your pelvis is angled forward, such that your tailbone is tilted upward slightly, it can be harder to sense the tanden. The sensation feels a bit like a string tethered to the spine that is slightly pulling the navel area back. If this connection is not happening for you yet, don't fret; you can still do the following exercise while focusing your attention on the space an inch or two below your navel and a couple inches under the surface of your skin.

Exercise Eleven: Joshin Kokyuu-Ho Breathing Technique

Note: This exercise is not recommended for people who are pregnant or have high blood pressure. If you feel light-headed at any point, stop immediately and return to normal breathing.

To begin joshin kokyuu-ho, inhale through your nose and envision drawing Reiki into your body through your crown chakra, which is at or slightly above the crown of your head. You might feel the Reiki entering as tingling, heat, vibration or waves and/or you can visualize it as white light. Envision pulling the breath and the Reiki down to your tanden with this inhale.

On the exhale, visualize the Reiki streaming out through your fingertips, the palms of your hands, the tips of your toes, and the bottoms of your feet.

With each successive inhale, focus your awareness on Reiki drawing down into your tanden, followed by Reiki expanding and permeating your entire body on the exhale.

Now that you've explored various treatments for connecting with Reiki, let's put that energy to use! In the following section, you'll learn the traditional hand positions for self-healing, and you can use them anytime you want to give yourself a Reiki treatment.

The Basic Twelve Positions for Self-Healing

1. **Front of the face:** Place both hands over your face with your fingertips resting on the forehead so the upper part of your palms are over your eyes.

2. **Sides of the face:** Place both hands on either side of your face, fingertips resting on the temple, palms curving over the jaw. Alternate position: Bring the fingertips together along the midline at the top of the skull. Your palms will fold along the sides of your head, above your ears.

3. **Back of the head:** Bring your palms to the back of your head, forming a triangle with your hands—index finger tips and thumb tips touching. Your palms will be cradling the base of your skull. Alternate position (and one I especially like): Place one hand over your forehead, fingers parallel to your eyebrows and the other hand on the back of your head, opposite the front hand.

4. **Throat:** Bring the heels of your hands together and bring them close to your throat, fingers wrapping gently around either side of your neck. No need to strangle yourself; a light, gentle clasp is what you're aiming for.

5. **Thymus:** Bring your palms up to your chest, fingers resting on the hollow between your collarbones, palms angled down and out to allow a comfortable position with your arms.

6. **Upper stomach:** Place your hands, fingertips touching and horizontal, right under the breasts.

7. **Middle abdomen:** Move your hands just below position six.

8. **Lower abdomen/tanden:** Move your hands lower on the abdomen, just under the navel. Alternate position (and another that I'm quite fond of): Place one hand over the center of your chest at heart level and the other hand just below your navel.

9. **Upper back:** Reaching over your shoulders, place your hands on your upper back. Depending on your shoulder mobility, your fingertips will rest somewhat higher or lower between your shoulder blades.

10. **Middle back:** This can be a bit difficult to reach, depending on shoulder mobility, so keep in mind that Reiki will go wherever it is needed, even if your hands can't reach. If comfortable, bring your hands back and around your sides, placing them on

your midback. Sometimes it helps to lean forward a bit, and you can also do one hand at a time.

11. **Lower back:** Bring your arms around and back, placing your hands on your lower back. Your fingertips will brush the tops of your hips. As with position 10, feel free to do one hand at a time if that's more comfortable.

12. **Sacrum:** The sacrum is a bone at the base of your spine. The tip of the sacrum is commonly known as the tailbone. Reach around your back and place your hands over your sacrum. It's usually most comfortable to angle the fingers down, palms angled up and out, forming a V-shape.

Hands-On Healing for Others

While the primary focus of this book is *self*-transformation, Reiki is, of course, a wonderful tool for offering healing to others, so let's learn the basic framework for conducting a healing session for another person.

The most important thing you can do to prepare is to connect with your True Self, and you can use any of the techniques outlined in this chapter to come into a state of calm, presence, and greater connection with the Self. Simply feeling your feet firmly planted on the ground and enjoying the sense of stability and groundedness traveling up your legs, into your trunk, and all the way up to your crown, can work wonders. You can also imagine sending tree roots down through the soles of your feet and into the earth, giving you a firm and stable connection. To center, you might focus your attention on your tanden and connect with this as both your physical center of gravity and your energetic center. Rock back and forth, and side to side on your heels to get a sense of this gravitational center. And of course, deep, intentional breathing as you do any of these exercises (and throughout the healing session) is always a plus!

I typically start sessions with the recipient laying face up, with the Reiki practitioner seated at the head of the table. You can place a round, cushy bolster underneath the person's knees to relieve pressure in the low back. When placing your hands in the various positions, allow them to hover just above or a few inches above the skin or clothing, or lightly rest your hands on the person's body. The decision to touch or not to touch depends on several factors:

- The recipient's comfort. Let the person know what to expect, including which areas of the body will be touched as part of the treatment, and obtain their consent before doing so. Someone might have a history of trauma or other reasons why they don't wish to be touched in specific areas and you'll need to modify accordingly.

- Never place your hands on areas of privacy, such as the groin or the female breasts. When working over these areas, hover the hands a few inches above the person's clothing. Be aware of your own body and clothing, not just your hands. You might be leaning against the person unintentionally or your forearm could be in contact with the underside of a female client's breast even though your hands are on her abdomen. Be aware of all places where you are making contact.

- On certain areas, such as over the eyes, it can be more comfortable for the person if you hover slightly above the skin rather than resting your palms directly on their face. Try placing a folded, clean tissue over the eyes before lightly placing your hands on the area to prevent the sweaty, clammy feel of skin to skin contact.

- Presence of injuries. If the recipient has a wound or other injury, it's probably best to hover over the skin instead of making direct contact. And of course, if the injury is acute, send them to a medical facility and/or call 911!

Wash your hands before the session and pay attention to your hygiene. It can be distracting and unpleasant for the recipient to smell body odors throughout the session, including bad breath. If you smoke, please be aware that the smell can linger on your hands, breath, and skin even if you wash your hands and brush your teeth, and it may be much more noticeable to a non-smoker than it is to you. I have not returned to a practitioner simply because the smell of smoke was so strong on their hands that it detracted from the healing experience.

If you do choose to make skin or clothing contact, remember to use a light touch. You aren't massaging the client, you are merely allowing energy to flow. Be aware of your body and the pressure of your hands at all times. I have had practitioners unwittingly leaning into me with increasing intensity as the session progressed (as they were presumably getting tired of standing), and in certain areas, such as the back of the knee, this can be uncomfortable and even harmful depending on the degree of pressure. If you find yourself getting tired, consider offering shorter sessions, using a chair, and/or doing movement and energy practices outside of sessions to build up your stamina. Using the recipient's body as a support post is not ideal!

The twelve hand positions for self-healing described above can be modified slightly for giving Reiki to others, but don't feel locked into the sequence. When I'm working, I tend to follow my intuition, and you might find that when you're using Reiki your intuition kicks in sooner than you think, even if you're brand new to the practice. That said, if you're busy second guessing yourself and your ego is trying to think its way through everything, you might find it more difficult to sense your intuitive promptings. In these situations, the traditional hand positions can be very helpful by providing you with a set sequence that will allow your mind to relax. Then, if intuitive guidance appears, you can deviate from the sequence as needed.

When your hands are placed on your own body or another person, you might feel a slight energetic tug in your hands that leads you toward the next position, or perhaps you might hear the name of that body part or see it in your mind—that's your intuition kicking in. You might notice that the heat or tingling in your hands suddenly fades, or you'll have a sense of "it's time to move on." With practice, you'll learn what your individual cues are, so pay attention to the sensations you experience during Reiki sessions.

The Basic Positions

1. **Front of the face:** Drape a clean tissue over the client's closed eyes, then place both hands over the person's face with palms gently cupping over the eyes and fingertips resting on the cheekbones. You can also forego the tissue and hover over this area without touching.

2. **Temples:** Place both hands on either side of the head, fingertips over the temples, palms curving around the sides of the skull, possibly meeting at the crown of the head, depending on the size of your hands and the recipient's head.

3. **Ears:** Hover your hands in a cupped position over the person's ears. I prefer to hover along the sides of the head as opposed to covering the ears, as the latter can feel constricting. Feel free to experiment and check in with the recipient's preference.

4. **Back of the head:** Place your hands on either side of the person's head with the backs of your hands resting on the treatment table. Gently rock their head to one side, enough to allow you to slide the opposite palm under their head, and repeat with the other hand so you are cradling the back of their skull in both hands. Make sure you aren't wearing jewelry on your hands or wrists that could dig into their scalp.

5. **Throat:** Two variations for this one, depending on the recipient's preference and comfort. You can lightly place your fingers over the front of the throat on both sides. Your fingertips

will meet in the center in line with the sternum (breastbone). Be very aware of the amount of pressure you are applying as a little can feel constricting in this sensitive area. A second variation that I prefer is to place the pinky-edge of the hands on the clavicles (collarbones) so the fingertips meet at the sternum and palms are facing the underside of the person's chin. You are able to send energy to the throat region without applying pressure to the throat.

6. **Heart:** Hover your hands over the heart region. You can overlap your hands in the air so that the palm of one hand partially covers the fingers of the other or you can stack them on top of each other. Hopefully this goes without being said, but do not touch female client's breasts.

7. **Ribs:** Working on one side of the body at a time, place your hands side by side (e.g., one hand closer to the recipient's head, the other hand closer to the hips) over their ribs. You can move to the other side of the table to treat the other side of the body or simply move your hands if you are tall enough to do so without straining or overreaching.

8. **Lower abdomen/tanden:** Place one hand above the navel and the other just below the navel.

9. **Hips:** There are two variations for this position. You can place your hands on either side of the body on the sides of the hips or placed on the front of each hip bone (where the front pockets of jeans would be) avoiding the groin. You might find it more comfortable on your wrists to place one hand with finger tips pointing up towards the person's head and the other hand with finger tips pointing down towards their feet.
Remove the bolster from beneath the person's knees and bring up the face cradle on the treatment table. The recipient will roll over to their stomach, placing their face in the cradle.

(Face cradles should be covered with disposable paper or reusable and washable fabric covers with a fresh one used for each person.) Check to see if the cradle needs to be adjusted for comfort. The bolster can be placed under the recipient's ankles in this position.

10. **Upper back:** Use the same staggered hand position as described for the heart area, this time placing your hands just above the scapulae (shoulder blades). Move down the back, placing your hands over the scapulae.

11. **Middle back:** Move down to the middle of the back.

12. **Sacrum:** The sacrum is a bone at the base of your spine. Place your hands at the uppermost part of the sacrum, right above the top of the gluteal cleft so you're not handling their glutes.

13. **Knees:** Place your palms over the backs of the knees. This is an area where you need to be sensitive of your pressure. There are nerves that can be compressed if you are bearing down on the backs of the knees.

14. **Ankles:** Move to the foot of the table and gently wrap your hands around the ankles.

15. **Feet:** Place your hands over the soles of the feet, from the toes to the middle of the foot, depending on the size of your hands.

To conclude the treatment, gently sweep your hands over the person's aura, usually about a foot to a foot and a half above their skin, starting at the crown of the head and ending at the feet. This constitutes one sweep. Walk back up to the head of the table, repeat with a second sweep, and conclude with a third aura sweep. Remove the bolster from beneath the ankles to make it easier for them to get off the table;

provide assistance and/or a stepping stool if necessary. Offer the person a cup of water and the restroom if needed. You can use the Dry Bathing technique on yourself to completely end the session. If you made contact with the clothing or skin, wash your hands between clients.

Now that you have a solid foundation for using Reiki to perform hands-on self-healing and healing for others, let's return to our seven-step journey of transformation, picking up with the second step, Submersion, in the next chapter.

—5—

SUBMERSION

The next step in our self-transformation process involves wading into the waters of the unconscious mind, and in doing so, forging a connection between the conscious, associated with the One Mind, and the unconscious, associated with the One Thing. If you recall from chapter 1, we want to bring these two internal forces together, as the Hermetic creation story illustrated, because in doing so, we ignite our full creative capacity, which includes our ability to create a state of health. We're going to start with an exercise, and it's important that you complete this exercise before reading the rest of the chapter, as this will allow you to approach the exercise with less interference from your ego. which might otherwise try to alter the experience to fit the material presented later in the reading.

Exercise Twelve: Explain Your Position

Choose a recent situation in which you felt strong emotions. It's often easier to start with unpleasant emotions, as these tend to readily trigger unconscious material.

Write a description of the situation, including any backstory or other contextual information that you feel is relevant. Imagine that you will be handing this paper to someone who will then judge the situation and the people involved to determine what part each person had to play in the event. Your job is to describe the event in a way that you believe accurately reflects what took place so the judge can properly do their job. Don't filter yourself; commit to paper everything you feel is relevant.

When you're done, put the paper in a safe place and leave it alone for at least three days, during which time you can continue with the chapter's readings.

Submersion and the Unconscious

To understand the process of Submersion, recall the encounter with one of your inner protector parts during the first step, Illumination. With the Illumination exercises, you began to transform your relationship to this part, which has been influencing your thoughts and actions, likely on an unconscious level, like a computer program running in the background. In Submersion, we are going further by wading into the waters of the unconscious to understand more fully why these protector parts exist in our psyche—what are they here to protect?

In the language of Internal Family Systems, the protector is guarding a part known as an exile, another character in the psyche that has sustained wounding and has remained trapped to some degree in that original wounding scenario. By entering the waters of the unconscious and gaining access to these exiles, we can heal them while also releasing the protector from its need to protect. Both of these parts are then free to fulfill healthier roles within the psyche. This is in keeping with our work with Reiki, in which we seek to remember our True Self. The more we heal these inner parts, the less they will feel the need to overthrow the Self in an attempt to protect us from perceived (or actual) threats, and the more we can remain anchored in our True Self.

The Lure of Projections

One of the most common ways protectors do their job is by shifting our focus away from the wounded exile and toward something else. While there are a variety of methods for attention shifting, we're going to focus on a very powerful and common method: projection. This concept was introduced in the step of Illumination, and we'll be taking this work deeper with Submersion.

In order for this work to transform us, we must address a common belief: the belief that we are somehow immune to projection: "other people do it but not *me!*" The irony, of course, is that this is itself a projection. I have never met a person who does not engage in projection, myself included, so unless you're a unicorn (and who knows—maybe unicorns are masters of projection), accepting that this process is occurring in your life is a prerequisite to transformation.

One aspect of projection that I find particularly interesting is the human tendency to unconsciously seek out in others the very things we are projecting. It's as if we know deep down that we need these energies to feel whole. If we cannot bear to see these qualities in ourselves, we will instead find ourselves encountering infuriating people again and again who "hold" these qualities for us. To use a simplistic example, if we deny ourselves the right to feel and express anger, we might routinely find ourselves yoked to an angry partner or boss. Can you see how we get trapped? With projection, we are locked in seeing the issue as being "out there." We say and think things like, "if only the other person would stop doing such and such, things wouldn't be like this ..."

or "If I could just get her to see that she needs to change, things would improve…"

We tell ourselves that what we're experiencing is the annoyance or pain of dealing with the other person's faults—their anger, inconsiderate behavior, and so on—but the deeper pain is about being disconnected from these potent energies within ourselves and feeling trapped in unsatisfying relationships with people who are carrying these energies for us. If we cannot see this pain, we will continue to project the source of our misery onto others and work ever harder to change it all the while feeling unable to shake the unfulfilling relationship patterns. Even if we leave a relationship with one person we've labeled as angry, we'll eventually find ourselves in another until we do the work of calling these projections back home.

Our freedom thus lies in seeing our projections for what they are and retrieving them from the person who is serving as a mirror for what we don't wish to see in ourselves. In doing so, we reclaim these energies that are integral to our sense of wholeness, and we'll begin this work in the next exercise in which you'll see a projection in action.

Exercise Thirteen: Seeing Projections, Part One

Get out your written description from Exercise Twelve: Explain Your Position. Go through and highlight or underline any phrases that refer to what another person is doing, thinking, or saying, such as:

- Denise turned her reports in late again.

- Jim talked over everyone at the meeting, and people are really getting sick of it.

    When you're done, put the paper down, close your eyes, and take some time to focus on your breath. Begin to lengthen your inhales and really feel your body expand as you fill with life force, then stretch out the exhales to release anything you don't need to carry into the next moment.

Place one hand over your heart and one hand over your belly. Allow Reiki to flow through your hands, pouring into your body and energy field. Feel yourself coming to center as you vibrate ever more strongly with the energy of love. Give yourself at least a few minutes to enjoy this feeling. When you're ready, thank Reiki and open your eyes.

Return to your paper. Are there a number of phrases marked? This can indicate a shift in focus away from your own experience to the experience of others. There's no judgment here; just hold this in your awareness while connecting with the feeling of love and centering you've just cultivated.

Next, choose one of the marked phrases and read it silently to yourself. Identify the action you are attributing to the other person ("Denise turned her reports in late"), and brainstorm why you think this other person is behaving this way. In this example, why do you think Denise is turning her reports in late? Because she's lazy? Does she not care about the rest of the team? Maybe she doesn't understand why the reports are important? Does she think she's above the rules? It's not important to know objectively, factually why Denise is missing deadlines; for this exercise, that's irrelevant. What is important are the reasons *you are attributing* to Denise's behavior. No one will see this but you, so don't be afraid to let it all out. Don't worry about sounding like a jerk; trust that this process will yield rich rewards *only* if you're unflinchingly honest while remaining connected to the energy of self-love.

If the process starts to feel intense, return to hands over your belly and heart, let Reiki flow, and perhaps use statements like, "Even though I think Denise is super lazy and does the bare minimum to keep from getting fired, I deeply love and accept myself." The format is, "Even though [insert challenging statement], I deeply love and accept myself." There may be many reasons that arise. Capture them all on paper, taking as many Reiki breaks as you need to stay connected with the energy of self-love. Remember, no matter what you dig up in this exercise, none of it has the power to mark you out as a bad person. You may interpret this information as proof of your badness, but that does not make it so.

When this process feels complete and you've listed all of the reasons you can think of, take a break from the exercise for at least forty-eight hours. Invite your True Self to offer its wisdom in the interim by saying to yourself, "I ask my True Self to retrieve any information from my subconscious and conscious mind, as well as from any other sources that will help me grow in response to this exercise. I seek to know myself in all my parts. So mote it be." If anything comes up that feels relevant, even if you can't verbally or intellectually validate how it relates, write it in your journal. Pay attention to your dreams, thoughts, or sensations that arise when you're spacing out, and so on. Allow your subconscious to deliver valuable information by remaining open. Don't discount anything because it doesn't make sense. The subconscious plays by different rules that seem nonsensical to the conscious mind but doesn't make information any less valid or useful.

Exercise Fourteen: Seeing Projections, Part Two

After at least forty-eight hours have passed, it's time to move deeper with the exercise.

Bring yourself into a meditative state (page 26).

Place one hand over your belly, one hand over your heart, and allow Reiki to flow into your body and energy field. Connect with the sensation of being centered while vibrating with the energy of love.

When you feel ready, open your eyes and pull out the paper from the previous exercise. Starting with one of the reasons on your list, begin to explore how this quality manifests in your life. For example, if one of your reasons for Denise's tardiness is "she tries to do the least amount of work possible without getting fired," ask yourself, "Are there areas of my life where I give less effort than I'm capable of?" See what arises. Don't discount any thoughts, words, memories, and so forth that pop up. Write them down in your journal.

Let's pause for a moment and introduce self-compassion by clarifying our intent. We're not doing this exercise solely for the sake of self-judgment. Let's say you identify an area where you're not giving your full effort: get curious; ask yourself why. Possible reasons include feeling uninspired by the work, which opens up important follow-up questions: Is this something you can stop doing? Is it indicative of a larger theme, such as choosing less challenging or less meaningful work because you doubt your capabilities? Maybe you're carrying resentment for someone else involved and are trying to get back at them by withholding your efforts. Or perhaps when you identify an area where you feel you aren't doing your best, it sheds light on your impossibly high standards. You're not doing your best (nor do you perceive anyone else as doing so) because your best is unattainable. This realization in turn could lead to seeing how you set sky-high standards that you know you can't meet as a way of justifying less effort. If you can't ever get the gold star, why bother? This line of questioning could then lead deeper as you ask yourself, "What do I think will happen if I don't get the gold star? Or if I do?" All of this is incredibly valuable information, and you will glean the most benefit if you can breathe yourself back to center and away from the urge to shame these internal parts into hiding.

Sometimes the reasons you listed for Denise's tardiness reveal an *opposing* quality in yourself. For example, if you judge Denise as being lazy, this might speak to a tendency to drive yourself into the ground with to-dos and deadlines. In short, you resent what appears to be

Denise's ability to operate at a more relaxed pace because it is something you deny yourself.

The projection exercise can be a tough one. It's challenging to look at ourselves in this manner because what we find isn't always comfortable to bear. When we don't engage in self-reflection, however, we hold this energy in our subconscious where it can influence our thoughts, words, and actions in *incredibly* powerful ways. As Jung said, "Until you make the unconscious conscious, it will direct your life and you will call it fate" (Jung 1967, 265). If like most of us you have issues that crop up again and again, such as bosses who overshare their personal life or romantic partners with a penchant for lying and can't understand why you keep encountering these people again and again (and again), exploring projections is your key to liberation from these cyclical experiences.

Archetypal Energies and Projection

As we go further with projections, it's helpful to deepen our understanding of archetypes and how these energies are relevant to our lives. We explored them on a more cosmic scale with the Hermetic creation story in chapter 1; now let's make them intimately personal. In Jungian psychology, archetypes–the prototypes upon which all other things are based–are considered to reside in the collective unconscious, which can be thought of like a huge soup pot of energetic information that we're all swimming in. When these archetypes are floating around in the giant soup pot, they exist as pure potential. For example, we have the archetype of the Mother or the Saint or the Victim, and each of these archetypes represents the sum total of all the different ways the energy of the Mother, the Saint, or the Victim can be expressed and experienced. And these are just three examples; there are countless others: there's an archetype for Love, Power, Justice, Earth, Fire, Water, and the list goes on.

You can think of these archetypes as a universal paint palette. We all have access to the full set of paints, but how we use them dictates whether we experience our life as a smeared finger painting or a multi-dimensional masterpiece. I love this definition of archetypes taken from the novel *The Seed Collector*: Archetypes are "every possible shape an ego can inhabit" (Thomas 2015, 249). To relate this to our internal parts exercises, archetypes represent the available roles our internal parts can play, and each part has the ability to combine different archetypes into one character. For example, you could have an Angry Intellectual or a Strategizing Mother. The types of archetypal energy we choose to channel and the ways in which we channel it determine the shape of our ego in any given moment, so understanding these energies is extremely important. While there are many, many ways to explore archetypes—magick, therapy/psychology, religion, ritual, meditation, myth, and astrology being just a handful of examples—the next exercise will guide you through a method that connects archetypes to our deepening understanding of projections.

Exercise Fifteen: Internal Activation

Start by entering a meditative state (page 26).

Recall the last time you fell in love or in lust with someone. Really try to put yourself in that space where you couldn't wait to see this person, where your thoughts were consumed by them, where you felt electric and alive in their presence. Give yourself time to really embody this experience. And if you're in this place right now, lucky you! This exercise will be even easier for you.

Identify one quality in the other person that you really, really love about them. If this is someone from your history and that love is now in the past tense, recall back to the honeymoon stage and identify one of the qualities that made you fall for them.

Imagine yourself in a situation when this person exhibited the desirable quality. If it was their sense of humor, imagine being with them as they're making you laugh. If it's their ability to listen, imagine them listening intently to what you're saying.

Staying in the scene, shift your focus internally and take your time as you home in on what, in you, is being activated by the other person's amazing quality. Perhaps their sense of humor activates in you a feeling that life is fun or safe or enjoyable. Perhaps their ability to listen activates in you the feeling that you're interesting or smart or worthy. If you're visual, you can imagine this quality traveling in the form of colored light into your body. See what happens when it enters your energy field. See how you feel. Do any images or memories come to mind? Any thoughts or sounds? Any physical sensations?

When the experience feels complete, return from the meditation and write down your impressions in your journal.

Let's look more closely at what was happening in this exercise. A common way by which we interact with archetypes is projecting them onto other people and events. While there are a host of reasons, my personal experience leads me to believe that one key reason is that it feels safer and more manageable to perceive these qualities as residing "out there." If they're projected onto another person or situation, we don't have to interface with the full energetic potential of these archetypes, including developing the skills, resilience, awareness, and other tools required to embody and express these energies in healthy ways. For example, when we're in the honeymoon stage of a relationship, it's easy to project archetypal images onto the other person and selectively filter out anything that might contradict this ideal. Though these idealized images have very little (and at times, absolutely nothing) to do with who the other person actually is, they have much more to say about who we want to be. Notice that I didn't say who we want the *other* person to be but rather who *we* want to be.

When I met my husband, I wanted to feel safe and secure not merely because this is a pretty standard human desire but because my past was anything but. My internal world felt like a chaotic brew of fear and instability most days, and my external world was a mirror of this internal state. I wanted to find my safe harbor in the storm. I projected that stability and calm onto my husband, who was the rock in the relationship...until he wasn't. My husband, of course, is human. He can't always be stable and calm, nor should he have to be in order for me to feel stable and secure within myself. He's his own person, not a projection of who I want him to be or more to the point, who I want to be but am afraid to own. By projecting the archetypes of Safety and Stability onto my husband, I absolved myself of the responsibility of activating and cultivating those energies within myself. And therein lies the trap of projection: sooner or later, the repository of our projections reveals themselves to be a person in their own right, someone who exists far beyond the bounds of our tidy ideals, and the illusion shatters. Where we become stuck is in assuming that what we're seeing can be entirely explained by the other person's shortcomings. *He's such a jerk. He isn't who I thought he was.* To paraphrase Joseph Campbell, when the honeymoon period ends, we often snatch back our precious projections and go off to find someone else to project them onto. But when we recognize our projections we can then ask ourselves where these qualities are lying dormant within us, yearning to be awakened. In my example, how can I create my own sense of Safety and Security, rather than expecting my husband to activate or "carry" that for me?

When we take back our projections, we are then able to see other people as people in their own right, and while I'm not sure that we can ever get to a state completely free of projections (while we're physical beings leading human lives, at least), my experience is that the more projections we reabsorb and integrate, the more empowered we feel, because we're owning our ability to interact with and channel these powerful archetypes ourselves without an intermediary. We become better able to love others for who they are and not merely for their ability to mirror back the qualities we want to see in ourselves. In the same way, we own the projections that represent less desirable qualities, like Selfishness and Hate, and gradually resolve our unconscious need to keep close at hand people who carry those undesirable traits for us.

A powerful way of working with projections is to use what I call the Button Pusher metaphor. Imagine that you have a giant console of buttons and controls inside your head. If you've seen the movie *Inside Out*, you have a ready-made visual. When we feel something, we are pushing buttons on our internal console. Here's the key—*we* are the ones doing the button pushing. No one else has the ability to climb inside our heads and wrest the console from our control. If a button is getting pushed, you can know with *100 percent certainty* that the finger on the button is yours.

Now, taking back your projections doesn't mean that other people are automatically pure, innocent saints who can do no wrong and you're simply projecting negative qualities onto them. This line of thinking doesn't lead to any more clarity than does projecting all of our experiences onto others. When we take back our projections, we do this in order to see ourselves and other people more clearly and to unravel the tangled threads of blame-shifting. To use Denise's late reports as an example, you might see that Denise is bringing some baggage to the situation and using her lateness to get back at coworkers she resents *while simultaneously* you're bringing a need to do other people's work for them because you assume they won't do it right, along with a subconscious activation of the Martyr archetype. When you call back your projections, you increase your chances of seeing your assumptions, archetypal activations, and what lies beneath them. You can then work with this valuable material and might find yourself less triggered in the future when Denise turns in a report late, or—and this isn't a guarantee, but it can happen—perhaps Denise's baggage is no longer being triggered by your unspoken assumption that she'll do a poor job, and she "miraculously" starts turning in reports on time. Either way, you become clear on what is yours and what belongs to the other person, and you're able to make empowered choices to focus on your internal work over micromanaging other people.

To connect this with Reiki, recall Reiki's ability to reintroduce our original blueprint to our system, reminding us of our True Self. This blueprint is comprised of a unique blend of archetypes we can consider our "archetypal fingerprint." Learning how to connect to and channel these energies is part and parcel with embodying our True Self. The archetypes are universal sources of immense power, available to each of us. The more we explore our personal relationship with these powers, the more we are able to channel them in effective ways. We're able to paint the picture of our life with more brilliant colors, and in doing so, feel whole and integrated. We're no longer scattering these powers around us, projecting them outward and hoping that other people and events will be the way we want them to be in order to maintain our relationships with the archetypes. Instead, we bring these powers within. We cultivate our archetypal relationships from the inside out and reclaim our wholeness in the process.

Our Longing for Archetypes

Archetypes don't simply crop up in our lives by happenstance; they are in our lives because we possess an inherent, deep longing for them. Again, these archetypes are the sum total of the potentiality of any given quality, so, for example, the archetype of the Mother is all the ways we can experience the energy of Mother. It's the nurturing and containing, the creative and life giving. It also includes the shadow aspect of the Mother, such as the ravenous, devouring Mother, like the Earth that we return to after this life comes to an end: the Mother of Death, the symbolic representation of She who is both Womb and Tomb.

The ways in which we experience this archetype depend largely on our past experiences (which I believe encompasses past lives) and the energetic channels created by those experiences. For example, if your human mother was neglectful and resentful of your needs, certain energetic channels become established in your psyche; even science has shown how biological pathways in the brain are formed by repetitive experiences. Thus, the energy of the archetypal Mother gets funneled through these channels and makes it difficult for you to experience this energy as anything other than that of neglect and denial of your needs. In spite of this, we don't simply lose our desire to experience the Mother archetype, so we strike a subconscious bargain: "Neglect and denial of needs is better than not experiencing the Mother at all, so I'll take it." As a result, we find ourselves in situations that replicate the original sensations of neglect and need denial, representing what we believe is our only shot at being able to experience the fuller, richer experience of the Mother, with her more positive attributes: the nurturing and creativity, the safe container and unconditional acceptance, et cetera. We share a universal need for these qualities that is impossible to eradicate from our psyche, so the solution is not in denying that these needs exist; the challenge is to forge new channels through which to experience the Mother and other archetypes. This recalls our discussions of Reiki healings and attunements as powerful means of clearing our energetic "pipes," allowing for a less obstructed flow of energy, including the energies of the archetypes.

I think we choose the family that we are born into (a contentious idea if your relationship to your birth family is challenging), because by experiencing these more limited representations of the full-bodied archetype, the acute sensation that something is missing can lead us to seek the true wholeness that these archetypes represent. This is an apt prelude to our work with recovering and healing inner exiles, because these exiles are often created in response to the very same wounding events that give shape to our narrower view of the archetypes. By healing these exiles (covered later in this chapter), we also reshape our experience of the archetypal forces.

Archetypes and Life Skills

Another layer to our understanding of archetypes is to look at the many ways these archetypes find expression in our lives through different life skills. Let's take the archetype of Love and imagine this archetype as arising from the "soup" of the collective unconscious, the ground substance from which all experience arises. It's a matrix that we are intimately connected to because we are formed from this matrix, hence even though we might lose our conscious memory that this matrix exists as our Source, we subconsciously remember and yearn to experience merging with this matrix once more. Notice the parallels and the Hermetic creation story with the One Mind seeking to return to and merge with the One Thing, the formless chaos from which all forms arise.

This is especially relevant to our work with Submersion, because this is the process of submerging ourselves in the unconscious to return to the matrix, so to speak, so we can remember what union with this Source feels like. The ego is opposed to this union because the ego, by definition, is the part of us that exists in seeming separateness from the matrix. As part of the development of our consciousness, we needed to separate from the matrix, just like the One Mind leapt up out of the One Thing. This sense of separateness allows us to function in ways that we could not conceive of if we were in a state of permanent merger, so while separation is not the enemy, we do need to remember that this state of separateness is but *one* aspect of a larger truth.

Returning to our example archetype of Love, when we were one with the matrix we were also one with the archetype of Love. When we came into this world and began to develop an ego, a sense of separateness, our experience of Love became less direct. Instead of coming straight from the source, Love was mediated through our unique energetic channels, channels that are continually shaped and rerouted according to our life experiences. If we have healthy experiences with the energy of Love, our channels get routed in a particular way; if we have unhealthy experiences of Love, our channels get routed another way.

These energetic channels have a corollary in our behavior. In essence, we behave the way we do because energy is running through our unique channels and activating certain thoughts, reactions, physical sensations, beliefs, and so on that are then translated into the fabric of our lives through our actions and the choices we make. If my Love channel consists of a few twists and turns shaped by a parental connection that left me feeling like I had to earn love and was not innately worthy of receiving it, the archetypal energy of Love gets funneled through that twisty channel into my life, and the chances that I will gravitate toward situations in which I feel I have to prove myself worthy of love increases. If I encounter a situation in which love is freely given without my having "earned" it, I might not recognize it as love because it doesn't match up with my energetic pattern, and/or it might make me so uncomfortable that I end up rejecting it.

We are then brought to the connection between archetypes and life skills. If I want to transform my energetic Love channels, part of that healing process involves learning new skills. The first step is recognizing that the pattern exists, exploring how that energetic channel was shaped, and seeing how it leads to certain thoughts and actions in daily life, which is what our work with Illumination and Submersion addresses. However, simply knowing we have these patterns is not enough to fully release us from their grip. As psychologist Anita Johnston writes:

"Coping with the 'real problems' [and not merely the symptoms] requires skills that you may not have, and resolving them may seem an impossible task…When you embark on a journey to uncover and resolve underlying conflicts and feelings, and don't allow yourself to be fooled by any illusions of what is truly troubling you, you may learn something important about the function of your [addictive pattern]. You may discover how it helps to distract you from the issues in your life that overwhelm you, that you haven't yet learned how to deal with effectively. And you may discover how effectively [the addiction] distracts you, moment to moment, from the fear of facing things head on, from the pain of past hurts" (Johnston 2000, 29).

Another obstacle to learning these skills is the shame of not possessing them in the first place. This shame and belief that we "should" already know how to do these things can prevent us from seeking out the necessary instruction and support. Or we might obtain the instruction but are too ashamed to apply it because like anything else, these skills take practice and we're probably not going to nail it right out of the gate. The fear of failure has us retreating to our tried and true behaviors, even if we're tired of the lackluster or even destructive results.

One of the ways to help alleviate this shame or simply be present with the shame without allowing it to dictate our life choices is to recognize that the life skills we have now made sense at the time we learned them. If we had an emotionally abusive parent, the life skill of shutting down and not letting people in made perfect sense. While it might not serve us now, we didn't develop this skill because we're inherently bad. As a therapist once described it, "we came by it honestly." There's no shame in whatever life skills you currently possess, and you now have the opportunity to expand your skills to include ones that are a better fit for your life today. Chances are that even within the life skills you've outgrown are sub-skills that can be repurposed. For example, the skill of shutting people out can be transformed into the ability to set and maintain healthy boundaries. You're not taking out the trash and starting from square one; you're transforming through radical self-acceptance the skills you already have.

Projections, Protectors, and Exiles

We now return full circle to our initial discussion of internal protectors and the exiles they serve to protect. We learned that one of the ways protectors carry out their role is distracting us from the exile's pain, and projection is a common method of distraction. Throughout the chapter's exercises you illuminated some of the projections active in your life right now, and in the next exercise, it's finally time to make contact with one of your inner exiles. In order to do so, you must first get permission from the exile's protector, and this exercise will walk you through this process. Exiles often carry intense emotions and stores of pain, so before you embark on this exercise, let's talk about ways to stay grounded during the experience.

During Exercise Three: Illuminating Ego Constructs, you practiced remaining in self while interacting with internal characters, and you will do the same here. First, learn how to recognize when you are blending with an internal part. While you are in Self, you will feel some mixture of compassion, curiosity, and openness. If you notice other emotions or attitudes arising, it's likely another part has appeared and you are blending with it to some degree. As the name suggests, blending refers to stepping into the shoes of a part that takes you away from the perspective of Self. For example, if you notice your curiosity is becoming tinged with impatience, an impatient part has entered the stage and you are beginning to identify or blend with this part.

To unblend from a part, ask the part to step aside so you can get to know it. You can visualize yourself standing some distance away to reinforce the unblending. Once you are unblended, you should find yourself once again in a state of Self: curious, compassionate, and/or open. If that's not the case, check for any new parts (perhaps an inner judge or an angry part) and repeat the unblending process. If a part is resistant, ask it what they are concerned will happen if they unblend and address their concerns. For example, if they're afraid you'll leave if they unblend, assure them you will not.

Remember this process as you begin to work with an exile. If you notice yourself starting to take on the emotions of the exile—and they can be intense—pause and follow the unblending process. I also highly recommend using Reiki because it brings you back to yourself, which is where you want to be when interacting with these parts. For example, place your hands over your belly and heart and allow Reiki to flow.

In the following exercise, you will begin the journey of getting to know and heal one of your inner exiles, a process we'll continue in later chapters. Before you begin, go over your journal entry from Exercise Three, and refresh your memory of the Focus Part; this is the protector you will be contacting in this exercise.

Exercise Sixteen: Encountering an Inner Exile

Enter into a meditative state (page 26).

Bring your awareness to the container of your body. Feel how your body contains you, how it provides the space in which you live. Run your awareness over the entire surface of your body from crown to feet on all sides. Say to yourself three times, "My sacred container is healthy and balanced on all levels."

Breathe into your body, feeling the contained space expand to hold more air, then release, noticing the changes in your container as you exhale all of the air out. Repeat for a few breaths.

Bring your awareness to your inner fire. Locate where in your body you feel the fire most intensely, and see your inner campfire burning. If it helps you connect, place your hands over this part of your body while you deepen the image of the sacred campfire in your mind.

See yourself sitting down next to your inner fire. Give yourself time to attune to its energy, breathing as you gaze into the flames, feeling your deep, unbreakable connection to this sacred flame.

Now bring to mind the Focus Part from Exercise Three and invite it to join you near the fire. You might call it by name, visualize it, envision the meditation in which you first met, or use any method that allows you to reconnect with this part. Maintain the image of the fire and you sitting beside it and wait for the Focus Part to appear.

When you feel or see or otherwise sense the presence of this part joining you by the fire, allow it to sit with you for a while. Simply breathe, acknowledge it with a nod and a smile, and maintain your open awareness and curiosity. If needed, unblend from the Focus Part or any new parts that arise and place a hand on your belly and heart, allowing Reiki to bring you back into Self.

When you feel ready, speak with the part and ask it to show you when it first appeared in your life. Allow any images or direct knowing to unfold. If the protector is allowing you access to the exile, you will likely be shown a literal or symbolic scene from your life in which you will meet the exile, or the exile part will simply appear. If this doesn't happen, check back in with the protector by the fire. Ask its permission in seeing when it first appeared in your life. If it has concerns or objections, address those concerns from the Self. For example, if it's afraid that the pain of these memories will be too much for you to handle, assure it that you will stay in Self; you aren't seeking to flood yourself with this pain, you want to witness it from the grounded place of Self. If the protector still will not give you access, don't force the process. This could be a sign that you have slipped out of Self and are now blended with, say, a judgmental part, and the protector senses this. In this case, ask the judgmental part to separate from you, and allow Reiki to help you recenter in Self before trying again. Alternatively, you may need to focus on building a deeper relationship with the protector before it trusts you enough to allow access to the exile. In this case, continue asking questions to get to know the protector, such as, "What do you need me to know about you?" and "Is there anything that you need from me?"

If you are granted access to the exile, get to know it, just as you did the protector. Ask it what it wants you to know about it. Ask it to tell you its story. Ask what it needs from you. Check in as needed to see if you are blending with the exile, then follow the steps for unblending, and place your hands on your belly and heart to allow the flow of Reiki to assist you in returning to Self.

When this process feels complete, invite the protector, exile, and any other parts that appeared to stay by the inner campfire. Tell them you will be back to see them again soon and thank them for being here and sharing their experience. Say your goodbyes and prepare to come out of the meditation. Gradually let the image of the campfire fade until the screen of your mind is empty.

Return yourself to a normal state of consciousness (pages 25–26).

Journal about your experience, and if you met an exile or any other new parts, write down as many details about each part that you can remember. Imagine you are creating an internal directory of these parts, making it easier to contact them in future sessions.

In this chapter, you made contact with the waters of the unconscious, bringing the healing power of awareness to previously hidden aspects of yourself, parts that may have been trapped at earlier stages of development. This is powerful stuff, and by bringing Reiki into the process, you have invited the Divine to guide you, infusing this work with infinite healing potential. In the next chapter, you'll move on to the third step of self-transformation, Polarizing, which is designed to supercharge your internal battery.

—6—
POLARIZATION

The next self-transformation step is Polarization. Here, we deepen our awareness of the internal polarity that serves as our creative engine. Like the two poles of a battery, we contain the duality of active energy and receptive energy, and their interaction generates the battery's charge, giving rise to our creative powers, just as the One Mind (active) interacted with the One Thing (receptive) to create the world. You can think of these principles we're about to learn as operating instructions. If you were given a machine, it would be of limited usefulness unless you knew what it was for and how it worked. Similarly, we are all given this internal polarity but if we don't understand how it works (or are unaware of its existence), we'll have a much harder time utilizing our full potential.

A Hermetic text called *The Kybalion* describes the Principle of Polarity as "Everything is dual; everything has poles; everything has its pair of opposites" (Anonymous 2017, 18). All experience exists on a spectrum that ranges between opposites: love/hate, hot/cold, high/low, and so forth. The power lies in understanding how to work with this spectrum more consciously rather than denying the existence (and power) of a side that we're less comfortable with. Returning to the metaphor of the battery, each of these opposites is required in order to create the battery. If we try to eliminate one, we decouple the battery and it no longer produces a charge, and in practice, one of the most common ways we decouple our battery is by projecting one pole onto others. For example, if we can't own our anger, we project it "out there" and see an angry world, and in doing so, we weaken our internal charge. Now, to be clear, this doesn't mean that our charge comes merely from allowing ourselves to be full of and acting from a place of anger. It means that instead of denying when we are angry, we allow our emotions to arise, creating space for them to simply be without getting overly caught up in the ego's narratives about why we're angry, why we have a right to be angry, and on and on. We let the stories float by, returning our focus to our sacred container, the space in which the emotional energy is flowing, and we trust that the intensity will pass, knowing that we are improving our health on many levels by allowing our emotions to exist. In doing so, we have an opportunity to witness and feel our internal polarity. We can feel the energy flaring at one pole—anger—and naturally finding its way to a place of balance, perhaps settling at calm or acceptance. We might still feel anger, but our energy has shifted from the intensity of one extreme to a more blended position on the spectrum.

We'll focus here on active and receptive energies because these two forces are the ingredients necessary for creating everything in your life from your physical and financial health, to your relationships, moods, job, and so on. Learning how to work with these energies is one of the most powerful life tools I have found, and my experience has led me to identify five active powers and five receptive powers I collectively call the ten Divine powers.

The Ten Divine Powers

The five receptive powers:

1. Gestational sleep
2. Receptive listening
3. Spiritual synthesis
4. Selfless support
5. Labor of love

The five active powers:

6. Restorative sleep
7. Courageous championing
8. Self-sovereignty
9. Conscious clearing
10. Purposeful procurement

Gestational sleep is the ability to move inward and allow yourself to truly rest, both in the form of physical sleep but also mental, emotional, and spiritual rest. In this state of quiet enfoldment you are able to gestate your creations—the seeds of what will eventually sprout and bear fruit in your life. Without gestational sleep, your creative capacity is short-circuited; you might feel devoid of ideas or describe yourself as not very creative, while in truth, we all are divinely creative beings. You might feel stuck and unable to envision new possibilities, or the mere thought of pursuing those possibilities exhausts or overwhelms you before you even begin.

Receptive listening is being able to listen in conversation as well as a deeper listening that comes in many forms such as listening to your body and your higher wisdom, to the Divine perhaps in the form of communicating with guides, and being open to new ideas and lessons. When we are unable to tap into our receptivity, we block change, growth, and blessings from entering our life. If you hear yourself repeating the same stories again and again or thinking the same thoughts on repeat, this is a clue that your internal state is one of recycling. Not a lot of new energy is coming in, so you're continually churning around the same old, same old in a relatively closed system. Additionally, if you feel like everything rests on your shoulders or others can't be trusted to do things right, this is a signal that your receptive abilities need to be activated.

Spiritual synthesis is the ability to see common threads running throughout your life and all existence. Synchronicity is a form of communication with the Universe, and the power of spiritual synthesis allows you to tap into this conversation and access a wisdom far beyond the confines of your individual mind. It also helps you take this information and integrate it in daily living, which is how true wisdom is cultivated. If we were to ground this power specifically in the area of physical wellness, for example, spiritual synthesis can help you sift through the overwhelming barrage of conflicting health information in order to create a holistic wellness plan that works for your unique body. We can take this synthesis a step further by integrating not only your physical efforts but also your spiritual practice and emotional and mental health into your wellness plan.

Selfless support came to me intuitively as the archetypal relationship of Mother and Child. The Mother is fully engaged in supporting the Child, rather than competing with the Child out of a fear that the Child's success will upstage the Mother. The paradox is that this divine selfless support arises from the deep knowing that we are all One, so when the Mother is supporting the Child, she is simultaneously supporting herself. This power expresses itself not only in our relationships with others but also in how we relate to and care for ourselves. When mastered, this power heals dysfunctional expressions of this energy: codependency, a martyr complex, and narcissism in some of its forms.

The phrase "labor of love" refers to the creation of something from a place of pure love. It's easy to grasp when we look at ways to birth something that are *not* arising from this place of love. Someone might want to have a child because their intimate relationship isn't satisfying and they're hoping a child will fulfill their unmet needs. Or perhaps someone creates a business solely because they want to make money (not that making money is unhealthy, but a creation that arises solely from a place of need rather than love will be imbued with different qualities). In contrast, a labor of love is birthed because the creator simply cannot help it; the creation is bursting forth spontaneously as a result of love. You might think of an artist who can't help but paint; they have ideas within them that simply must come out.

Let's shift now to the five active powers, and then we'll discuss where the real magic happens: in the interaction between the two.

The first active power is restorative sleep. If the active energy is perpetually on the go, it will become depleted. It needs time to rest and recharge, and as we'll talk about shortly, connect with the wellspring of receptive energy, its source of inspiration and nourishment. Without this connection and nourishing fallow period, the active fizzles out. If you find it easier to start projects than to finish them or have a lot of enthusiasm that doesn't seem to lead to productive action, you might be in need of restorative sleep. As with the receptive form, this refers as much to the physical act of sleeping as it does to emotional, mental, and spiritual times of rest.

Courageous championing is the power of living in the world and asserting the value of your gifts, which are a product of your receptive and active energies working together. Recall in chapter 3, Joseph Campbell's assertion that the journey of retrieving treasures from our depths is merely part of the challenge; often the most difficult step lies in bringing those treasures back into the world and having the courage to share those gifts with others. For example, if you create a business but the energy of courageous championing is not activated, you might undercharge for your services or fail to do any marketing. The end result is that your creation—the business—falters or fails because it is not being championed and its value goes unrecognized.

Self-sovereignty is the inner seat of true power. When this energy is dysfunctional, it seeks to attain a sense of rulership by domination of self and others. When healthy, it no longer needs to go around dominating everything in sight because it rests in the assuredness of its own inner power, which cannot be taken away by any external force. If this power lies untapped within you, it might manifest as being very controlling of yourself (strict diets, punishing habits and self-talk) and controlling of others. It might seem paradoxical, but this controlling behavior is usually paired with equally out-of-control behavior—for example, adhering to a rigidly strict diet interspersed with bouts of binge eating. Again, this is a result of being disconnected from true inner power (feeling out of control) and the backlash that follows (attempting to regain control by being overly rigid).

Conscious clearing is the power of removing obstructions, of clearing the path so that the outpouring of your creative energy isn't blocked or impeded. If you have good ideas, but seemingly insurmountable obstacles routinely appear, this is often a sign that the channel is blocked. Here's an example of this in action: An acquaintance was explaining a business idea, and while it was clear that they had a lot of passion and weren't lacking in energy or motivation, their description was so convoluted I could barely figure out what, exactly, the business would be offering! I see this as an idea traveling through clogged pipes, backtracking this way and that as it tries to find a clear route, leaving one in a state of confusion and stuckness.

Purposeful procurement is the act of engaging with the world, identifying and procuring what you need in order to fulfill your soul's purpose. Our active energies are wired to seek out and merge with their complement, our receptive energies, but when the bridge between the two is damaged, the active energy's seeking can become obsessive.

What it seeks takes on the form of a mirage, always just out of reach, and the dysfunctional active energy spends its life trying to close the gap by seeking more stuff, more relationships, more events on the social calendar, and so on, while never actually merging with the receptive energy it desires. When the power of purposeful procurement is activated, however, we are able to move through the world seeking and finding what we need to further our evolution rather than mindlessly amassing more and more stuff that simply clutters up our channels and blocks us from true satisfaction.

Now that we have a basic grasp of the ten divine powers, let's talk about the importance of the dialogue between the two: the divine marriage. We can look at this interaction in various forms: one way to envision it is to imagine the active energy protecting and supporting the receptive so that the receptive energy can focus on what it does best. In turn, the receptive nourishes and supports the active so it can focus on doing what it does best, and around and around the cycle goes. For example, the active energy engages with the world, performing its outward-projecting functions (recall the thought rays of the One Mind traveling outward), freeing the receptive energy so it can turn inward and do deep, creative work (the One Thing gestating and creating the world). Here's an example of what can happen if this dialogue between receptive and active is thwarted: Let's say the active energy isn't "pulling its weight" (which can happen when this energy isn't well developed within us and/or when we're projecting these energies instead of owning them), so the receptive energy has to work overtime and perform both receptive *and* active duty. When receptive energy tries to fulfill an active role, this action assumes less functional forms because this isn't the receptive's strong suit. If we're asking our receptive energy to carry out the active power of purposeful procurement, the receptive will move outward and try to procure what we need but in a manner that has a distinctively receptive flavor to it: that of nurturing and giving. In practice, this might manifest as the receptive striking a bargain to nourish and give in exchange for getting what it needs.

In contrast, active energy goes out, identifies the necessary ingredients for the soul's path, and procures them without apology. Take a squirrel hunting for acorns to satisfy its hunger and stay alive. When it finds one, it doesn't feel guilty (as far as we know) about taking the acorn; it just takes it. After eating the acorn, the squirrel will eventually give back to the ecosystem in the form of fertilizing squirrel poo. When the squirrel is in active-energy mode gathering acorns, it isn't worried about when it's going to "pay back" the tree for eating the acorn. The active and receptive energies are in communication, and the squirrel knows that one will naturally follow the other—no bargaining or apologizing needed.

How does this energetic power use look in human terms? One way this behavior manifests is through codependency. A person needs and wants certain things but for various reasons may not know how to go about getting needs met in a healthy manner, so instead they do things for other people with the subconscious expectation that the other person will reciprocate. In simpler terms, let's say Mark wants to feel appreciated but he either doesn't know this about himself or isn't comfortable expressing this need. Instead, he lavishes appreciation on his boyfriend, Alex, subconsciously (or consciously) hoping that Alex will return the favor. If Alex doesn't pick up on Mark's unexpressed needs, Mark will feel unappreciated and resentful: the markings of a codependent relationship. Contrast this to Mark clearly expressing his needs (his active energy courageously championing for his receptive need) and Alex gladly reciprocates because he is no longer expected to read his boyfriend's mind. Mark's receptive energy is then able to receive this appreciation, and together they can build the foundation for a healthier, more nurturing relationship.

Another example: Let's say the active is disconnected from the receptive, thus it feels separated from the infinite wellspring of creative potential and nourishment that the receptive represents and instead exists in a state of fear that it's not enough. It responds with the very active tools at its disposal: by going out into the world and aggressively attempting to obtain these wellsprings for itself, essentially seeking to own these sources of nourishment and "enoughness." This manifests as trying to exert power *over* instead of developing power *within*. In practical terms, we see this in the devastating trauma of rape, both of people and of the Earth, and in war and tyranny. This is not true sovereignty; this is a controlling force that is attempting to recreate the lost feelings of empowerment and connection by exerting dysfunctional power over others. The cycle continues when the active, now so cut off from the capacity of the receptive that it no longer trusts in these powers, starts to devalue receptivity, equating it with weakness. When the active no longer values or trusts in the immense power of the receptive, it seeks to suppress receptive energies and obtain "power" through the harmful means mentioned above.

On the flipside, the receptive in this scenario no longer trusts or feels protected by the active, and so the receptive feels that it too has to fulfill both energetic roles on its own, leaving the receptive depleted and unable to create to its full potential. This could manifest as working long hours and fighting for a promotion from a place of fear that there will never be enough (i.e., the receptive is unable to count on the active for support), such that there is little if any time for self-care. This person's receptive energy starts to wither and dry up, and because the receptive is a source of nourishment for the active, their actions are unsustainable and eventually lead to burnout and collapse. To postpone the inevitable collapse, they might seek shadow forms of "nourishment," such as coffee, sugar, recreational or prescription drugs, unhealthy relationships, or excessive TV watching or Facebook checking, none of which leave them feeling truly replenished.

It is not enough to have well-functioning receptive energy and well-functioning active energy in isolation; they must exist in productive dialogue. A simple exercise illustrates this well: Walk in a straight line, allowing your arms to swing freely at your sides. As you move, notice that when your right leg steps forward, this movement is paired by your left arm swinging forward. Now try disrupting this pattern by moving both your right leg and right arm forward at the same time, followed by the left leg and left arm moving forward. No doubt you feel (and look) like a toy soldier, mechanically jolting forward with each awkward step. This walk wouldn't be made any less awkward by increasing the strength of your arms and legs; you need the opposition of right and left to bring fluidity and ease to your forward movement, and your energy is much the same. In order to tap into your full power, the active and receptive energies must be in healthy dialogue, partnered together in the divine marriage. When this communion takes place, you are able to birth a life of purpose and passion in a way that is sustainable and satisfying, not draining and depleting. You are able to move forward in life with fluidity and grace.

Working with the Divine Powers

We're going to work with each of the ten powers through meditation and daily life practices. As with the Reiki techniques in chapter 3, the idea is to really pay attention to what you *feel* as you do the exercises, because you're learning what these energies feel like for you. This is more important than simply going through the motions and doing it "right," although again, there's nothing wrong with going through the motions with intention until the feelings kick in.

Many of the following exercises ask that you establish a flow of Reiki through your crown chakra and into your tanden as described here. Refer to these instructions when indicated in future exercises.

Establishing a Flow of Reiki

Bring your awareness to your lower belly, to your tanden, and begin to breathe in through your nose with the tip of your tongue lightly touching the roof of your mouth. Exhale through your mouth, letting your tongue release.

Continue this pattern for a few more rounds, then with each inhale, start to bring Reiki down through your crown and into your tanden. On the exhale, maintain the Reiki in your tanden, letting it swirl and build in this lower belly energy center.

Continue with the rest of the exercise.

Gestational Sleep

The metaphor of the seed or egg is really useful, because gestational sleep is carried out with the intention of paving the way for future growth and expansion. Our creations need time and space to gestate, time to stew and brew as they develop into their full expression, like a seed that needs time and space to sprout. Just as you wouldn't be angry at a seed if it didn't sprout immediately, acknowledging that our own creations need time allows us to be patient when on the surface, nothing much seems to be happening. A powerful way to deepen your connection to gestational sleep is to recognize that you possess the power of creation. This is not a power that resides somewhere called "out there" you must somehow earn or obtain. What is necessary is embracing this innate power and nurturing it. When we're convinced that what we're seeking is external, we remain blind to the potent creative capabilities within lying dormant. To open a connection to the energy of gestational sleep, let's do a simple meditation.

Exercise Seventeen: The Golden Egg

If you like, burn an earthy incense like patchouli for this meditation.

Bring yourself into a meditative state (page 26).

Establish a flow of Reiki (page 125).

Visualize this energy coalescing into the shape of a golden egg in your tanden. Take your time, and once you have conjured this image, hold it in your mind as you breathe naturally. If the image falters, simply bring the golden egg back into focus.

Say to yourself three times, "I fully activate my creative powers in a way that is correct and good for me." Continue to breathe and focus on the golden egg.

Say three times, "I attune myself with the power of gestational sleep."

Let any sensations or feelings arise in your body, mind, and soul as you simply sit and breathe for a few more rounds.

When the experience feels complete, release the image of the golden egg. If you're feeling lightheaded or spacey, bring your awareness to your crown chakra and set the intention to return to a normal, balanced state for you. If needed, visualize any excess energy flowing into the earth through the base of your spine or the bottoms of your feet, leaving you energized but without any jitters from an overabundance of energy.

Bring yourself out of the meditative state (pages 26–27).

Give yourself time to journal about the experience, in particular making note of any sensations that will help you get a feel for the energetic qualities of gestational sleep. Was there an energetic weightiness or a sense of turning inward? Did you feel more rooted to the earth? Did your internal landscape feel darker, quieter, or lush? Begin to learn what this power feels like so you can more easily cultivate it when needed and recognize it when you are experiencing it.

For your daily life practices, focus on the quality of your sleep, particularly your ability to carve out time for needed rest. Are you staying up too late watching Netflix or scrolling through your Facebook feed? Are you over scheduling yourself socially? Are you trying to fit in early morning workouts when what your body really craves is more rest? In order to tap into and sustain our creative capabilities, we must be fiercely protective like a mama bear of our down time. If you have social plans every single day this week, next week carve out *at least* one day for yourself. If we are constantly surrounded by other people, it's hard to connect to the dark stillness within, our fertile inner ground in which to plant our creative seeds, so it's important to consciously carve out solitude, particularly if the power of gestational sleep feels out of balance within us.

This brings us to another important quality of gestational sleep: silence. When we are in constant communication with external forces, be it in the form of media, friends and family, or other stimuli such as shopping or being stuck in traffic, we can lose focus on what matters to us and only us, those personal desires cradled in the seat of our soul. And when we lose touch with these deeply personal desires, we feel aimless and more easily swept into other people's ideas of what it means to find success. In this disconnected state of being, it's all too easy to get caught up in seeking approval and external validation because we aren't connected to our own metrics of happiness and well-being; we're locked into achieving external awards, honors, and pats on the back to feel like we're on the right track. In gestational silence, we reconnect with our soul truth and learn how to cultivate the fertile soil for this truth to take root and blossom in our lives.

Gestational sleep, like all of the divine powers, is far vaster in scope and more multidimensional than we could possibly tackle in the allotted space, but here are some additional ways to explore this power in your life.

- Practice allowing energies to build before releasing them whether in the form of money in a savings account, creative ideas prior to manifestation, or emotions before choosing a mindful course of action. Cultivate a gestational pause of silence and see how this transforms the events that follow.

- Play with the power of silence in situations where your inclination is to talk. For example, if you're excited about a new project you're working on, spend a few days simply enjoying the excitement and containing that energy before releasing it in the form of talking. On the flipside, if you're feeling frustrated and have the urge to gossip or complain, try sitting with the thoughts and emotions for twenty-four hours and seeing how they transform before deciding whether or not to speak.

• If you find yourself worrying about something, write it down on a slip of paper to get out any thoughts and concerns you might have. Put the slip of paper in a box with a lid. Place the box somewhere dark (not under your bed), such as a closet, wrapped in a blanket, or buried shallowly in the ground and say, "I call on the power of gestational sleep to transform this situation." Wait three days, during which time do your best to release any worries or thoughts that arise; remind yourself of the box and know that your concerns are securely held and are gestating, "solving" the problem for you. At the end of three days, open the box and take note of how you feel about the situation. You can then burn the paper and bury the ashes in the earth.

Receptive Listening

There are many forms of listening and receptive listening, in particular, asks us to remain truly open, to remain receptive. We often bring our preconceived ideas with us in conversation with another, in our internal dialogue, or in the ways we look at and process our experiences of the world. When we become more aware of these preconceived notions (something our work with projections helps us do), we can consciously set them aside even if just for the span of a conversation and adopt a mental, physical, and spiritual posture of openness. In this space, we learn. We grow. We change. We aren't simply recycling the same thoughts and ideas; we're actively receiving new ways of being in the world.

As healers, this ability is especially important because each client is unique; if we simply overlay our previous ideas onto a client's experience, we are limiting our ability to see an individual for who they truly are. Many of us move through life having relatively few experiences in which another person is truly listening, genuinely focused on witnessing our authentic expression without judging, waiting for their turn to speak, or evaluating our expression to determine whether or not they agree. To provide a space where your clients can feel deeply seen and heard is in and of itself the very stuff of healing. Providing this sacred space is the single most transformative technique, more than any other energy work or fancy bells and whistles. Treat people like a book containing fascinating secrets and deep wisdom that require patience and receptivity to reveal. In this space, their soul will feel safe enough to converse, and that's when you know you're really getting somewhere not distracted by small talk or symptoms and you're making contact with the heart of how they need and want to heal.

To help ourselves and others reconnect with wholeness, we must remain open to the immense variety of possible expressions of that wholeness, even when they seem contradictory in nature. As Hugh Milne writes, "Go beyond the analytic mind. Go for what is present, not what you would prefer to be there. Incorporate the complexities of contradictory truths into your being. Only then will you be present in all of your quiet energetic splendor" (Milne 1998, 135). The more you are able to cultivate this presence within yourself and bear compassionate witness to those numerous complexities of contradictory truths within yourself, the more you will be able to provide this space for others.

Another aspect of receptive listening is being aware that we take in information from a variety of sources, a fact that becomes clear when we expand our notion of information as strictly the currency of rational, linear thinking. Functional medicine doctor Mark Hyman encourages us to think of food as information. When you eat a piece of kale, what information are you sending to your genes, to your endocrine system, to your brain? What about when you eat a Twinkie? Energy worker Cyndi Dale writes that "energy is information that vibrates," and when we expand our definition of information, we see that there are many forms of receptive listening. We can listen with our hands while giving Reiki (Dale 2009, 18). We can listen with our third eye when we're tuning into intuitive guidance. We can listen with our heart rate and notice when it's racing due to stress and use our breath to bring our heartbeat into a gentler rhythm.

One concept in nature I find particularly interesting is mycorrhizal associations, which are partnerships of vast networks of fungus in the soil and plant roots through which plants can communicate with each other. The phenomenon has been dubbed the "wood wide web" by some scientists, and according to the BBC, "by linking to the fungal network [plants] can help out their neighbours by sharing nutrients and information—or sabotage unwelcome plants by spreading toxic chemicals through the network"(BBC Earth, 2017). The image of a network of roots and fungi communicating across vast distances, provides the foundation for our next exercise in receptive listening.

Exercise Eighteen: Listening Through the Roots

Bring yourself into a meditative state (page 26).

Establish a flow of Reiki (page 125).

Focus on the base of your spine, and imagine roots extending from this base, deep into the earth. Allow the image to expand: a single root branches into many. Appreciate the complexity of your roots, the vastness of the network tethering you to and making you one with the Earth.

Allow the stream of Reiki entering your crown and gathering in your tanden to travel out through your network of roots, absorbing into the Earth. Allow the Reiki to continue to flow but release your focus on it. Set the intention to receive via your roots the information that is correct and good for you at this time, then allow the experience to unfold.

Maintain gentle awareness of the root network and allow any thoughts and sensations to arise. You might see images, hear words, notice thoughts pop into your head, and so forth. Allow the information to flow into you.

When the experience feels complete, give thanks as feels appropriate to you, and gently allow the stream of Reiki to taper off. Envision your roots reabsorbing into your body, and bring your awareness fully back to your center, your tanden.

Return to a normal state of consciousness (pages 26–27).

For your daily practice with receptive listening, experiment with this power both in conversation with others and within yourself. In conversations, really practice the art of giving another human being your full attention. Sometimes we become distracted from this practice because we're worried we won't have anything to say once the other person is done talking. In my experience, this is rarely the case because when we're practicing receptive listening, we're taking in so much information that there's actually an abundance of things to respond to, things that we might have overlooked when we were busy trying to think of something to say. If there is a pause, it's a powerful thing to be able to enjoy moments of silence with another person without frantically trying to fill them with something, *anything*. And yes, I know how uncomfortable this can feel at first. In many cultures, people are socially conditioned to view these pauses as awkward, but like all of our practices, it simply takes time to adjust to a new way of relating to the world, one that does not involve attacking every single moment of silence with a verbal hatchet. Use these moments as an opportunity to sit with the feelings that arise, possibly with a relaxed, open smile on your face that alerts your conversation companion that all is well and there's no need to panic.

This daily practice of receptive listening can be done internally by allowing for silence and pauses in your mental chatter. I find the breath helpful in cultivating these pauses, focusing my attention on the inhales and exhales and letting everything else drop away, even for just a few breath cycles, perhaps while waiting for tea to steep or sitting in traffic. In those moments of silence, set the intention to listen receptively and be open to receiving information through myriad ways: physical sensations, thoughts and memories, desires, images, the refrain from a song you haven't heard in a while, a bird landing on the windowsill, et cetera. The universe is in constant communication with you, and receptive listening is a powerful way to interact with this web of synchronicity. The web is here to guide you in step with your soul, and the more we stay present with open eyes and an open heart, the more we become aware of what is *actually* occurring, over our ego's interpretations, and from this vantage point we are led to wiser choices in matters big and small.

Additional ways to work with the power of receptive listening:

- The next time you are faced with a decision, give yourself some time to tune into your bodily sensations. Resist the urge to use your mind to analyze the situation. Focus instead on how you feel in your body. When you bring the decision to mind, do you feel a sense of expansion or constriction in your body? Does your sense of temperature change? Do you notice a ringing in your ears or the first twinge of a headache? Do you get excited butterflies in your stomach? Based solely on bodily sensations, what option feels best?

- For the next hour, pay attention to your thoughts without judgment, resisting the urge to get engaged by agreeing, disagreeing, or otherwise latching onto them. Just notice what they are. Really listen to your internal dialogue. Would you say these things to someone you love? If not, what sorts of things would you like to hear instead?

- Experience being in a safe space blindfolded for a short period of time. What do you notice when you can't rely on sight?

Spiritual Synthesis

I find that one of the more challenging aspects of spiritual practice is surrendering to divine flow without knowing where the flow goes beyond, perhaps, the next one or two steps. As a recovering control addict, I like to have everything mapped out, but living a soul-led life is an entirely different animal. This doesn't mean I can't plan at all, but I am more keenly aware of the limitations of those plans. Plans are a nice starting point, but rarely do things unfold precisely according to them, and if I attempt to force events I generate more stress for myself (and others) while limiting the abundance I can experience.

We talked earlier about using synchronicity as a guide like lights on the riverbanks of divine flow that ensure we stay in tune with the river. With spiritual synthesis, we interpret daily experiences through the lens of synchronicity using the details of our life as lights guiding our way. Using receptive listening, we learn how to engage in constant dialogue with the universe, paying attention to a bird that swoops over our path while we're out for a hike or an insect crawling on our windshield as we load groceries into the car. We make note of something a friend says that really strikes a chord or the lyrics to a song that stick with us all afternoon. We listen to our dreams, our inner voice, our bodies' signals. And through spiritual synthesis we begin to see the common threads and weave them into a life of magic. That cardinal reminds us of our dream last night in which we were caught in a house, ablaze with bright red flames. At lunch, we tune into a twinge of heartburn that again reminds us of fire, and we feel inspired to look at natural ways to heal heartburn by adjusting what we eat. And that night in meditation we receive intuitive urging to look at the emotional and symbolic meaning of "heart burn." What pain are we harboring in our heart that is yearning to be honored and transformed? How does it relate to our dream of the burning house?

This is the art of spiritual synthesis: seeing the common threads in our dialogue with the universe and using those threads to guide us on our path, one step at a time. Using the above example, rarely will we get one giant chunk of information that maps out everything we need to do to heal our physical and emotional heartburn. We will, however, get bite-sized chunks of information that we can use right now. When we use them, we are then given more. We get stuck when we postpone taking action until we know the entire plan and refuse to engage with step one because we don't know what step ten will be. This is a habit we must learn to break because it will have us waiting a very long time, indeed. Life is more like a divine scavenger hunt, each clue leading to the next, and we'll never move past clue one if we're not willing to engage with the mystery. And not to be morbid, but if we truly require an answer to what the end holds in terms of this physical lifetime, we already know: death. We're all heading in that direction, so we might as well make the steps in between as memorable and rich as possible.

Exercise Nineteen: Divine Scavenger Hunt

For a full day, you will undertake a divine scavenger hunt. The night before, choose a question on which you wish to receive guidance. A couple of guidelines: be specific and avoid simple yes/no questions. The clearer your question is, the clearer the guidance. Replace this: "I don't know if I should take the job downtown or if the one out in the suburbs will be better for me. I hate getting stuck in traffic, and I guess downtown traffic will be worse that time of day, but…" with this: "Which job is most in line with my soul's calling: the downtown position, the suburb position, or another option that I'm not aware of yet?" You'll often receive information with greater depth when you're not expecting a simple "yes, do this" or "no, don't do that." Remember that as Life Alchemy Reiki practitioners, we are consciously choosing to co-create our lives with the divine; we're not simply looking for top-down orders to blindly follow. We want information that will challenge us to grow, change, and deepen our wisdom on multiple levels—a tall order for a simple yes/no question to fill.

Once you have your question, write it down. Read your question aloud or to yourself with intention first thing in the morning. Follow it with, "Today, I am open to receiving guidance in response to my question in ways I am able to understand. Thank you!" It can be easy to lose sight of the hunt as the events of the day distract us, so let's establish some helpful structure to keep us engaged.

Bring your journal so you can record any guidance you receive.

Every time something resonates with you (in a positive or negative way; either lighting you up or triggering you), make a note of it, such as a quote that grabs you, a bird that catches your eye, a comment from a co-worker that irks you, and so on. If it resonates, treat it as a clue on your scavenger hunt.

Throughout the day, every time you change locations (moving from the office to a restaurant for lunch, from your desk to the restroom, and so on), mentally recap your time at the location you're vacating and make a note of at least one thing that resonated with you.

If more than two hours go by without a location change, set an alarm on your phone and carry out the same process: mentally recap the last two hours and make a note of at least one clue.

This structure should provide enough reinforcement to keep you engaged with the process even amid your busy day. This training is important, because how often do we get to escape to a serene mountaintop or monastery to do this work? If you're like me, not very, so we must train in receiving guidance in the lives we are actually leading, instead of waiting for our future fantasy monkhood in which to feel connected with divine wisdom. With practice, you won't need this kind of structure; you'll naturally make note of clues no matter where you are or what you're doing. Building this habit now is a great way to exercise the power of spiritual synthesis.

At the end of the day, give yourself time to look over your clues. Do you see any themes, even if you can't fully explain them through logic and language? Do any intuitive knowings arise, possibly in the form of thoughts, memories, bodily sensations, or emotions? Step away from the clues for ten minutes, then return and ask your question again. If you make the assumption that these clues somehow add up to a response like a divine word jumble, what might that response be? You can also look up some of your clues in books or online. Perhaps you saw a cardinal on your way to work, and when you look up cardinal in the field guide the phrase that resonates with you is "accomplished songster." As you muse on the words, you're reminded of your desire to take voice lessons. Just for fun you decide to look up local voice teachers, and lo and behold, there's a teacher two blocks from the downtown job. The thought of taking voice lessons two nights a week after work fills you with excitement, and this leads you to see other aspects of the downtown job that feel like a good fit right now.

Engage with the clues. Meditate on them. Ask for clarification if you're not sure what they mean. But most of all, practice receptive listening. Quite often, we're receiving guidance, but we're so worried the guidance isn't coming that we drown it out with fear-based mental chatter and the tendency to over-analyze. Make the assumption, even just for this exercise, that the guidance is flowing. Don't panic if you can't hear or see it quite yet; use this opportunity to practice receptive listening and trust that it will come. "Waiting involves 'simply' being present, attentive, and mindful…It is as if you consciously create a vacuum [within yourself], which nature will therefore fill. There are some laws of physics we do not know about, and there are some laws of grace that are seldom experienced" (Milne 1998, 138).

Other ways to engage with the power of spiritual synthesis:

- Meditate or journal on this passage: "We may feel fearful and deny or hide ourselves from the challenges of the unknown that lie ahead. Into this new 'unknown' we project our fears of what is worse than familiar discomforts. Indeed many of the fears, guilts, thoughts, and conclusions we hold are defenses against not knowing. Thus the ability to tolerate not knowing is a sign of psychic strength. It attests to the development of basic trust in the [Source] and its meaningful processes. Such trust enables transformation" (Perera 2001, 269).

- Begin to blend your spiritual practice into more aspects of daily living. Perhaps devote your exercise session today to a spiritual being or deity and use this time to open to their love and guidance. While cooking, focus on qualities like love or an openness to change, imagining them entering the food as you stir or sprinkle just like physical ingredients. What are other ways you can coax out the magic hidden in the mundane?

Selfless Support

To tap into the power of selfless support, we are going to focus on seeing and feeling the connection between taking care of yourself and being of service to others. As healers, it's far too easy to put self-care *after* the care of others but this simply isn't sustainable, nor are we able to bring our best to our healing work when we do this. Remember, we cannot give to others what we are unwilling to give to ourselves, so if you push yourself with the whip of an inner tyrant, this energy is affecting your interactions with others, even if you consciously strive to be gentle and accepting of their struggles. The easiest way to ensure we're not unloading our own psychic baggage onto others is to take care of ourselves.

Like all divine powers, selfless support has a shadow side: codependency and a martyr complex. When our natural desire and ability to care for ourselves is stunted, we don't lose our need for self-care; instead we try to achieve it through less direct means, like codependently supporting others in the hope that they will return the favor or playing the martyr or victim with the desire that someone will take care of us in the ways we aren't caring for ourselves. There are many reasons we do this that typically reach back to childhood. If our primary caregivers were unable or unwilling to give us adequate care rather than assume it was because they were lacking as caregivers (to a child, this notion is terrifying) we think there must be something wrong with us, making

us undeserving of care. Trauma and abuse also thwart healthy channels of self-care in profound ways. And as women living in a culture
that idealizes the selfless mother and wife, most of us have internalized
to some degree the damaging message that we are selfish if we don't
put everyone else's needs ahead of our own. In addition, in the West
it's hard to completely escape the messages of spiritual suffering and
martyrdom that Christianity holds in high esteem. Even our secular
culture is steeped in the energy of heroes who sacrifice everything for
noble causes, and to buck this trend can make us subconsciously feel
like we're choosing the path of a degenerate narcissist. Needless to say,
there are many reasons self-care can be a challenge, but in order to be
effective healers and happy human beings, it is vital to care for ourselves
with love and compassion.

Another dimension to selfless support is the belief that we are all
one. If you subscribe to this belief, you cannot create positive change
in the world if you are treating yourself like crap. The way you treat
yourself is the way you treat others and the world around you (particularly on a subconscious level), so let's do a meditation to activate
selfless support.

Exercise Twenty: Love Expansion

Bring yourself into a meditative state (page 26).

Establish a flow of Reiki (page 125).

Continue to build Reiki energy at your tanden, bringing in
more on each inhale, and with each exhale see the glowing ball
of Reiki at your tanden expand, gradually filling your entire body.

Continue as you expand the Reiki out to the edges of your
aura. Take a few moments to notice what it feels like to vibrate
so fully with Reiki. Know that you are engaging in an act of
profound self-care. Reiki naturally flows in through your crown
chakra and suffuses your entire energy field as you continue
breathing more naturally.

With the Reiki flowing freely, begin to extend its reach by visualizing it spreading outward from your aura, filling the room you are in. Imagine the furniture, the floor, the walls, being infused with light.

Continue to breathe as you expand even further to fill the entire building with Reiki. Feel yourself as a channel of limitless Reiki. Continue to expand, filling the entire block. Perhaps shift your inner view to an aerial perspective, and see Reiki expand to fill your entire town. Keep breathing.

Expand to fill the entire state. Then the country. Finally, see Reiki suffuse the entire globe. If you want to keep going, send Reiki out into the cosmos, using whatever visuals or sensations work best for you.

Breathe for a few more cycles and feel your connection to everything. Feel how this act of self-care, this time that you have taken to love and support yourself, is beaming forth and showering love on the entire world. Feel yourself at the center of this energy expansion. Know that you are a vital part of this process, that you are a vehicle for Reiki entering the world. Thank Reiki and honor yourself for taking this time to cultivate the love within and share it with others.

When you feel ready, release your energetic focus on the expanded energy. Don't call it back in, let it continue to expand outward, but consciously bring your awareness back to ever smaller scales—back to your country, your state, your town, your block, the building, this room. Bring your awareness back to the edge of your aura and feel your center in your tanden.

Focus your energy back in your body and return to normal consciousness (pages 26–27).

For your daily selfless support practice, carve out time *every single day* to do something just for you, whether it's a short walk on your lunch break without checking your phone, a yoga class after work, a hot bath before bed, or an hour to curl up and read with no distractions. If you live with others, explain your plan for self-care. If they're resistant, let them know why this is important without getting defensive. Practice what you're going to say ahead of time so it's easier to remain neutral in your tone. Remember, you don't need to convince anyone of your right to self-care, so if they seem intent on disputing this right, perhaps respond by mirroring back their concerns followed by reinstating your intention: "I hear that you're concerned I won't have as much time to spend with you. Spending time with you is super important to me too, and I know I'll be better company if I'm taking care of myself. I'm going to take an hour after work to read and take a bath." Remain loving yet firm. If there are practical considerations, such as who will cook dinner, pick up the kids, et cetera, address those while remaining committed to your self-care plan. If you're accustomed to doing all of those things yourself because "that's the way it has always been done," ask for support.

It's also a good practice to respect other people's needs for self-care, perhaps by honoring their private time or requests for reasonable support. You're modeling what it looks like to practice selfless support, which is incredibly powerful. This world needs more of that to balance the abundance of images of overwork and self-sacrificing martyrdom.

Other Ways to Engage with Selfless Support:

- If you find yourself worrying about what someone else is thinking in a situation ("Do they think I'm stupid?" "Are they going to leave?") or what they're feeling ("Are they mad about what I just said?" "What can I do to make them happy right now?"), shift focus. What are *you* thinking right now? What are *you* feeling? For many of us, we must retrain our bodies and brains on a deep, energetic level to return to center rather than scramble around trying to please and appease the world. Trust that by getting in tune with your own internal landscape, you will be better poised to make choices that truly serve the highest good of everyone involved.

- Allow yourself to receive as an act of service, both to yourself and the giver. Have you ever given someone a gift, compliment, or assistance and it brought you joy? By opening to receive, you are allowing others to enjoy giving. Soak it up with love and joy; express your wholehearted appreciation. Allow the energy exchange to flow freely instead of blocking it by deflecting the compliment or shutting down when someone offers support.

- Practice giving freely without expectation of return. If you're unlearning codependent habits, a fun way to practice is by leaving anonymous surprises in public places. That way, it's not possible to monitor someone else's behavior to see whether they'll reciprocate. Try leaving notes on park benches with happy affirmations or leave a book in a coffee shop with a note to its future owner mentioning a part you especially liked and the hope that they'll enjoy the book, too. Get creative and play the Giver Fairy around town!

Labor of Love

This divine power speaks to the distinction between birthing something in order to fill a perceived lack versus birthing something because the creation is naturally bursting forth from a place of love. We can think of this birthing process in many contexts. For example, parents might have kids to assuage a sense of loneliness, save their marriage, or live vicariously through their kids, pushing them to do things they themselves did not have the opportunity or the courage to do. Admittedly, this doesn't paint a cheery picture of parenthood, and certainly there are many wonderful reasons people choose to have kids, but these reasons can and do come into play at times. Another example is birthing a song, a book, or a painting. An artist might force themselves to create to feel deserving of love and acceptance, bolster their sense of self-worth, or fulfill their idealized self-image of what it means to be an artist.

Just so our view of human motivation does not slip into overly dreary depths, let's look at the flipside of this: creation as an expression of love: the parents who are excited to welcome a new person into the world and support this child's development as a unique expression of self; the artist who is bursting with images that simply must be committed to canvas; the writer who loves language and can't help but express herself. When we are tending our inner fire through self-care, we activate our innate ability to be a sacred vehicle for labors of love to enter the world. This doesn't mean the process is always effortless, although certainly it can feel that way at times when we are so engaged in the task that we enter a state of flow. We might feel the *labor* aspect of this power more acutely at times, but the creative act itself remains an expression of love. We're not laboring away at something because we think we "should"; our soul is yearning to find expression and we are devoted to paving the way for that outpouring of soul energy. That is the labor of love in action.

A clear sign that we are blocking this power is resentment. When this emotion crops up, take this as a cue to step back and engage in self-exploration. What exactly do you feel resentful about? Why are you doing this thing that generates resentment? What are you afraid would happen if you were to stop? What might be some positive effects of stopping? Use resentment to illuminate areas of your life where your soul is feeling cramped. These clues are not invitations to dig your heels in deeper and "grin and bear it," they're invitations to explore where you've been compromising the full expression of your soul so you can choose to expand instead.

Exercise Twenty-One: Giving Birth to Love

Think of a hobby or interest you feel passionate about. Even if it's something you haven't done in a while, no judgment—just choose an activity that you feel or have felt passionate about.

Enter into a meditative state (page 26).

Establish a flow of Reiki (page 125).

Call to mind a setting in which you can engage in your chosen activity. If painting, imagine a pleasing room with natural light, plenty of supplies, and a canvas. If dance, picture a place where you would love to dance. If teaching, imagine yourself in a setting where you can share your knowledge with others. Take a few minutes to build out the scene, creating any details that feel important. Notice your choices and the feelings that accompany these choices, such as joy, excitement, or peace.

Shift your focus back to the flow of Reiki and allow it to infuse the scene as you birth your creation. If you're dancing see or feel Reiki moving with and swirling around your body as you move, like an energetic dance partner. If you're painting, see Reiki flowing down your arm, into your hand, and out through the brush as it moves across the canvas. If teaching, see Reiki flowing from your throat chakra, from your heart chakra, from your hand chakras as you share this light with your students. Give yourself time to explore the experience, allowing the Reiki to flow through your creative expression. Take note of what you create and how it feels, notice any details, any sensations that arise. Soak it all in.

When the experience feels complete, thank Reiki and allow the image to gradually fade.

Return to a normal state of consciousness (pages 26–27).

Take some time to journal about your experience. What did you create? Did it take shape in ways that differed from your expectations? What other details did you see, hear, smell, taste, feel? What emotions arose as you gave birth to your labor of love?

In the days that follow, think of how you can integrate this meditative experience in daily life and take action. Carve out time to paint, close your office door and dance on your lunch break, volunteer to mentor at an after-school program, or teach a class at your local community center. Start a blog. Cook a healthy meal. Dust off those hiking boots. Engage in an activity that is an expression of love, an outpouring of the pure joy of creating. The more you do this even in the littlest of ways, the more you activate this divine power and transform daily events from things to check off your to-do list to experiences that engage, awaken, and transform you. Make your life a labor of love one choice or moment at a time.

Other ways to explore the labor of love power:

- Honor unique expression in someone else. Help them see and appreciate their unique passions and offer encouragement to follow them. Never underestimate how powerful it can be to have your passions and gifts witnessed by another. Love is contagious—spread it!

- When you create something, give yourself time to bask in the afterglow. Too often, we jump right to the next project without soaking in the pleasure of our efforts. Before starting something new, carve out time to really steep in the experience of your creation. Get comfortable cozying up to your labors of love. Intimately explore what they feel like, look like, sound like, smell like, and taste like. The more connected you are to these sensations, the easier it will be for you to consciously cultivate the labor of love power.

Restorative Sleep

When I first discovered the ten divine powers, I wondered why there were two forms of sleep but none of the other powers are so obviously paired. A couple days after posing this question, the following passage from *The Sleep Revolution* by Arianna Huffington stopped me in my tracks:

> Pre-industrial sleep differed from our own not just in the reverence attached to it but in the nature of sleep itself. In most cultures, sleep wasn't the uninterrupted stretch of time it is now. Throughout most of human history, night was divided into two separate periods of sleep, known as segmented sleep. One of the earliest references to this practice of segmented sleep is in *The Odyssey*, where Homer wrote about "first sleep." Between the two sleep stages was a period of wakefulness, which would last up to several hours … [and] was a prized and valuable time … 'No other period afforded such a secluded interval of darkness in which to absorb fresh visions of solace, spirituality, and self-revelation.' The quiet relaxation of these special hours, without the distractions of daily activities, allowed people to become aware of subtler things and digest the unique insights that so often occur in that transition state between waking and sleeping (Huffington 2016, 72).

I have a strong sense that these two sleep-related powers are directly tied to our ancestral sleep stages, and by comparing and contrasting gestational and restorative sleep we can deepen our understanding. Both powers are clearly a form of rest; they are activated when we are disconnected from the faster pace of wakefulness and the distractions of the outer environment. While their form is similar, however, their purpose is somewhat different. Gestational sleep is a state of containment. Here we have all that we need in order to create, and the process simply requires time and stillness to unfold. Restorative sleep is a state of refilling our inner stores. If we look at the receptive and active qualities of these two powers, we see that gestational sleep relates to the receptive state's ability to create new life given the time and support to do so. In contrast, restorative sleep is a time when the outward-reaching active energy takes a break and reconnects with its source, the receptive wellspring within.

Restorative sleep's active energy takes a much-needed pause to retreat from the outer realm of *doing* and reconnects with a deeper state of *being*. During this fallow time, stores can be replenished, wounds healed, and baggage released. There's a fascinating corollary in our biology. A *Scientific American* article explains:

> Every day the brain eliminates a quarter of an ounce of used proteins that must be replaced with new ones. The waste-disposal process traffics half a pound of detritus a month and three pounds a year, equivalent to the brain's own weight. The glymphatic system, [a pathway in the brain for…cleansing fluids to effectively sweep away waste products], may become a critical target for treatment of neurological diseases such as Alzheimer's or Parkinson's that result from the buildup of toxic proteins that are not cleared from the brain (Nedergaard and Goldman 2016, 46–49).

And when is the glymphatic system most active? Yep, during sleep. Not only does this system remove waste, it has also been shown to deliver nutrients to brain tissue. Studies are underway to see whether the brain may rely on the glymphatic system to maintain the structural integrity of brain cells. To support the myriad functions required for daily life, we need the interplay of gestational and restorative sleep on biological, emotional, mental, and spiritual levels. So now let's couple our earlier exercise for gestational sleep with an exploration of restorative sleep.

Exercise Twenty-Two: Held by the Darkness

Enter a meditative state (page 26).

Introduce the flow of Reiki (page 125).

On the exhales, feel Reiki suffuse your body, gradually spreading outward to fill your entire aura with each successive breath cycle. Establish the sensation of being a channel and a container for Reiki as you prepare for the next stage.

Bring your awareness to your inner campfire, perhaps placing your hands over that area of the body to connect more fully. Conjure the image of the inner fire as you envision approaching its warmth and crackling energy. Sit next to the fire and gaze into the flames for a few minutes.

With love and intention, allow the flames to subside gradually. You can use a poker to separate the burning logs or simply use your intention to bring the flames down until you are left with warm, glowing embers. Notice if any thoughts or fears arise as the fire goes down—perhaps fears that you won't be able to get the fire rekindled, that it might be completely extinguished. Notice without judgment.

As you sit by the glowing embers, prepare a comfortable bed for yourself a short distance from the coals, conjuring up a fluffy sleeping bag or whatever feels most delightful to you. Curl up and allow your inner self to close their eyes. Feel the darkness around you and know that it is safe. This place holds, supports, and nourishes you in whatever forms you need most. Open to this nourishment and remain in a state of rest and receptivity for as long as you like. If your mind wanders, gently refocus on the intention of opening to nourishment.

Notice if any images, memories, colors, or other sensations arise during this period of restoration.

When you feel ready, thank the wellspring of the receptive for its nourishment and support. Gently awaken the inner you, perhaps stretching and yawning before climbing out of your bedding.

Return to the fire and rebuild it with intention. Ask that the fire reach an intensity that is correct and good for you at this time. You will find everything you need (kindling, logs, et cetera) to build the fire, and soon it is crackling and dancing with renewed vitality. Thank your inner fire for its passion and guiding light.

When the experience feels complete, allow the image to gradually fade, and return to a normal state of consciousness (pages 26–27).

Take some time to journal on this experience, making note of any information that came through at various stages: while you were seated next to the fire, as you began to dampen it, while you rested, as you rebuilt the fire.

Other ways to engage the power of restorative sleep:

- Research adrenal fatigue. Do any of the symptoms resonate with you and your current state of health? If so, look into holistic approaches to healing. In a related fashion, if you suffer from insomnia, begin to experiment with ways to balance your sleep, perhaps avoiding electronic devices for at least an hour before bed, changing the temperature of your bedroom, giving yourself a Reiki treatment before bed, writing down any stressors or worries from the day to get them out of your head and onto a piece of paper, cutting back on sugar and caffeine, and so on. Sleep is one of the most precious resources we have for our overall well-being— nurture and protect it!

- This week, remove at least one non-essential task from your to-do list. If you're really feeling motivated, remove at least one thing every day for the entire week. Notice how you feel as you remove each task from your list and check in at the end of the day and at the end of the week. Do any fears come up, perhaps that you're not doing enough, that things will fall apart without your efforts? Explore these without judgment.

Courageous Championing

This divine power is all about asserting your needs and inherent value in order to carry out your soul's mission. This power is vital if we want to experience balance between ideas and manifestation, and one of the primary obstacles to full expression of this power is a misconception regarding our worth. If we don't believe that we are innately worthy, we may find it difficult to assert the value of our gifts and contributions. Lack of self-worth can also manifest as false bravado and "used car salesman"-type techniques. When we fear that we're not really worthy but pretend to be so, we often feel that we have to resort to manipulation or gimmicks to get people to acknowledge our shaky sense of self-worth, and we may struggle with feeling like a fraud or the fear that we'll be "found out" at any moment.

Thus, courageous championing relies on a diligent practice of self-care that routinely self-affirms our inherent worth. When we take care of ourselves, we are sending a powerful message to all levels of our being that we are worthy of care. When we break self-care commitments or when we don't even make commitments to ourselves in the first place, we are sending the message that we're not worth the effort. Let's change the channel and start sending messages that are reflective of our worth as divine human beings. In doing so, we activate the power of courageous championing.

Exercise Twenty-Three: Your Inner Knight

Enter a meditative state (page 26).

Establish a flow of Reiki (page 125).

Bring your awareness to your inner campfire. You might place your hands on this area of the body to connect more fully. Conjure the image of the inner fire as you envision approaching its warmth and crackling energy. Sit next to the fire and gaze into the flames.

Ask to meet your inner knight, your inner champion. Repeat the request three times and settle into a receptive state.

Who approaches? What are they wearing or carrying? Introduce yourself and ask if they have any messages for you. Listen to the response. Give the experience time to unfold.

Next, your inner champion offers to outfit you with the armor of a knight to shield and protect you as you courageously champion the value of your soul's gifts in the world. What does the armor look like? Is it made of metal, fabric, or tree leaves? What colors and textures do you notice? Take in the details and see how it feels as you put it on. Are there any areas that seem more defended than others? Is it comfortable? Ask the knight any further questions you might have.

When the experience feels complete, thank the knight and slowly allow the images to fade.

Return to a normal state of consciousness (pages 26–27).

Take some time to journal on this experience. Really establish the memory of what it feels like to wear your knight's armor. When it's time for you to engage the power of courageous championing in daily life, mentally don your armor and feel the energy of this divine power infuse you, enabling you to carry out your task with assertiveness, wisdom, and grace.

On a practical level, can you identify an area in your life where you have expended creative energy but the power of courageous championing was not fully employed to assert the value of that creative output? Championing does not occur only in the context of helping other people see the value of your efforts; we also employ the power of courageous championing when we assert within ourselves the value of our expression. How often do you hear people say, "Oh, I'm just not that creative"? We are all creative, and that energy might find expression through avenues we don't value as such. Many of us think of creativity as strictly the domain of fine artists, but we are creative when we garden and cook, when we think of new ways to approach a relationship or work situation, when we interact with nature, when we parent, when we're choosing our outfit for the day, when we journal, during a yoga pose, when we dream, and yes, when we paint, sing, sculpt, and dance. Learn to see the many beautiful ways that creative expression exists in your life and honor them. Celebrate your creativity and resist the urge to describe it in diminishing terms. Own your power and courageously champion your gifts.

Other ways to explore the power of courageous championing:

- Learn something new about marketing. Some excellent, non-sleazy sources include MarieForleo.com, IttyBiz. com, and AlexandraFranzen.com. Even if you don't consider yourself to be an entrepreneur, we can all benefit from learning how to convey the value of our gifts more effectively, and marketing is a field that explores precisely that topic. There is a new wave of marketing experts who are casting aside the "used car salesman" techniques in favor of authentic expression of value with the goal of connecting your unique gifts with people who will truly benefit from them. Even if you don't use this know how in the context of getting paid for your gifts, these techniques can help you get clear on the value of your offerings and how to communicate that value in many contexts, be it in relationships, in a volunteering situation, or simply within yourself.

- Explore the energy of this power through physical movement. Courageous championing is all about moving into the world and engaging. While that movement is sometimes more symbolic than literal, we can still connect with this symbolic power by physically moving with intention and getting comfortable with what that feels like. What does it feel like to mindfully move from one yoga pose to another, to hike up a hill or swim a lap with intention? If you have different movement abilities, explore the feeling of movement however you're able, perhaps moving your arms and hands into a yoga mudra, such as prayer hands at the heart. Marvel at the power of intentional, courageous movement.

Self-Sovereignty

We've already explored this power in great depth with the Tara tests of the Celtic High Kings, but let's look more deeply at one specific aspect, that of the beneficent sovereign versus the tyrant by exploring whether we were allowed age-appropriate choices as a child. Some parents adopt the "my way or the highway" approach, but in order to develop the ability to make wise decisions, it's paramount that we're given the opportunity to practice through age- and developmentally appropriate choices (e.g., at age four, we get to choose from two or three healthy-ish snack options, not whether or not to drop out of kindergarten) over having our lives dictated to us. By honoring our choices, parents help us relate to our needs, internal cues, and intuition as valid sources of information, not as shameful or wrong simply because they are inconvenient or pose a challenge to the adult's authority. Many of us did not grow up in environments that respected our ability to know what we were thinking, feeling, wanting, and needing and to make choices based on that information. Instead, many of those choices were made for us, and in that process we were stripped of valuable practice time and instruction in the art of self-sovereignty.

As adults, if we still have not developed this skill, our internal decision-making "apparatus" or inner ruler may be modeled after the archetypal bully, dictator, or tyrant. We don't know how to make decisions in any other way, so we create a part within ourselves that replicates the domineering parent, telling us what to do even if those directives contradict what our thoughts, feelings, and intuition are saying. As far as the inner dictator is concerned, "it's my way or the highway," a refrain we've been trained to heed. This figure is constantly vigilant against the presumed chaos and destruction of emotions and other nonlinear states of being. The problem (one of *many*) with this approach is that this dysfunctional power is shaky; we must expend incredible amounts of life energy maintaining its brittle structure. We're left with a nagging fear that things will fall apart if we're not 'round-the-clock vigilant. And because many of our other parts are being suffocated under this stifling rulership, they often rebel. We might see this in our lives when we attempt to stick to rigid diets because we fear trusting our body's rhythms and natural hunger, and then we rebel in the form of cheat days and binging, only to have the inner tyrant come down twice as hard. So much of our energy is tied up in the violent back and forth between heavy-handed oppressive control and self-destructive rebellion.

To heal this energy-sapping cycle, we must relearn how to make wise choices and give ourselves the time and space to practice. As we build our skills in this area, we must allow the True Self to lovingly repattern the inner tyrant, repurposing that energy away from pursuits related to control and dominance toward creating healthy structure and support.

Exercise Twenty-Four: The Power of Choice

Enter a meditative state (page 26).

Establish a flow of Reiki (page 125).

Bring your awareness to your solar plexus. This is the energetic center most associated with your ability to execute the power of choice. It can feel energetically closed down, constricted, dense, entangled, or otherwise off balance when our ability to choose has been routinely compromised. Notice what this area feels like for you, perhaps placing your hands over your upper abdomen to help concentrate your awareness. Do any images, thoughts, memories, or sensations arise?

Think of a time in your youth as far back as you can remember when your ability to choose was denied. It doesn't matter if your adult self thinks the adults were justified in denying you this choice, perhaps for your safety. For now, simply bring a situation to mind that feels intuitively relevant. Recreate the situation, building the setting in as much detail as you wish.

Imagine yourself as a child and see if you can feel what it was like to have a desire for choice that was denied. Do you notice sensations in a particular area of your body? If so, which area and how would you describe it?

Now imagine your caregivers allowing you the option to choose. If it feels too triggering to picture your actual parent(s), choose an adult figure who feels more neutral or benevolent; even a character from a book or movie will do. Imagine them kneeling down to meet you face-to-face. With patience and openness, they listen to your choice. If your inner child is feeling overwhelmed or throwing a fit, the adult waits without judgment and offers support.

When you feel ready, switch your awareness to the adult and offer your inner child whatever comfort, support, and guidance you wish you had received. At any point, feel free to switch back to the perspective of your inner child and feel what it's like to receive that comfort and support.

When the experience feels complete, maintain awareness of the image while you bring attention to your physical
hands. Feel the flow of Reiki through your palm chakras and
place your hands over your solar plexus. As you do so, imagine
Reiki showering the entire scene and infusing it with Divine
consciousness.

When you feel ready, thank Reiki and your Higher Self. Say
three times, "I honor my right to choose. I make wise, empowered choices." Let the image fade as you bring your awareness
back to your breath.

Bring yourself out of the meditative state (pages 26–27).

For your daily self-sovereignty practice, you will create an environment in which to practice the art of wise decision making. Start small,
perhaps focusing on choices regarding what to eat for lunch or which
book to read next. Don't minimize these experiences, though, because
when done with intention, these seemingly trivial decisions are a powerful way to reconnect with all the internal cues that help you make
sound decisions, cues that you may be accustomed to overriding or
ignoring. Start to tune into how your body feels when you *don't* want
something. Do you feel more closed off or constricted? Do you physically pull away, even subtly, from the thing or situation you don't want?
What does it feel like when you *do* want something? Do you feel more
open and expansive, more curious and exploratory? Be your own inner
detective and start to identify your unique cues.

Journal about your experience so you can see patterns over time.
Make a note of decisions, which option(s) you chose, and the result. Do
you notice any common threads? For example, perhaps you notice that
when you take that churning feeling in your gut as a negative cue, those
are always times that looking back, you're glad you said no. Perhaps you
see that when you overrode that cue and said yes, you didn't enjoy the
experience as much. Begin to build your own sensory vocabulary that
will help you make decisions that incorporate the consensus of your

whole being rather than allowing yourself to be whipped into submission by the domineering voice of an inner tyrant.

Other Ways to Explore the Power of Self-Sovereignty:

- Do you find yourself apologizing if you bump into someone or for other minor interactions in which you haven't actually done anything that warrants an apology? Women in particular develop the habit of chronic apologizing, so releasing this habit is a powerful way to move into self-sovereignty. This tendency can mask a belief that we don't have a right to be where we are, take up space, have wants and needs, or to be seen and heard. Explore whether this is true for you by challenging the impulse to apologize. In many cases, simply saying nothing is an excellent alternative. If you bump into someone, try saying "excuse me" with a smile. What comes up for you in these situations? We might feel exposed, overly brazen, or any other emotions that can surprise us with their intensity. Observe without judgment, and just as you did with your inner child in the preceding meditation, practice soothing the part of you that's feeling overwhelmed with compassionate inner dialogue and Reiki.

- Pay attention to your thoughts. Are there times when you speak to yourself like a tyrant? Do you make demands and threats or use scare tactics to get yourself to act the way you think you should? For example, "If you don't go to the gym, you'll be disgusting"? Or "You'll get this work project done today, and you're not going home until you do!" Bring awareness to these moments. Breathe, give yourself some Reiki, and ask what's underneath the noise of the inner tyrant. What are you afraid will happen if the inner tyrant isn't in control right now? Explore those fears. Are they realistic? If those fears were realized, would they really be that bad? How might you respond if the inner tyrant's worst fears became a reality? Many of our fears begin to deflate when we face them. Their power lies in their ability to take on any shape and to shift into new forms to keep us anxiously on guard. When we see them for what they are, they're usually incredibly limited and often unrealistic. Even if what we fear is possible, our actual fears themselves are often not nearly as difficult to handle as we once thought.

Conscious Clearing

In order to bring our thoughts and ideas into the manifest world, we need a channel. The degree to which this channel is clear and free from obstruction in large part determines how easy manifestation feels to us. If we have great ideas but the process to bring them into reality feels overwhelming and exhausting, there's a good chance the power of conscious clearing needs activating. How do our pipes get clogged? We've touched on this already in our earlier discussion of Reiki. The short answer is: life. As we move throughout our days adopting beliefs, forming opinions, and creating ego structures, our piping system gets more and more complex and can become cluttered with debris. To a certain extent, this is unavoidable. Our brains have evolved to create beliefs and mental maps that provide shortcuts. For example, we don't have to consciously think about the process of brushing our teeth in painstaking detail. Our brain helps us automate the process so we can expend energy on other things. While this automation is necessary for less laborious functioning in daily life, it can also lead to autopilot assumptions that exert major influence over our days. For example, we've evolved to remember negative occurrences more easily than positive ones not because we want to make ourselves miserable but because we want to stay alive. If our ancestors saw a tan lump behind a tree and thought, "Yikes, that could be a predator. Time to skedaddle!" those cautious ancestors were more likely to survive and pass on their cautious brains, even if nine times out of ten that tan lump was only a rock. The ancestor who saw the same tan lump and thought, "I'm just being paranoid! That's probably a rock," might have been lion lunch more often than their cautious neighbor, thus our predisposal is a survival mechanism to more fatalistic thinking. However, today that thinking doesn't always serve. Most of life's challenges are not as life-or-death as a hungry lion, but we tend to treat them as such and let our negativity bias run unchecked, stewing over that rude comment someone left on Facebook or that "stupid" thing we said at our work meeting.

We also develop beliefs that inform our sense of self-worth. Let's say we hold the belief that we have to be the best at something in order to earn love and affection, and so we compete with others, even if working together would be more in service of our ultimate goal. In doing so, we end up feeling more isolated, reinforcing the belief that we're unworthy of love. Then, imagine we're given an opportunity for a position that meets all of our dream-job requirements with the exception that we'd be working on a close-knit team—in other words, in a situation where we'll have to radically adjust our competitive MO. We might talk ourselves out of the job for unrelated reasons that we then build up in our minds: "I'll have to drive across town in rush hour traffic" (never mind that we're already doing that for our current job) or "There aren't any vegetarian restaurants nearby for lunch" (never mind that the office has a well-equipped kitchen and we can bring our lunch). The real reason is that we don't want to challenge our belief that we must be the best in order to earn love and affection. It feels like we're giving up our only shot at ever experiencing love if we release this belief, so cooperation is out of the question and we turn down the job.

The power of conscious clearing in partnership with the other divine powers helps us to identify what's *really* going on; we can see the clogs in our pipes and develop the courage to transform those clogs. This paves the way for learning new life skills because these beliefs often serve as a crutch, preventing us from learning new ways of operating.

It can be incredibly liberating to finally admit that you don't yet have a particular skill rather than using energy-intensive workarounds to compensate and then to give yourself the time, space, support, and compassion to learn that skill. Forgiving yourself is a major piece of recovery from addiction. And even if not the more overt form of substance abuse, it's my opinion that most of us struggle with addiction. Whatever we're hooked on acts as a substitute for true satisfaction of the deeper need *and* development of the life skills that can help us meet that need in healthier ways. For example, I was intensely addicted to sugar for decades—it was a substitute for the "sweetness" of unconditional acceptance and maternal nourishment I was craving, as well as a substitute for learning life skills that would enable me to satisfy those legitimate needs in more life-affirming and less self-destructive ways.

An important facet of conscious clearing is trusting that our needs are legitimate. Our core needs are often masked by more superficial wants but the underlying needs must be sought out and honored if we are to heal. The inner tyrant would have us wield willpower and shame in the hopes of eradicating these deeper needs, but our needs are not the enemy. When we learn how to satisfy them in more soul-aligned ways, they help guide us, and they infuse our life with depth and richness. Often our pipes get clogged because we disavow our true needs. This denial creates roadblocks in our energy channel but because the need still exists, it also spawns twisty side roads and back alleys in an attempt to find other means of getting them addressed. These side roads and back alleys create the experience of being scattered, confused, and unable to gain traction, so let's do an exercise that will help you return to a more clear and focused state.

Exercise Twenty-Five: Clearing the Way for Flow

Enter a meditative state (page 26).

Introduce the flow of Reiki (page 125).

Bring to mind a river and find yourself standing at its banks. Notice the quality of the water—is it moving? If so, is the current fast or slow? Can you see to the bottom of the river or is it cloudy? What other details do you notice in the river or along the banks?

Walk along the river until you see a rock, log, or other obstruction in the water, and start to explore the nature of this obstruction. Conjure up any tools you need to feel safe while you explore the obstruction, such as an inner tube securely tethered to the land, the ability to fly, extra-long arms, and so on.

Touch the obstruction. Is it hard or soft, smooth or rough, hot or cold? What is it made of—stone, wood, plastic, something else? Are there other objects trapped in it, such as toys, pots and pans, books, et cetera? If so, explore them. Ask the obstruction and any trapped objects what messages they carry.

If you wish, swim below the surface of the water to explore the submerged portions of the obstruction. Is it connected to the riverbed or free floating? Is it made of different materials than the exposed upper portion? Continue to explore and ask questions.

When you feel ready, prepare to send Reiki to the obstruction. Place your hands anywhere on your body that you feel intuitively drawn and allow Reiki to flow into the obstruction. Notice if the obstruction changes in any way.

When the experience feels complete, thank Reiki and your Higher Self. Thank the obstruction for teaching you. Return to the banks of the river if you are still in the water, make note of any final details that arise, and gradually let the image fade.

Return to a normal state of consciousness (pages 26–27). Give yourself time to journal about your experience.

For your daily practice, bring awareness to situations that you perceive as being complicated, confusing, or overwhelming. Start with one rather than trying to work with a dozen situations at once. Begin by writing down what feels confusing about the chosen scenario. Commit it all to paper, then wait twenty-four hours. Next, pretend that a total stranger handed you this paper and is asking for your help in brainstorming solutions. Imagine that you have zero attachment to the people involved, including yourself, and write down possible responses and solutions for each confusing aspect. For example, in response to "I can't look for another job, so I'm stuck with this one," you might make the following note: "Why can't you look for another job—what do you perceive as blocking you from doing this?"

Give yourself time to make an initial pass over the list of confusing aspects and make notes as you go. Then go back and address any questions or comments in your notes if you wish. In the above example, you could explore what you perceive is blocking you from looking for another job. Perhaps it's fear that you aren't capable of landing a better position and you'd rather not confirm this fear, or maybe your ego is churning out unsubstantiated opinions and presenting them as "facts" such as you'll never get paid as much as you do now (is this true? And if so, is it actually important to you?), you'll have to work longer hours (again, is this true? Is it important?), and so forth. Our egos have a limitless supply of reasons to keep us from exploring, but when we step outside of our comfort zone and start fact checking the ego's assertions, often things don't add up.

Get in the habit of questioning your ego. To create those mental shortcuts we talked about earlier, the ego will create obstructions based on past experience to reroute energy. For example, if we were shamed as a child for singing because an adult had a headache, our ego might reroute any energy connected to singing down different channels, putting up a barricade at the channel entrance connected to the shaming experience. This can clutter up not only our ability to sing but to express ourselves in general. Your ego thinks it's helping by keeping you safe from reexperiencing the original wound but the ego's definition of safe is not always synonymous with happy, healthy, and spiritually alive. Your ego is a tool and can be helpful as such, but it takes self-awareness and questioning to make sure you do not become a tool of your ego.

Other ways to explore the power of conscious clearing:

- The next time you feel intense emotions, don't try to halt their flow. Practice being present, perhaps closing your eyes and focusing on your breath, placing your hands on your belly and feeling your hands move with your breath. Remind yourself that you are not your emotions. You are a channel through which they are flowing, and they will pass. When this process feels especially difficult, identify more strongly with the channel than the flow of emotions; perhaps imagining yourself as a strong, indestructible tube through which emotions are flowing like colored water. Notice how emotions pass of their own accord—they don't last unless we try to stop them, cling to them, or otherwise impede their flow.

- Be mindful of situations in which you complicate things in order to stay stuck/safe, perhaps by thinking you have to know the next ten steps before taking action. Trying to map out the entire plan often causes us to swing back and forth between wanting to feel prepared and having so much information that we're stuck in analysis paralysis. When you find yourself procrastinating because you don't know how things will pan out, ask yourself, "What's the next step?" Then do it. And repeat: "Now, what's the next step?" Do it. Keep moving, one step at a time. Instead of "Write a book, get an agent, and land a publishing deal," why not try "Set aside two hours every day this week to write a rough chapter outline of my book." Then do it. Liberate energy that has been trapped in stuck pipes, and you can reroute the flow of your entire life.

Purposeful Procurement

As someone who has used shopping as a way of self-medicating in the face of fear, self-doubt, and other uncomfortable emotions, I am particularly interested in the power of purposeful procurement. I struggled for a long time with over buying books and courses as a substitute for writing my own books and teaching my own courses, and when I am feeling overwhelmed at the prospect of writing or teaching, it feels easier to superficially scratch that itch by shopping. What's interesting is how buying books and taking courses made it more difficult for me to live my soul's calling, because I was so busy reading other people's books and taking their classes! This is purposeful procurement gone awry. Notice the parallels with conscious clearing and identifying and honoring the underlying needs. At this point in my life, it does feel like a genuine need of my soul to write and teach, but how I go about getting that need met determines the quality of my life in relationship to that need. I can binge on distractions and substitutes or actively engage with writing and teaching.

When the power of purposeful procurement is activated and healthy, we aren't throwing up self-made obstacles to pursuing our soul's calling. We're not apologizing for taking up space, for being seen and heard, and for expressing our truth; we're too busy living to worry about those things. Remember the squirrel from earlier in the chapter: When the squirrel finds a nut, it snatches it without hesitation; it doesn't spend ten minutes apologizing to the oak tree and promising to pay the tree back. We might imagine that the squirrel has an instinctual spiritual awareness of the cyclical nature of things, that the nut will be "repaid" in the form of fertilizing squirrel poop and, eventually, fertilizing squirrel body.

While there are limits to this metaphor in terms of human inter-actions—I'm not advocating snatching up resources without a second thought—it's nonetheless useful to examine the ways in which we keep ourselves small because of a perceived debt we can never hope to repay. By its very nature, living consumes resources; we cannot escape this fact of life. We can, however, learn to become finely attuned to the call of our soul so that our resource procurement and consumption serves the purpose of our soul's mission and not merely the whims of the moment. Will buying another book or taking another course help me fulfill my soul mission? Sometimes, but not always. And it is here discernment is required to procure purposefully. There are not one-size-fits-all rules. We must check in with our changing selves in the moment and see what's really going on. What deeper needs are calling out for atten-tion? Are we procuring things that actually address these needs, or are we grasping for anything available to fill what feels like a gaping void? Let's do an exercise to explore this power further.

Exercise Twenty-Six: Communing with Your Higher Self

Enter a meditative state (page 26).

Introduce the flow of Reiki (page 125).

Bring your awareness to your heart. Feel your heart beat-ing. Then, expand your heart awareness to encompass your soul. Feel your heart and soul beating as one. Notice if your heart rate feels rapid. Breathe slowly and deeply into your heart and soul as you say, "I love and accept you."

With your attention still on your heart, imagine the secret garden from our earlier meditation. Ask now to enter the secret garden of your heart and make your way inside. Take some time to look around. Make note of any plants or animals, the season and time of day, and any other details that appear.

Ask to meet with your Higher Self. Breathe and wait until you feel a connection with your Higher Self.

Ask your Higher Self to show you what your soul most needs right now. Remain open to answers. You might hear phrases or sounds. Your Higher Self might show you objects or scenes, you might have memories or thoughts, you might notice sensations in your body. Be open to different forms of communication. If you feel confused, don't be afraid to ask for clarification. Are you getting a sense of what your soul is seeking right now? Answers you receive don't have to be immense or epic; they might be simple, like more leafy, green vegetables in your diet or time in nature. Remember that we are often given a step or two at a time, and that's all we need.

When you have a clear sense of what your soul is trying to procure right now, place your hands over your heart and send Reiki. Say to yourself, "I activate the power of purposeful procurement in my quest for _____." *(Fill in the blank with what your soul is needing right now.)*

When the experience feels complete, thank Reiki and your Higher Self. Let the image of your heart garden slowly fade as you bring your awareness back to your breath.

Return to a normal state of consciousness (pages 26–27), and give yourself time to journal about the experience.

In daily life, activate this power by purposely procuring what your soul needs.

Other ways to engage with the power of purposeful procurement:

• Meditate and journal on this passage from Joseph Campbell's *Romance of the Grail: The Magic and Mystery of Arthurian Myth:* "The eyes are the scouts of the heart. They are looking for an appropriate object of beauty; that is to say, they are selective. This is discriminative … this is personal choice, and having found their image, the eyes recommend that image to the heart—not just to any heart, the gentle heart, the heart capable of love; this is not a case of sheer lust. When these three, the two eyes and the heart, are in accord, love is born ... The eyes quest in the outer world for the object of inspiration, and the heart receives the image" (Campbell and Smith 2015, 26–27).

- For twenty-four hours, as much as possible before you buy, eat, or otherwise consume anything, including media, food, sex, and so on, check in with yourself. Is this something you genuinely need to procure? Does this feel in alignment with your soul or are you merely filling space? Often, creating space is precisely what we need in order to make room for deeper fulfillment. Be mindful of rushing to consume things simply because they're available and you don't want to feel empty. Explore what emptiness feels like for you. Does it contain hidden needs that have something to teach you?

Infinite Power Within Finite Reality

One of the key aspects of working with the ten divine powers is to understand that ultimately, these powers are one. In the same way that the All differentiated into the One Mind and the One Thing to recombine and create, we are teasing apart the ten powers in order to recombine and create with them. So although we must develop all of the powers within ourselves, rarely are we using all ten powers simultaneously. The ten divine powers are infinite and archetypal, but we are experiencing these powers through a physical vessel that is finite. Thus we have the unique challenge of channeling infinite energies into finite reality, which requires discernment. By definition, finite cannot have or be everything at once—it must pick and choose. Mastering our finite aspect is synonymous with mastering the art of discernment. You can see this challenge expressed in someone who is trying to do it all.

Their finite resources are stretched so thin that they often appear to be running on fumes, always a smidge (or a lot) late with a thinly veiled impatience in their dealings with others and themselves. They have not accepted the limitation of finite existence and hence cannot master it. Instead, limitation masters them. You can hear this sentiment in oft-repeated phrases such as, "I never have enough time," as if time is being portioned out by a miserly boss and the person is always last in line. Paradoxically, when we accept and come into an aligned relationship with our finite aspects, we tap into the infinite: we seem to have all the time and all the resources we need.

We cannot manifest all possible outcomes simultaneously; we must choose which outcomes to channel our energy into, and so it is with the ten divine powers. Channeling these powers effectively into the physical world means learning how to discern which power is most relevant in any given moment. Do we need to channel courageous championing and spiritual synthesis right now? Or perhaps we need to devote everything to conscious clearing, at least for the next ten minutes. This is where true mastery unfolds, and there's an interesting biological parallel to this process of discernment and selective focus, and its effects on our sense of self. In his book *Head in the Game: The Mental Engineering of the World's Greatest Athletes*, Brandon Sneed writes:

> We've all heard the myth about how we use only 10 percent of our brains. The truth is that our brains are generally running close to 100 percent—except for when…flow has taken over and we've gone automatic; in those moments, most of the brain actually shuts down, except for only the most necessary parts. When Eminem raps about "lose yourself in the moment," there's scientific basis for that. On automatic, one of the primary parts of the brain that shuts off is the neocortex…This is the part of the brain that makes mammals, and humans in particular, so unique…Among other things, the neocortex is the part of us that is aware that we

are "someone," that we have a "self." In flow, the neocortex shuts down, and we forget about ourselves. And so worries about ourselves disappear (Sneed 2017, 67).

It's fascinating to ponder the connection between the narrowing of focus, the selective shutting down of certain parts of ourselves, and a feeling of expansion and transcendence of our individual self. It's as if by honoring our finite aspect and the reality that all things cannot happen simultaneously, we are given access to our infinite nature—the two sides of the same coin reaching their full potential when their opposing natures are fully honored. When we aren't forcing the finite to be infinite by multitasking ourselves into the ground, for example, and when we're not forcing the infinite to be finite by, say, expecting archetypal Love to never change within the context of a finite human relationship, each aspect of our dual experience can shine in its full glory.

We've covered a lot of ground in this chapter, all under the step of Polarization, the third in our series of seven steps. By learning about the ten divine powers, we've explored the inner polarity of active and receptive energies within us, a polarity that, through its interactions, creates the very stuff of our lives. With our internal battery charged and primed, let's return to our exploration of Reiki principles.

—7—
MERGING

It's time to explore the fourth step of self-transformation: Merging. In our previous step, Polarization, we gained awareness of our inner "battery" by exploring the ten divine powers, five receptive and five active. Through exercises, we got a sense of the energetic flavor and feel of each of the powers, and we also discussed how the interplay between them is more important than any one power in isolation. It is this interplay that we will work with more deeply in Merging, for this is the step in which our inner receptive and inner active come together in the divine marriage, or *hieros gamos*. The product of this union, the Divine Child, is not yet strong enough to go forth on its own, and it is vital at this stage that we learn how to nurture this "child" and support its development.

What does this mean in less arcane terms? As we learn how to use our receptive and active energies together, the result of that powerful interplay will likely feel new, and at times, awkward. It is important to support ourselves as we learn new ways of being and relating during this stage. We must cultivate compassion and patience as we experiment, make mistakes, and try again. We will set ourselves up for frustration if we approach this step with the expectation that we'll transition overnight with perfect execution. Just as we wouldn't expect a child to instantly learn something new and punish them if they needed to practice and made mistakes, so too must we be kind and patient with ourselves, and we must consciously create safe space in our lives in which to do this exploratory practice.

During polarization, you gained a sense of what each of the ten divine powers feels like to you as a unique being. This awareness is immensely useful, because when you know which of the powers you are exhibiting most strongly in any given moment, you can use your intuition and your rational mind in partnership to provide a sort of gentle checks and balances, inquiring whether this particular power is what is truly called for right now or if it's simply what you're used to resorting to in these situations. Or perhaps you'll see that, yes, this power is called for but also needs to be tempered or even activated with the addition of another power, after which you can call in that complementary power to balance or ignite your current energy state.

Let's say you're arguing with your partner over who pulls more weight when it comes to household chores. The two of you are locked in a tug o' war because each of you believes you're contributing your fair share while the other person is slacking. You can sense that the argument is escalating without heading toward a resolution, so you both decide to take a ten-minute break to calm and collect yourself. As you're splashing cool water on your face and focusing on your breath, you notice that your jaw is feeling locked and tense. You ask this tension to share its insights—why is it so tense? Is it trying to protect against something? At this point, you're feeling less invested in who does which chores and more curious to know what your tension has to share with you because you've switched to an internal focus instead of trying to figure out how to change your partner. You call upon the power of receptive listening, and your energetic senses open. You recall a memory from when you were eight and were told to take the garbage out. You forgot, and your mom was furious; she refused your allowance that week and you were grounded for the night. You had completely forgotten this incident, and as an adult your initial reaction is, "What's the big deal? That couldn't possibly have had that much of an impact." But your tension recalled this memory for a reason, and as you tap into the power of spiritual synthesis, you begin to see the common threads between past and present.

You recall how you felt like you were often walking on eggshells as a child, how the littlest thing could set your mom off. You never knew when something would be no big deal or a trigger for World War III. You can see now how her behavior made it difficult for you to discern the magnitude of events. While magnitude is partly subjective, of course, there is a measure of objectivity as well: not taking out the trash is not equivalent to burning down the house. You feel a little silly admitting this, but it's difficult for you to tell the difference sometimes, especially when you're stressed or neglecting self-care. In those moments, you're more likely to respond to trash-removal forgetfulness with house-burning-down intensity. This leads you to wonder if your partner might actually be pulling their fair share when it comes to chores, but the rare occasion when they do forget feels huge...and overtakes the times when they remember.

You then call upon the power of self-sovereignty, your kind and just inner ruler, who suggests a simple support, a structure that will help you and your partner create space to practice discerning the difference between a one on the magnitude scale versus a three or a ten. You decide to create a list of weekly household chores on a whiteboard with two columns: one for you and one for your partner. Each week, you decide together who's doing what, and once the chore is done, the doer checks it off. This tally creates a structure that's not being imposed by one person or the other in the form of nagging or arguing; it's a structure you co-created and in which neither is being appointed the chore police. If someone forgets a chore, you can use this as an opportunity to practice refining your sense of magnitude. If you forget to vacuum and your internal dialogue is harsh enough that you'd think you'd murdered someone, you can practice moderating this response with compassionate self-talk: "It feels like it's a really big deal—a nine out of ten on the magnitude scale—that I didn't vacuum this week. Even so, I love and accept myself." After a few rounds a breathing and perhaps a little hands-on Reiki, things may shift: "When I think about it, it seems like this is more of a two on the scale, so I'm going to use this as an opportunity to turn down the intensity dial so it reflects what I know about this situation more accurately." You can even picture a control panel in your mind labeled "MAGNITUDE" and see yourself moving a dial from 10 to 2. This is just one example of how we can tune into the powers that are dominant in any given moment and call upon the balancing and supporting effect of other powers as needed.

Divine Power Alchemy

To replicate this process regardless of the details of the situation, start with an intention: the intention to identify which power or powers are dominant in the present moment. I like to pose the question to my Higher Self: "Which of the divine powers are most dominant for me right now?" I take five minutes of quiet reflection to receive the response, which can come in the form of images, sensations in the body, memories, fully formed thoughts, smells, and so on. Over time, you will learn your own intuitive language and how to interpret it, and the more you practice, the deeper your understanding will become. And remember that if you do the exercises from chapter six in which you explore each of the divine powers individually, you'll create your own frame of reference, your internal Rosetta Stone. The exercises get you in touch with what each energetic power feels like, allowing you to compare and match those sensations with the energies you're experiencing in any given moment.

Once you've identified the power or powers that are currently activated, use both your rational mind and intuitive faculties to assess. Given what you know about the situation, does this seem like the most effective divine power to use right now? If not, which power might be more effective? To kickstart this assessment process, here are some examples of when each of the powers are most and least effective. This is by no means an exhaustive list so use these pointers as tools while you develop your own wisdom, not as fixed rules.

Gestational Sleep

Gestational sleep is most effective when you're nursing the idea for a fresh start or a new project, whether it's a physical project, a personal growth commitment, a new relationship, a new way of looking at things, or any new beginning. Gestational sleep might be needed when you're feeling a lack of creativity or decreased motivation to change and grow or when you're feeling overwhelmed or confused as to where to begin. It's also helpful when you have ideas that seem strikingly similar to ones you've had in the past that didn't seem to lead anywhere fruitful. In this case, gestational sleep can help you take stock and discern whether the idea lacks spark because it's something small and safe (or so you believe) that's keeping you in your comfort zone, or if it feels big and scary because it's challenging you to step out of this zone and your ego is throwing up defenses in the form of false boredom and apathy.

Gestational sleep might be less effective if your idea is already fleshed out and you have most of the tools you need to get started but are hesitant to dive in. In this case, you might be more in need of labor of love power (the near-unstoppable passion to birth something from the heart), self-sovereignty (the creation of inner and outer structure to make time for and apply peaceful discipline to the project), or courageous championing (the inner knight who believes in your idea and will champion it with gusto, even in the face of self-doubt).

Receptive Listening

Receptive listening is most effective when you feel like you're going around in circles: your thoughts feel repetitive, you hear yourself repeating the same complaints or rationales, or you feel like every possible solution is destined to become a dead end. Receptive listening might be needed when you feel overburdened, like everything depends on you and other people aren't pulling their weight or can't be trusted to do things properly. Receptive listening can help you re-attune to the Divine radio frequency and allow you to receive fresh, new information from a source beyond the ego. It helps you realign with the flow of your soul's energetic path rather than fight your way upstream using outdated methods of the ego.

Receptive listening might be less effective when you already know what your next step is but you find yourself asking friends for more advice, doing more tarot readings, researching "just a little bit more," and otherwise going into analysis paralysis. In this case, the information you already have (albeit incomplete, as our information will always be no matter how diligently we research) needs to be transformed into knowledge through action. The near-unstoppable passion to birth something from the heart (called a "labor of love"), conscious clearing (mindfully releasing obstructions to taking action, including the ego's fear that you must know everything in order to take the first step), and courageous championing (the inner knight who believes in your idea and will champion for you through real-world action) are all powers that can be helpful in this circumstance.

Spiritual Synthesis

Spiritual synthesis is most effective when you've done the intuitive and logical research and now you need a glimpse of the big picture to help inspire and guide your actions. It's also helpful when you sense that you're engaged in an unhelpful pattern and want to uncover its roots to learn the lesson and move on. Spiritual synthesis might be needed when you feel disjointed or as if your work, spiritual, social, and other lives are at odds or battling for limited time. One red flag is feeling like you have to be different people in different areas of your life. The power of spiritual synthesis is also useful when you have a lot of information but don't know how the parts relate to the whole and what to do with it all. It can also help when you're caught in information-gathering mode but are struggling to see the personal significance of what you're learning. For example, if you're aware of synchronicity in the form of animal messengers and meaningful dreams and other clues that resonate with you but haven't gone deeper with these clues by meditating or journaling on the common threads, spiritual synthesis can help.

Spiritual synthesis might be less effective when you're working on taking a one-step-at-a-time approach in relation to a situation that feels big in some way whether it be emotionally overwhelming or a situation involving a lot of people or complex factors, most of which you can't control. While it can sometimes be helpful to see the big picture in these situations, it can also add to the overwhelm. It's more effective at times to simply stick with what you can do right here, right now, and let the rest unfold as it will.

Selfless Support

Selfless support is most effective when you're suffering from a comparison hangover: in other words, you're spending too much time comparing your ideas and efforts to other people's and generating a downward spiral of envy and self-doubt. It's also useful when you feel alone, unsupported, and overwhelmed by the immensity of your current tasks. Selfless support might be needed if you notice that you're feeling hypercritical and it feels hard to stop fixating on what isn't working and any mistakes that have been made, either by you or other people. It's also useful when you feel trapped by other people's expectations or what they might think of you. If other's opinions weigh heavily when you're making a decision, selfless support can remind you that self-care is the foundation upon which all your service to the world rests, and it is the best metric when making a decision: Would doing X be loving to myself?

Selfless support might be less effective when you're finding it harder than usual to release internal stories that cast you in the victim or martyr role. In this case, calling on restorative sleep (recharging your batteries and reconnecting with self-care practices), purposeful procurement (getting crystal clear on what you need and taking *direct* steps to meet those needs, rather than trying to covertly rope others into meeting them for you), and self-sovereignty (reclaiming your inner seat of power and moving out of victimhood) can be helpful.

Labor of Love

Labor of love is most effective when you're ready to give birth, whether in the form of creating a work of art, birthing a baby, embarking on a relationship, launching a new product, and so forth. This power helps you effectively channel your energy and focus your efforts on ushering your love project into the world in a way that is simultaneously supportive of yourself and your creation. This support will be unique each time you give birth, e.g., creating ideal conditions in which to finish the painting you've been working on will be different than creating the ideal conditions to feel supported as you ask someone new out on a date. Labor of love is also useful when you're bursting to create, yet you're worried that other people might think you or your creation aren't good enough or they won't understand what it is you're creating and why. Labor of love helps you reconnect with your insatiable passion that won't settle for holding back out of fear. This love is bursting to come into the world, come hell or high water.

Labor of love can be less effective when you're struggling to identify what you need and consciously own those needs. When we aren't clear on our needs, we sometimes divert the labor of love energy through less productive channels in order to get our unexpressed (and possibly unconscious) needs met. For example, we launch a new product with the unexpressed need for approval, and the labor of love energy gets shunted down approval-seeking pipes rather than flowing freely through our creative channel. In these cases, calling on purposeful procurement (getting crystal clear on what you need and taking *direct* steps to meet those needs), conscious clearing (releasing outcomes and expectations that are beyond your control or at cross purposes to the spirit of your creation), and restorative sleep (tending to your inner fire, so you are fulfilled and can give birth to your creation freely, without expecting an immediate, or any, return) can be helpful.

Restorative Sleep

Restorative sleep is most effective when you're feeling depleted and burnt out, particularly if these feelings are accompanied by a world weariness related to feeling like there's never enough time, resources, ideas, or support to go around. When you can't seem to connect with a sense of abundance, restorative sleep can reunite you with the infinite wellspring within, a sustainable, ever-flowing source of nourishment. Restorative sleep is also useful when you're physically ill or otherwise low in energy and is great after you've finished a project and find yourself stuck in go-go-go mode. Allowing your body, mind, and soul time to decompress and process in between bursts of effort and energy establishes a more sustainable pattern and helps to ward off ailments like adrenal fatigue and headaches.

Restorative sleep can be less effective if you feel like you've been in hibernation mode and you're struggling to get moving. It can be helpful to get therapeutic support, like speaking to a counselor to see if you might be experiencing depression, or a holistic practitioner to see if a physical issue is siphoning away your energy. In addition, calling on the powers of selfless support (prioritizing self-care, even while you are out in the world taking action), receptive listening (tuning into your body, mind, and soul to uncover the root causes of your flagging energy), and courageous championing (honoring the value of your unique self-expression and offering it to the world) can be useful.

Courageous Championing

Courageous championing is most effective when you have something you want to share with the world and you're unsure how or are feeling insecure about doing so. Whether you're starting a business, asking for a raise, building awareness for a cause you feel passionate about, or simply finding avenues to share your gifts and be of service, courageous championing can help. Courageous championing is also useful when you're struggling to recognize the value of your receptive energies, as it is a challenge many of us face as a result of living in an extroverted, action-oriented culture. If you associate receptive energy with being weak, "overly" emotional, or irrational, for example, courageous championing can help heal this misperception and assert the value of the receptive.

Courageous championing can be less effective when you feel like you're pushing and striving to make something happen, and you're not getting the results you want. In this case, it's often more helpful to step back and reevaluate rather than forge ahead. Call on the power of receptive listening (quieting ego chatter and tapping into deeper insights), gestational sleep (allowing new ideas and perspectives to bubble up from the wellspring of the unconscious), and self-sovereignty (the calm inner ruler who cultivates patience and wisely assesses, even when the ego wants to force and rush).

Self-Sovereignty

Self-sovereignty is most effective when the desire for control gets in the way of creative and free expression. If you're afraid things will fall apart if you release rigid control over yourself (perhaps by denying your needs or emotions) or are excessively anxious or irritated when you don't have control over external circumstances and other people, self-sovereignty can bring you back to your inner seat of *em*powerment and help you release the need for power *over* self and others, which can drain your energy and squelch collaboration and support. Self-sovereignty is helpful when you feel beset with inner conflict, as if there are warring factions within you. Your inner sovereign is capable of taking seemingly opposing wants and needs and finding the deeper, core needs that crave fulfillment by all parties; from there, you are better able to move forward with purpose and inner coherence. It's equally helpful when the metaphorical warring factions are external, i.e., you and other people.

Self-sovereignty can be less effective when your need to control yourself and others is tied to chemical addiction, process addictions (such as disordered eating or obsessive-compulsive behavior), or other behaviors that feel too difficult to release on your own. In these cases, it's wise to seek support from a therapist or mental health professional to assist as you learn how to differentiate between your Higher Self and the inner tyrant and inner rebel. In conjunction with professional support, calling on the powers of purposeful procurement (learning to discern between wants and needs and identifying which of these are truly in service of your soul's work), receptive listening (attuning to your deeper needs over trying to find satisfaction through superficial fillers), and spiritual synthesis (identifying self-defeating patterns and self-supportive patterns so you can consciously choose the latter) can be helpful.

Conscious Clearing

Conscious clearing is most effective when you're feeling confused as to what to do next, when you have a lot of ideas and no clue how to pick one and get started (for example, if you have no idea which of these ten powers to start working with first!), or when an issue feels so complex that it seems impossible to find resolution. Conscious clearing can help you identify where and why your energetic pipes are clogged, allowing you to learn from and eventually release the obstruction, rather than subconsciously creating elaborate workarounds to redirect the energy, leaving you feeling scattered and lost. Conscious clearing is also helpful if you're having trouble communicating effectively, whether speaking or listening. If other people seem to misunderstand you or if you often misunderstand others, conscious clearing can help you release communication blocks, assisting the energy in flowing clearly from one party to the other with less potential for misinterpretation.

Conscious clearing can be less effective when you have trouble seeing things through to the finish line. In this case, it can be more transformative to see what makes it hard for you to sustain energy and interest, rather than simply making a fresh sweep and missing potential lessons. Calling on the energy of receptive listening (illuminating hidden fears and other elements that can cause us to abandon ship prematurely), restorative sleep (self-care that provides the steady nourishment required to cross the finish line), and spiritual synthesis (discovering how choices and effort in the present create the future and weave the overall tapestry of your life) can be useful.

Purposeful Procurement

Purposeful procurement is most effective when you have clarity on the next steps of your soul path and you need resources, whether it be time, information, money, or support to take action. Tap into this power to get clear on what you need and what you don't so you're not bogging yourself down with unnecessary baggage or getting waylaid by quests for the irrelevant. Purposeful procurement can also be helpful when you feel overburdened by stuff, yet every new thing you encounter feels, in the moment, like something you genuinely need or at least something you truly want and think you'll enjoy, and only later do you see that it was unnecessary filler. This power can help you discern between wants and needs and sift out desires that will bring joy versus desires that are masking a deeper need that cannot be fulfilled simply by acquiring more stuff or experiences.

Purposeful procurement can be less effective when you struggle with self-worth in such a way that it's hard for you to justify procuring anything—for example, if it's difficult to spend money unless it's to benefit someone else. If you struggle with deep feelings of guilt when you take care of your own needs or wants, the energy of purposeful procurement can be misdirected and used to justify even more stringent habits and unhealthy abnegation. It can be helpful to balance this with receptive listening (opening up to the deeper, core needs that are calling to be met and the reasons why you feel that you are undeserving) and selfless support (recognizing that taking care of yourself is a gift to those around you because you're not subconsciously shifting the responsibility of meeting your needs onto others). On the flipside, if you find yourself consuming in excess, the power of spiritual synthesis in conjunction with purposeful procurement can help you see the larger pattern of unmet needs so you can go about addressing the core desires rather than chasing superficial satisfaction.

Going Deeper With the Powers

You should now have a firm foundation upon which to experiment with the ten divine powers. Learn to recognize which power or powers are dominant in any given moment and assess whether the addition of a different power helps balance or activate your current energy state. Remember that what's covered here is just the tip of the iceberg; each power contains a universe of nuance that is up to you to discover for yourself. The more you work with these powers, the deeper your understanding will become.

Here are other ways to deepen your relationship with the powers:

- Meditate on a power. You can choose a character that embodies this power for you (such as a figure from literature or the tarot) and seek to interact with this figure in your meditation. You might step into a tarot card scene or imagine meeting this character at a cafe, a clearing in the woods, or another inspiring location. Next, ask questions. Listen,

watch, receive. Meditate on the same power multiple times
and see how the interactions change and deepen. You can
also use this technique to see how different powers interact by personifying two powers and asking to see how they
relate with each other, both beneficially and detrimentally.
Journal about your experiences.

- Ask to be given information regarding a particular power
(or a combination of powers) in your dreams. Upon waking,
immediately jot down whatever you can remember about
your dream. You can also extend this experience by later
meditating and returning to the dream to get additional
information, to experiment with altering the course of
dream events, to ask questions of any characters in your
dream, and so on.

- If you have trouble connecting to a particular power, ask
Reiki for help. This process can be as simple or as elaborate
as you like. For example, you can charge a candle with Reiki
by holding the candle in your hands, allowing Reiki to
flow through you, and envisioning it filling the candle. As
you light the candle, set the intention that it will help you
connect with the power in a way that is correct and good
for you. You can then meditate in front of the candle, gaze
softly into the flame, free write in your journal, or leave the
candle to burn in a safe place while you do other things
about the house and stay open and receptive to insights.
If you want to play with a more elaborate technique, use
Reiki in conjunction with the first suggestion in this list.
If you are stepping into a scene, create a lantern, candle, or
other light source in your mind and imbue it with Reiki. In
essence, imagine that the light source *is* Reiki and will flow
wherever you direct the light. If there's anything you have

trouble understanding, shine the light of Reiki on it and see what changes. If you are creating a mental location in which to meet your character, you can create the scene with Reiki, such as making the windows and walls out of Reiki, marking out a path with Reiki, and so on. Get creative! See if meeting the personified power in a Reiki room changes the interaction.

- Write a letter to yourself as one of the powers, noting everything you think this power wants you to know about it. Let yourself write without censorship and you'll be surprised how much knowledge you contain, as if it was simply waiting for an avenue of expression. You can do a similar process through other mediums such as finger painting, working with clay, making music, or anything else creative.

- While embodying a power, you can walk, dance, or otherwise move your body (this can be done in a chair and using any movement expression accessible to you), seeing what it feels like to be this power. Do you make certain facial expressions or hand gestures? Does your body want to move in ways that feel out of the ordinary for you? Journal about your experiences.

- Call a forgotten power back into your life...by throwing a welcome home party! If you have friends who are also working with the divine powers, you can throw a party for everyone's long-lost powers. Make things as simple or elaborate as you like. The point is to have fun, enjoy connecting with these powers, and recognize that our lives are enriched by their presence. You can create invitations that briefly capture in words the intention for the gathering such as, "Join us for a celebration of purposeful procurement. Let's reconnect with our inner compass that knows just what our souls need to live fully and freely!" If you want, you can make foods that feel connected to this power and/or come up with activities like a spiritual scavenger hunt for purposeful procurement that will help you all celebrate this power in a new way. Let your imagination run wild; the more you engage your whole self as you explore and interact with these powers, the more real they will feel to you, and the easier it will be for you to recognize and call upon them when needed.

Becoming more mindful of the ten divine powers and how they affect your moods, behavior, thoughts, and energy level throughout the day is a powerful practice in self-awareness. By exploring which powers are easier or more challenging for you to activate, you can get a better sense of how energy is flowing through your life—including where it might be getting stuck. The simple act of bringing awareness to the energies helps transform unconscious influences into conscious material that you can work with more productively. In the next chapter, we return our focus to Reiki as we explore the five precepts and the first three Reiki symbols.

—8—
REIKI PRECEPTS AND THE FIRST THREE SYMBOLS

Part of Usui's original teachings included something called the five precepts, or Go-kai, which were recited by students every morning and evening. There are two titles for the five principles, and they're both quite wonderful: "the secret method to invite happiness" and "the miraculous remedy for all diseases." Here's a version of the Go-kai from Usui's memorial stone, the translation for which is provided by Hiroshi Doi:

> For today—**Do not be angry**
> **Do not worry—Be Thankful**
> **Do what you are meant to do—Be kind to others**
> Morning and night, with your hands in Gassho
> Put them in your kokoro and recite
> Improvement of Mind and Body
> Usui Reiki Ryoho
> Founder, Mikao Usui

The precepts are the five phrases in bold, and while there are slightly different translations of these principles depending on the source, the meaning is consistent. Let's look at each phrase individually and explore how these principles can help us on our journey of self-transformation.

For Today

This phrase is meant to modify all of the phrases that follow; for example, "For today, do not be angry," "For today, do not worry," and so forth. We are asked to focus on the present moment, which is where we are most effective. Focusing on the present introduces a healthy perspective check, especially when we're feeling anxious or overwhelmed. Quite often what is being asked of us in the present is fairly straightforward and well within our ability to do, but when we're spinning out into the past and future things rapidly start to feel more complicated. For example, if you're beginning a healing session with someone and are well grounded in the present, you will invariably get a sense of where to place your hands; however, you might worry that you won't know what to do next or beat yourself up for not practicing your Reiki more intensely the day before. Neither of these thoughts are particularly helpful in the present moment and are distractions from the greatest healing gift you can offer to yourself and others—full presence right here, right now.

I remember starting a session as a new therapist with the fear that I might screw everything up. A part of me recognized that this was not the most healing of mindsets, so while my client was getting prepared I left the room and focused on showering myself with love. I couldn't run through everything I knew about energy healing (nor do I think this would have been useful even if I could), and I knew better than to suppress my feelings. What I *could* do was accept my nervousness and fear and love the crap out of myself just the same. Here's where things got interesting: I began the session by placing my hands on the client's ankles. The entire time, I was internally showering *myself* with words of love, such as, "I love you so much. I am in the right place, at the right time, doing the right thing. I am loved. I am love." By the time I reached my client's head, I noticed that she had a very peaceful look on her face, tears were streaming out of the corners of her closed eyes, and her mouth was curved into a gentle smile. At the end of the session she said, "It was the most amazing thing. As soon as you put your hands on my feet, I had this overwhelming feeling that everything was going to be okay."

Even when we are feeling small and scared, we can have a profound healing effect on ourselves *and on others* by cultivating and practicing self-love. For this healing to happen, however, we must be anchored in the present moment and willing to trust that all we need is happening right here, right now, even if the present moment brings us in touch with our nervousness, fear, or vulnerability. Trust that even these so-called negative emotions are okay and that simply by being present with them, you're "doing it right."

Do Not Be Angry

Most of the traditional interpretations of this phrase are pretty straight-forward: do not be angry. Anger is seen as a potentially destructive force that we're better off transcending. While I certainly agree that anger has the potential to be destructive, I do not find the imperative "do not be angry" particularly helpful; when anger arises, it's easy to start the internal song and dance of shame and blame: "Oh crap, I'm angry. I'm not supposed to be feeling angry. Argh, if only so-and-so hadn't been such a jerk I wouldn't be feeling angry right now. Screw him! I'm *so* angry!" And on it goes. We've already worked a great deal with various practices designed to help us sit with and be present with our emotions, and these practices lay the foundation for what I believe is a more helpful approach to this principle. When anger arises, be present with it. There's no need to react to it internally by recounting events in our head, justifying our anger with stories casting us as the victim or righteous rebel, or shaming ourselves for our anger, *or* externally by taking it out on other people overtly or passive-aggressively.

When we are simply present, we start to feel the gap between our emotions and our reaction to them. Without this practice, emotions and reactions flow together so seamlessly that it might seem impossible to experience one without the other. Our self-sovereignty lies in re-establishing this gap, and one of the ways we do it is by focusing awareness on our body, the vessel through which the emotional energy is surging. We strengthen identification with *the vessel* as opposed to the energy it is temporarily containing by becoming aware of what our body is experiencing, perhaps making mental notes as sensations arise such as, "My hands are trembling. I feel heat in my belly. My breath is fast and choppy." Trust that you don't need to mentally figure out what to do or say. Just be present with your body and let the emotional energy run its course while you abstain from saying or doing anything. The one exception to the latter is if you find it helpful to move your body, like walking or following other intuitive guidance such as wrapping your arms around yourself or sitting on the ground and swaying back and forth gently (you might want to find privacy for that one, lest your coworkers or family get concerned). If movement helps, go for it. When I say abstain from doing anything, I refer to taking action to try "solving" or distancing yourself from your anger, such as calling someone and venting, getting on Facebook, eating sugar, or rushing to create an action plan.

With practice, our presence lessens the fear of our emotions. We see that they can indeed be quite intense at times (sometimes surprisingly so), but we also see that we have the tools to weather the storm, and the tools are always available: we always have our body—our vessel—and we always have the option of choosing to be present. This expanded resilience in the face of emotions liberates us; we become less and less concerned with trying to micromanage our internal and external environment (including other people) in an attempt to avoid triggering encounters. Instead we can simply live and trust that we can handle whatever arises.

Do Not Worry

There simply is no benefit whatsoever to worry. Not only does it pollute our state of mind, which then pollutes our energy field, it accomplishes nothing...nada, zip. If we are in the habit of worrying, we may find that it serves as a subconscious crutch when we examine this habit more closely. The crutch allows us to think we're doing something about the issue at hand (after all, we were up all night worrying about it) and helps us *stay* immobilized, absolving us of any real responsibility to face the issue outside of the confines of our worried mind.

We can become addicted to worry, or any other emotion and the cascade of chemicals released in the body, to the familiarity of the sensation (however unpleasant), and to the buffer it provides from learning and using new life skills. For example, I used to chronically and habitually worry about money. I'd stay up half the night, thinking about whether or not I was going to have enough and panic over all of the possible consequences if I didn't. The worry served as a distraction to actually looking at the patterns underlying my state of perpetual financial crisis and learning the skills necessary to cultivate long-term financial stability. Instead of sitting with my emotions, I instead temporarily ignored them and went shopping, a distraction that *clearly* wasn't in support of financial stability.

If you've been worrying for as long as you can remember, it can feel hard to break this habit. My suggestion is to practice what we've been learning throughout our entire journey thus far: proceed with open eyes and an open heart. If you find yourself worrying, pause and look closer without judgment. What are you worried about? If it helps, get the worries on paper as a symbolic act of getting them out of your head and into a more manageable form. Writing also serves to create the gap mentioned earlier between a trigger and a habitual reaction. Next, really look at your concerns. Circle the ones you can actually take action to address. For example, "I'm worried that if I don't hang out with Sarah on Friday, she'll think I don't like her…but I'm really tired and need to rest." Possible actions include sitting with the discomfort as it arises—yes, this is an action, and it can feel as challenging as running a marathon! You might also call Sarah to explain exactly what you're feeling. Sometimes examining your worries will illuminate previously hidden beliefs and self-imposed rules, such as, "I can't simply tell Sarah that I'm afraid she'll think I don't care if I don't come on Friday." Wait…what? Says who? When we do make the effort to express our feelings and show vulnerability, it almost invariably deepens the friendship while also opening the door for others to be honest in return. Opening this door is like letting a big, beautiful gust of fresh air into the relationship, and you can practically feel the mutual sigh of relief: "Oh, thank God. We don't have to pretend anymore!"

For those items on your list that you can't or aren't interested in taking action to address, let them go. If you don't plan on taking action—and that's totally fine—resist the urge to pretend you're doing something by worrying. Let it go intentionally. There may be many things on your list that you can't address even if you wanted to. Let them go with intention. Write them on a piece of paper and burn it. Try using the Serenity prayer like a mantra: "Grant me the serenity to accept the things I cannot change, courage to change the things I can, and the wisdom to know the difference." Amen to that!

Be Thankful

Gratitude is a game changer. We talked earlier about our mind's evolutionary predisposition to seeking out the negative, but we have a powerful antidote at our disposal: gratitude. There are many ways to incorporate more gratitude into your day, and as with all of the practices we're learning, doing them with intention is what really counts.

Start and end your day by saying three things you're grateful for either to yourself or to someone else. You could also journal your gratitude in a special notebook and flip through it whenever you're struggling to connect with gratitude.

Make the ritual fun. Years ago, my step-dad and I started a practice called LDS: Life Doesn't Suck. It began somewhat as a joke but years later we're still emailing or texting each other our list of reasons why Life Doesn't Suck on a regular basis.

Create a gratitude box, a twist on a piggy bank. Whenever you feel inspired, write down something you're grateful for and put it in the box (bonus points: decorate the box with glitter, collage elements, quotes, et cetera). When you're struggling to think of something you're grateful for, pull out one of your banked gratitude slips and "cash it in" for a helpful reminder of life's sweetness.

Explore finding gratitude even amid struggles. Let's say you're arguing with a coworker. You don't need to whitewash the situation and come up with sappy sweetness that doesn't actually resonate with you; instead, try something even more powerful: Find gratitude for your ability to make empowering choices even in difficult times and then exercise that choice. For example: "I'm grateful that I have a choice to go outside, get some fresh air, and collect myself for five minutes." Then do just that. You might even inject powerful vulnerability and authenticity into the situation by saying, "You know, I'm noticing that I'm feeling pretty scattered right now, and I'm not able to be as present in this conversation as I'd like. I'm going to go outside for five minutes and clear my head, and then I'll be back so we can talk about this."

Do What You Are Meant to Do

I particularly like the wording "Do what you are meant to do" as opposed to other translations I have read, such as "work hard," which in this go-go-go culture usually isn't something we need to hear any more than we already do. "Do what you are meant to do" evokes for me a call to find your purpose and live it one day at a time. It also brings to mind Don Miguel Ruiz's fourth agreement, "always do your best" and the helpful reminder that our best can change from day to day (Ruiz 2008, 75). As healers, this reminder is especially important. We cannot do our work sustainably if we are holding ourselves to unwavering standards that fail to take into account how we're feeling in the present. If you're tired, carve out time for rest. It serves neither you nor others to push through, trying to deliver the exact same level of effort day in and day out. By modeling self-care, you can inspire others to do the same.

There's another interesting aspect to releasing yourself from the pressure of unchanging performance: you leave room for surprises. When you honor your internal rhythms and cycles, you might see that doing your best takes on different flavors and nuance, depending on the day, the season, the time of month. For example, women might find they're especially intuitive right before their menstrual cycle and it brings something different to the energy work process—beautiful! Work with that. There are countless variations that exist in your unique cycles that will remain untapped if you try to conform to a rigid, perfectionistic standard.

"Do what you are meant to do" also challenges us to be authentic in our choices, whether that be in our choice of vocation, friends and lovers, the words we use, how we spend our time, and so forth. The more attuned we are to the voice of our soul, the more we know in our heart when we are doing something discordant. We know that we're shortchanging ourselves when we choose to gossip, indulge in worried thoughts, spend time with people who drag us down with jealous discouragement, or stay in jobs that drain us because we fear we can't find anything better. When we do these things, it simply doesn't sit right with us. The key is to use that information to move toward choices that are more soul-affirming, *to do what we are meant to do.*

Be Kind to Others

The more we deepen our connection to spirit, the more we feel on a deep level that we are all one. We *are* individuals and know that exploring and expressing individuality is important; consider, however, that growth is better served when we do so *while* staying connected to the truth that we are ultimately one. This connection helps balance the oppressive drive to compete, which is fostered through so many facets of Western culture. The compulsion toward competition can lead us to feel an uncomfortable mixture of superiority and insecurity as we constantly fight to maintain the false and slippery sense of being better than others. We can waste a great deal of our precious energy fighting this imaginary battle; indeed, our culture encourages this, especially in the areas of business, sports, and sexual relationships. We are more often blinded to the greater gains to be made if we work together.

Being kind to others serves to dissolve the barriers of false superiority that keep us feeling "safe" and separate; however, in order to do so, we must have healthy boundaries. Many of us were not taught how to create and maintain healthy boundaries in relationships and may have seen adults in our life model quite the opposite. If our early caretakers felt threatened, rejected, or inconvenienced when we explored our autonomy and healthy differentiation, they may have shut down our attempts to forge boundaries. Trauma and abuse are also devastatingly effective at destroying boundaries. If this has been our experience, we must learn new life skills and create boundaries. Without this skill, we will not feel safe enough to release the less healthy means—judging, chronic anger, depression, illness, body image issues, and so forth—of staking out our territory. All of these and many other self-destructive behaviors can act as a shield that keeps other people and aspects of ourselves at arm's length, but as we learn how to construct healthy boundaries, the need for these less functional protective methods begins to lessen and the habits are much easier to release. When we have healthy boundaries, it's much easier to feel compassion and choose kindness because we're not walking through life feeling like a resentful doormat.

Other Components of the Go-kai

In addition to the five precepts, the go-kai contains two evocative titles that sum up why one might wish to use the go-kai in the first place: to find happiness and improve their wellbeing. Following the five principles are further instructions:

> Morning and night, with your hands in Gassho
>
> Put them in your kokoro and recite
>
> Improvement of Mind and Body

Here we are given the suggestion to do these practices morning and night, which could be taken literally or more figuratively, as in do these practices *often*. The more you use them, the more you will benefit. The precepts conclude with:

> Usui Reiki Ryoho
>
> Founder, Mikao Usui

As we discussed in chapter 1, Reiki scholar-practitioner Frans Stiene writes that Usui Reiki Ryoho "can be read as: Usui's teachings (dharma) to cure and heal one's True Self." (Stiene 2010, 15) And he further explains, "Of course Mikao Usui is using a metaphor: to heal one's True Self. He knew that there was nothing to heal—we just need to remember our True Self" (Ibid.). As we continue to look at Reiki principles and learn the symbols and mantras, the different possible translations can seem overwhelming. It is valuable to do our best in learning the material accurately, particularly if we wish to teach this information to others, but it is equally important to actively engage with these concepts in our practice and in life. Beyond memorizing these principles, we must live them. The idea is not to know about Reiki, the idea is to *be* Reiki. Keep this idea in mind as we add more terms and concepts to the teachings.

Reiki Symbols

What are Reiki symbols and why do we use them? To explore this question, I'll compare and contrast what I was originally taught as the common Western perspective on the symbols with alternative viewpoints. Typically, Western students are taught three symbols as part of their Level Two training and receive the fourth symbol during Level Three or Master training. Since Reiki's inception, however, some have developed their own Reiki systems and symbols. Here we will be discussing only the four symbols that have been connected to Usui's original teachings (though some sources credit Hawayo Takata with introducing the Fourth Symbol). If you're interested in learning about the different types of Reiki and their symbols, Christopher Penczak's *The Magic of Reiki* provides a great overview.

I was initially taught that the Reiki symbols consist of both the image and the associated name. Using the symbols might involve drawing them in the air with the finger or mentally in one's head (or in some cases in the inside of the mouth with the tip of the tongue) usually while silently reciting the name of the symbol three times. The three symbols taught in Level Two are Symbol One (mantra: Choku Rei), sometimes referred to as the Power Symbol; Symbol Two (mantra: Sei He Ki), the mental and emotional symbol; and Symbol Three (mantra: Hon Sha Ze Sho Nen), the distance symbol.

Mainstream teachings describe the first symbol's primary characteristic as power. It can be used to amplify energy, for example, by tracing the symbol on the palms of the hands before giving a Reiki treatment or by tracing a very large version in front of and around the body. It is associated with activating, strength building, dispelling harmful energy, and bringing and sealing in Light. The second symbol's mainstream association is with mental and emotional healing; it is also connected to protection, balancing the left and right hemispheres of the brain, releasing attachments and habits, healing psychosomatic issues, and letting go of harmful thinking patterns. You might trace the symbol over someone's body to help heal any of the above issues. I was also taught that Symbol Two had to be followed up by Symbol One because it was too fragile by itself and needed to be "fixed" by the power symbol, but I haven't felt that to be true with continued practice. The third symbol's mainstream association is distance healing. It is used to send Reiki either to another place (including other dimensions) or another time. For example, you might use this symbol to establish a connection with someone in another location before you send Reiki. I was originally taught that Symbol Three was intended to be used with the other two symbols in this order: First Symbol Three, then Symbol Two, and finally Symbol One.

I certainly don't think the above associations for the Reiki symbols are useless—far from it—but I do think they're more of a starting point, not the whole picture. For example, I have found Symbol One to be quite good at helping me get in touch with my power current, but I've also found it to be useful in leading me to a clearer understanding of my inner truth, something that extends beyond its common associations. Let's look deeper at the possible meanings of the symbols, and then explore different ways to use them.

True Symbols

To start, we need to define what a symbol actually is. Many of us would consider a logo for a well-known company or a street sign to be symbols, but C. G. Jung argued that these are not true symbols because we know precisely what they stand for. When we see the golden arches, we know this stands for McDonalds. When we see a red sign with the word "stop," we know exactly what that means. A true symbol, on the other hand, is an image that serves as the best representation we have to point to something that is beyond our ability to capture with language and other mental constructs. The symbol doesn't neatly match up with any one definition; we use the symbol precisely because it's impossible for us to sum up the concept in any other way. In essence, the symbol is a signpost pointing us in a particular direction; it's merely a guide to the experience and gnosis of something that is beyond words.

While the symbol is not the thing to which it is pointing, this does not mean that the symbol itself is completely useless. As an occultist, I hold the belief that symbols are both signposts guiding us to something more expansive *and* energetic entities imbued with their own power. In my practice, Symbol One represents all of the common associations listed above as well as something bigger and more complex than any of those words could possibly capture. Additionally, I use the symbol (drawing or mentally picturing it) because I feel the image in and of itself causes a shift in energy. I think one contributing factor to their power is that many people have been using them intentionally and for specific purposes repeatedly. Repeated intentional use has created an energetic current associated with each symbol, like thousands of feet wearing a path in the earth. And just as the path makes it easier for others to travel along this route, the repeated use of a symbol makes it easier for us to tap into the energetic current it embodies. Furthermore, in the same way that the well-worn path isn't the only way to get from A to B, the symbol certainly isn't the only way to tap into a particular energy current; it's simply one way with built-up momentum we can use to our advantage.

Sacred Sound

Each symbol is also connected to a mantra. While in the West these mantras are sometimes considered to be the names of the symbols, Stiene teaches that the symbols are known simply by numbers: Symbol 1, Symbol 2, and so forth in Japan (Stiene 2010, 87). The mantras, or *jumon* in Japanese, are sometimes called *kotodama*, another Japanese word that means roughly, "the spirits that live inside a word and give it a special power" (Ozeki 2014, 98). According to the International House of Reiki, "Kotodama and jumon were ancient Shinto practises that used vibrations to interact with the natural environment. It was believed that the use of these sound vibrations would ultimately bring us to a closer connection with ourselves and the universe" (Various 2010, 7).

I like to think of mantras as a way of uniting our body, mind, and spirit. We are using our physical body to create sounds initiated by our mind to connect more deeply with spirit, weaving the three together; that spirit is in turn a spirit we share with all that exists, connecting us to the greater whole. Chanting the mantras can also help us connect with the tanden, our energetic center. When we fully embody the sound, we're likely to feel a vibration in this area a few finger widths below our navel, deep in our abdomen, close to the spine. Bringing our awareness to this space can increase our sense of grounding and centeredness, so these mantras are excellent tools to use when we're feeling scattered, anxious, indecisive, flighty, or otherwise disconnected. They bring us back into our physical vessel while also resonating with our mental and spiritual dimensions. It's like a three-for-one special!

To chant the mantras, you can intone only the vowels or the entire mantra. I would recommend experimenting with both to see if you get different results.

Choku Rei can be pronounced as follows:

CHO (rhymes with "show" and is pronounced with a hard CH sound as in "chop") KU (rhymes with "moo") REI (sounds like "ray")

An alternate method is intoning only the vowels. Any vowels that are next to each other are sounded individually, as shown below in the separate intonation of the E and I at the end of REI.

O (like the o in "slow") U (like the oo in "moo") E (like the ay in "pray") I (like the ee in "spleen")

To give you a better idea of the sound of the vowel-only chant when it's strung together, it would sound like:

OHHHH OOOOO AYYYY EEEEE

Sei He Ki can be pronounced as follows:

SEI (sounds like "say") HE (sounds like "hay") KI (sounds like "key")

If you're using only the vowels:

E (like the ay in "pray") I (like the ee in "spleen") E (like the ay in "pray") I (like the ee in "spleen")

And finally, the pronunciation of Hon Sha Ze Sho Nen:

HON (rhymes with "bone") SHA (rhymes with "blah") ZE (rhymes with "meh") SHO (sounds like "show") NEN (rhymes with "pen")

When using the vowel-only version of this mantra, you will often hear two consonants included, the Z and the N, but feel free to experiment by dropping both:

O (like the o in "slow") A (like the a in "tra la la") ZE (rhymes with "meh") O (like the o in "slow") NE (rhymes with "meh")

Using the Symbols

The symbols can be used in a variety of ways, and I encourage you to honor your intuition as you experiment. You can meditate on the image or the mantra, perhaps by imagining the symbol as a hedge maze or path in your mind's eye and walking the path in meditation. The symbols can be drawn in the air with a fingertip, inside the mouth with the tip of the tongue, on paper, or in your mind's eye, and you can do this in a variety of situations such as before or during a healing session, upon waking and before sleeping, before meditating or journaling, or before approaching a challenging situation. You can also get creative and draw them on your water bottle to infuse your water, create them with icing on a cake, draw them in bathroom mirror condensation—you name it! Regardless of the medium you're using there is a traditional pattern in which to create the lines composing each symbol, and some teachings indicate how to say the mantra so that it corresponds to specific points of the drawing process. Let's look at how this works for the first three symbols, and we'll cover the fourth symbol in a later chapter.

Drawing Symbol One: Follow the directional arrows, drawing line one, then line two, and spiral line three around the central shaft three times to complete the symbol.

Pairing the symbol drawing with the mantra, Choku Rei: When you reach Point A, intone Choku Rei once per each revolution around the spiral for a total of three times.

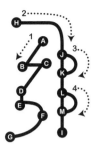

Drawing Symbol Two: Follow arrow 1, creating the entire left side line. Move up to the top and follow arrow two, drawing the line all the way to the base. Return to line three and draw the little hump, followed by line four and the second hump.

Pairing the symbol drawing with the mantra, Sei Heiki: Intone one syllable per line segment as follows: Sei as you draw from points A to B, He as you draw from points B to C, and Ki as you draw from points C to D. Repeat the mantra a second time: Sei as you draw from points D to E, He from points E to F, and Ki from points F to G. Then, start at point H and say Sei as you draw down to point I, He as you draw from point J to K, and finish with Ki as you draw from point L to M.

Drawing Symbol Three: Follow the directional arrows.

Pairing the symbol drawing with the mantra Hon Sha Ze Sho Nen: Say Hon Sha Ze Sho Nen, one syllable per line as you create lines one through five. Repeat with one syllable intoned per line as you create lines six through ten. Repeat the mantra a third time, one syllable per line, as you create lines eleven through fifteen. Then, say the numbers one through seven as follows: one (points A to C), two (points A to B), three (points D to E), four (points F to G), five (points H to I), six (points J to K), and seven (points L to M).

My Experience with the Reiki Symbols

It was Frans Stiene's teachings as well as my occult studies and practices that led me to explore deeper meanings to the Reiki symbols by chanting the mantras and meditating on the symbols. Interestingly, my meditative experiences had much in common with the material presented in Stiene's *The Inner Heart of Reiki*. While meditating on Symbol 1, I followed the trajectory of a large golden arrow through deep woods and was led to a cave, the walls of which were aglow with an orangey, red-pink light, like a giant amniotic sac. I knew I had to enter the sac, and once inside I saw myself in fetal form floating in the fluid. I asked, "Why did I come into this life?" The response: "I am a Waymaker." My body erupted in goosebumps—this was a word I'd heard in meditation a year before that deeply resonated with me for reasons I couldn't fully articulate at the time.

I compared my experience with Stiene's teachings on the symbols. Stiene believes they are signposts Usui employed to point students back to their True Self, while each symbol contains its own nuance, all point to the same place. Stiene translates Choku Rei as literally meaning "straight," "direct," or "correct spirit," and the practice of Choku Rei is one in which our aim is to remember or rediscover our True Self (Stiene 2010, 64). We can do this through self-reflection, through practices like meditation and journaling, and also by actually looking at our reflection in the mirror for long periods of time until our awareness shifts and we can sense a deeper level of being that is beyond yet mingled with our physical appearance. This can be very uncomfortable, which is a great reason to do it! Choku Rei also carries the quality of focus. It is not enough to get a glimpse of our True Self and then wander off. We must remain straight, direct, and correct with an unwavering focus on our True Self, like the arrow in my meditation. When we begin to wander, we compassionately gather our focus again. And again. The Reiki precepts are helpful in regaining this focus, because they alert us to potential distractions such as anger, worry, and a lack of gratitude. When we find ourselves experiencing these states, this is a reminder that we aren't focused on our True Self and that we need to adjust our focus.

Choku Rei is also associated with our vital connection to earth and our ability to be fully grounded. Choku Rei teaches that remembering our True Self is not about transcending our body; it is about connecting with our True Self and *embodying* this Self in the world. This has an interesting corollary to Rabbi Rami Shapiro's understanding of angels, which he describes as the aspect of humans that can interface directly with the Divine, unfettered by the ego. In Shapiro's view, angels are not entities separate from us, they *are* us. Spiritual energy, whether it be angels, Reiki, or any other form, cannot execute actions in the physical world without a physical vessel serving as a conduit for that energy. Thus, in order to make contact with our divine nature—our True Self—and carry out its work in this life, we must be grounded, we must have an intimate connection to Earth. This is another reason why it is so important to care for our bodies. It's not enough to meditate for hours on end, only to treat our bodies like crap. All of these teachings seem to parallel the details of my meditation, from the need for direct, one-pointed focus to lead one back to the True Self, represented by the golden arrow, to the earthy groundedness of embodying the Self in this life (the cave and the fetus), which then sheds light on what we're here to do (embracing the role of a Waymaker, in my case).

The following night, I meditated on Symbol 2 (Sei Heiki). The symbol formed a door, and when I stepped through I found myself in a quiet hall at dusk. There was a long mahogany table, and the room was completely empty. As I sat down, suddenly the table was filled with faces of all races, ages, and genders, and I felt a deep sense of connection and homecoming. In amazement, I asked, "How do we know each other?" and the group replied, "We are all Waymakers." These were my people.

I was humbled, filled with love, and overflowing with questions all at the same time. I spent quite some time in this meditation, asking questions and listening. When I left, I felt great clarity and a knowing that tied together so many seemingly disparate choices throughout my life.

Stiene's take on the mantra is that Sei Heiki heals the mental and emotional tendency to mistakenly see reality as dual in nature. (Stiene, 65) Non-duality is a large concept that can be thought of simply as the acknowledgment of a reality beyond the apparent world of this/that, black/white, body/spirit to reveal the unifying oneness underlying everything. The more we are able to connect with this oneness, the less tempted we are to label our experience in dualistic terms such as "This is good!" and "That's bad!" Instead, things simply are. In connecting us with the knowledge that all is One, despite appearances to the contrary, Sei Heiki connects us with our True Self, a Self that fully knows and *is* this Oneness. This state of being is associated with another quality of Sei He Ki—harmony—cultivated when we embrace the beautiful duality of our experience: our physical, earthly nature (Choku Rei) and our spiritual, "heavenly" nature (Sei Heiki). When we only perceive the differences between these two states of being and we cannot see their underlying unity, we lose the sense of harmony and Oneness symbolized by Sei Heiki. Stiene writes that "discovering our True Self…is really the heart of Sei Heiki. Without rediscovering our True Self, we will be attached to and create new emotional and mental habits all the time," habits that blind us to our innate Oneness (Stiene 2015, 76).

In my meditation experience was the contrast between being alone at first (the empty hall) and being joined by my soul family, and the fact that even though I might appear to be carrying out this work in my individual life, the work is connected to the web of my fellow Way-makers—and indeed all life—because of the underlying Oneness of all that is. Embracing and learning to live within this seeming duality helps weave together the fibers of our lives that otherwise might seem to be an incoherent tangle of threads. In this same way, rediscovering the True Self can unite the illusion of duality into the truth of Oneness.

Hon Sha Ze Sho Nen, often called the distance symbol in modern teachings, is typically used when performing healings where the recipient is not physically present. From the start, I had trouble with this symbol, as it didn't entirely make sense to me why distance was even a factor when it came to Reiki. It seemed that Reiki was more than capable of being where it needed to be regardless of distance without the need for a metaphorical bus pass. I then wondered why we are taught to place our hands on certain areas of the body *and* taught that Reiki will automatically go wherever it is needed. Why would it matter if my hands are on someone's knee or their ear? In using Reiki, my current understanding over the years is that Reiki is absolutely capable of being where it needs to be because it's already there—it's universal. There is no such thing as traveling for Reiki, because it is here—*and* there. To that end, it can be helpful for us as beings who are both universal and finite to focus if we have a place to put our hands and our thoughts, in effect. I don't think we necessarily need to focus in order for Reiki to do what it needs to do; the focus is more important in keeping the ego out of the way so we don't *hinder* Reiki. For example, if my ego thinks that all I have to do is place my hands on someone's knee and allow Reiki to flow, I will be less likely to start orchestrating complex healing plans in my mind. My ego will be pacified in knowing that I've done my part and can let Reiki do its thing. Our touch also brings the recipient's focus to the area; where attention goes, energy flows, allowing touch to aid in the self-healing process.

If Hon Sha Ze Sho Nen isn't really about distance, then what is this symbol here to show us? Hon Sha Ze Sho Nen is kanji, or Japanese writing characters, and we can get clues by looking at translations of the characters. The following are given by Stiene:

Hon: true, book, origin, real, to find the origin in

Sha: person, someone, the one [who/which], he/she who is

Ze: right, correct, just so, this, justice, perfectly, it is this

Sho: correct, true, straight, the basis of correct knowledge, righteous

Nen: thought, feeling, mindfulness, mind, memory, meditative wisdom, patience, forbearance

I encourage you to meditate on these translations and combine them in different ways to see what messages arise for you. One meaning that resonates with me is "meditating on the nature of the True Self allows us to reclaim our original wisdom." In other words, Hon Sha Ze Sho Nen acts as a signpost, guiding us back to our True Self. When we focus on our True Self, we will find genuine wisdom that has always existed within and needs only to be activated. This focus challenges the typical view—looking outside oneself and the drive to gather more and more information, to study with people considered experts, and to see our state of being as one of lack that must be rectified by filling it with external things we believe we are missing. When we make contact with our True Self, we are aware that we already are whole—we're not missing anything. We can still learn new things, embrace the wisdom of our fellow seekers, and otherwise engage our minds and hearts, but we do so for the pure joy of the experience, not to drown out a gnawing fear that we're lacking.

When we remember our True Self, we start to operate from the assumption that we are already whole, and from this mindset we have access to inner resources that we couldn't see. It's as if we switch out our "I'm broken and unhealthy" glasses that caused us to see the world as filled with validation of this faulty belief with "I am whole and healthy" glasses. Is it possible that seeing ourselves as either sick or well rigidifies energy that prefers to be more fluid? These labels turn healing into a state we think we have to *get to* rather than a state in which we *already exist*. When we think we are not healthy and must somehow get there, we make lists of things we think we must do (such as a particular diet or exercise) or ways we must be (wealthier, in a relationship, et cetera) in order to experience wellness. This black-and-white thinking creates rigid energy channels such that if life refuses to flow through these channels and we can't check off the boxes on our list of wellness requirements, we are convinced we must remain unwell. What's interesting is that these very beliefs make it harder to follow through on the things that could support our health, such as a healthy diet and exercise. If we're currently identified with a state of *un*wellness, doing things that make us well like eating healthy food or exercising feel wrong, like a mismatch to our current state. As a result, our efforts are harder to sustain.

To see how these concepts might connect with the interpretation of Symbol 3 as the distance symbol, consider one translation of Hon Sha Ze Sho Nen: I am Right Mind. Takuan Soho writes, "The Right Mind is the mind that does not remain in one place. It is the mind that stretches throughout the entire body and self. The Confused Mind is the mind that … congeals in one place" (Stiene 2010, 77). We could say that the Right Mind travels, in the sense that by remembering its Oneness with all things, it can be in all places and all times because it *is* all places and all times. It transcends our rigid labels in doing so. Perhaps when we are using the distance symbol to heal, healing comes in part from the realization that the distance itself is an illusion—you and I are actually One with all that is, and thus anything we think we're lacking—anything we perceive as separating us from a state of wholeness and health—is an illusion on some level.

This also speaks to an important facet of healing work: the ability to recognize this Oneness while simultaneously maintaining healthy boundaries. Recall the Hermetic creation story: The All (Oneness) wanted to know itself more fully, so it separated into the One Mind and the One Thing, creating the possibility for relationship and greater self-awareness. In the same way, you and I are like individual droplets of the universal ocean; we're made of identical stuff, but life looks different through your eyes than it does through mine. The view when we put our viewpoints together is greater than the sum of its parts, and this is only possible because we are honoring not only our Oneness but also our separation. This is especially important for us healers because it means that in spite of our Oneness, I cannot practically live your life nor you mine. We each have our own path, and healing does not entail me learning your lessons for you, forcing you to change, or trying to "fix" you. Healing requires both the compassion that springs from awareness of our Oneness and healthy boundaries that arise from honoring our separateness.

We continue our journey of self-transformation in the next chapter with the fifth step, Inspiration. This step will serve as preparation for your second Reiki attunement.

—9—
INSPIRATION

The fifth step of self-transformation, Inspiration, builds on our previous work and prepares you for your second attunement by taking the product created through Merging and completely changing its characteristics. This change is two-fold and involves allowing this product—what we will refer to as the Divine Child—to die and then breathing new life into it. Why kill off what we've put so much work into creating, only to bring it back to life? In short, this newly transformed product must die to the world of illusion in order to be reborn to the light of truth (enacted through your second attunement), and we'll expand on what this means later in the chapter. To accomplish this rather epic-sounding aim, we're first going to deepen our work with projection, starting with exploring how the act of projection is similar to the Hermetic creation story and how it's different. In doing so we will discover that our human tendency to project can be useful *if* we do it with intention and awareness.

Remember that the creation story begins with the All separating into the One Mind and the One Thing, driven by the All's desire to know itself more deeply. By looking at itself through different perspectives and by experiencing itself in the context of relationship, the All builds a more nuanced self-image. In a similar fashion, we can approach projection—a temporary "separating out" of aspects of our wholeness—as a way to expand our self-awareness. The creation story is not referring to something that happened once, way back when; it is referring to a constantly unfolding process. The *All* is all times and places, so its actions are occurring in all times and all places, including right now in all of us. Each of us is continually cycling through this creation story. In each moment, we have the ability to separate different self-aspects from one another and learn from their interactions—for example, by using the inner witness to observe your emotional experience or by using your body to sense the environment and processing that input with your mind. There are myriad ways to explore your experience and the *you* who is experiencing it, and this diversity allows you to create a more nuanced understanding of yourself.

Projection is one way of separating out and understanding our inner aspects. We project these aspects onto other people and situations, even the world at large. As we work to develop skills and strategies for dealing with those "external" forces, there is also the potential that we will learn how to deal with those aspects within ourselves. However, when we are not conscious of this projection and *only* see these qualities as existing externally, we get stuck in trying to make other people and external situations change to fit our view of what's right or in eradicating them entirely without increasing our self-awareness. The process of eradicating is also mirrored within (often subconsciously)—just as we seek to rid ourselves of the supposed external enemy, we are seeking to destroy that aspect within ourselves. We are harmed in this process just as much as our external enemies are, and this is an unavoidable result of engaging in this unconscious battle. We cannot wage war externally without waging it within.

Becoming aware of the material we are projecting helps us take responsibility for all of our parts, not just the sunny, happy ones. Rabbi Rami Shapiro writes, "The Devil symbolizes the dark side of the human personality. It is the devil we know because it is the devil we are. It is everything we are that we wish we were not. As long as we admit that we have a dark side, we have the potential to tame it. But most people do not admit this, and project their devil onto others" (Shapiro 2009, 138). He continues: "What then shall we do with the evil of which we are capable? Reb Nachman of Breslov, a nineteenth-century Jewish sage, saw the answer to this question in the command to 'love your neighbor as yourself' (Leviticus 19:18). While the plain meaning of the text is clear—one should treat others with love and respect—Reb Nachman saw another meaning as well. The Hebrew phrase ray-ah-cha, 'your neighbor,' could (given the fact that the Hebrew Bible is written without vowels) also be read as rah-ah-cha, 'your evil.' We should come to accept our dark side as part of our selves, no less part of our selves than our light or good side" (Ibid., 141).

How is it possible to love your evil as yourself? One of the most powerful ways I have found is to look beyond manifestations of evil and seek the underlying need motivating it. While we may find the outward behaviors abhorrent, it is often easier to relate to the underlying needs. Let's use an extreme example to see this in action. While it can feel impossible to relate to the *actions* of a serial killer, we might find it easier to relate to the underlying needs—perhaps the need to feel loved or safe from abandonment. We all want to feel loved, and we all have an innate, biological fear of abandonment because as infants we are dependent on our caregivers for our very survival. Abandonment could literally mean death. While the vast majority of us could not conceive of killing someone—thankfully—to prevent them from leaving us, we *can* understand the fear of being abandoned and by extension, the underlying need that is motivating the extreme and much harder to understand behavior.

Marshall Rosenberg, author of *Non-Violent Communication: A Language of Life*, writes, "Everything we do is in service of our needs. When this one concept is applied to our view of others, we'll see that...what others do to us is the best possible thing they know to do to get their needs met" (Rosenberg 2016, 206). What would change in your relationships and even brief interactions with strangers if you believed that other people's actions were not a personal attack nor a reflection of what they think of you but simply the best way people knew to fulfill a need? The way people treat us is a direct reflection of their relationship with themselves; an expression of their needs.

Let's look at these principles in action. Politically, I have a lot of opinions and sometimes strong reactions to world events; it gives me fertile (and frequently triggering!) ground for exploring my projections and finding ways to channel this energy more productively. At the heart of this struggle is navigating how to recognize my projections without attributing everything I see in the world to my own baggage. As I write this, the current president brings up such volatile feelings for me that it is difficult to even look at photographs of his face. Part of my work involves working on my projections, being present with my emotions, and returning to my own center in the midst of this whirlwind of triggers. However, I don't believe my work ends here. As a member of the human community, I want to contribute my time and energy to affecting change. How do I determine the course of right action (to borrow a Buddhist term) in the face of radically opposing views? Tending to my internal state is paramount; I cannot create peace in the external world if my internal state is one of strife and warfare because even when I consciously work to create peace, my methods for obtaining it will be defined by looking for enemies and fighting them in the name of "peace." Our internal environment mirrors the actions we take in the world, regardless of whether or not we are consciously trying to make a very different impression.

It's helpful to simply let myself feel what arises. I don't take action or make decisions from a place of disagreement; I simply allow the feelings to exist. Then, I work to get in touch with the need that is motivating me in this situation. If I am riled up about Issue A, I ask myself: "What need does this issue speak to?" or "If Issue A doesn't go the way I want it to, what need do I fear will go unmet?" When I feel ready, I then try to put myself in the person or people who are preventing me from solving the issue's shoes and imagine what need they might be trying to meet in this situation. Can I empathize with that need, even if I don't agree with the method being used to meet it? This process might take days or even weeks, depending on how attached I am to my views.

Finally, I explore ways that both parties could get their needs met. Even if the ideas seem far-fetched, simply considering the possibility that everyone's needs can be honored rather than trying to eradicate the opposition is a powerful, consciousness-expanding process. If our solutions carry the expectation that other people will somehow stop needing what they need, we will be waiting a very long time indeed. Jennifer Lehr writes, "Needs drive behavior. We humans need what we need. Needs aren't luxuries. If a [person] isn't responding to a reasonable request, then their behavior must be meeting a more pressing need" (Lehr 2016, 201). From this foundation, I can choose actions that are more aligned with the outcome I seek to bring about (such as peace) and am more open to different people arriving at that outcome in their own ways.

How does this relate to Inspiration and its power to affect deep change? At the risk of stating the obvious, change requires the addition of something new or a transformation of an existing state. We cannot exist exactly the same as we do now and experience change. Duh, right? And yet I often find myself wanting what I perceive as the benefits of change without having to experience any of the actual change itself.

I want all of the same comforts and touchstones in my life to continue just as they are but also want that annoying thought, feeling, person, or situation to just go away. If we return to our projection work, we realize there is no "away." *We must be willing to undergo internal change* if we expect our experience of life to be different: our experiences at work, in our relationships, in our body, in any area of our life.

Looking back at the previous step, we conjoined the inner active and receptive energies during Merging, and their union produced a new being, the Divine Child. Yet now here we are, letting this child die. Why? Pragmatically, we must become accustomed to allowing change, even—especially—in areas that feel near and dear to our hearts. On one level this step is challenging the natural tendency to get a good thing going and then try to set things in stone so they will never ever change and we will never ever lose the awesome result. Inspiration bursts in, entirely unplanned, scatters the papers of our concrete knowledge, and challenges us to confront who we really are and the inevitable truth that these awesome things will change and even die.

The Divine Child is the precursor to realization of our True Self that encompasses both the physical and the divine, but at this new stage our awareness and skills aren't yet strong enough to serve as a sturdy bridge between our physical and divine natures. At this stage, what we have is more like a rope bridge swaying in the wind, in danger of collapsing at any moment. The bridge must undergo further transformation in the form of death followed by rebirth. We can continue this metaphor by saying that rather than being transformed into a more permanent, concrete structure between the physical and the divine, the rope bridge is instead allowed to completely fall away in order that we can be reborn with the awareness that we don't need the bridge. Our True Self is simultaneously physical and divine—we don't need a bridge to get there. What is *really* dying is our attachment to the world- and self-view defined by separation between the physical and the divine.

This way of seeing life as either/or must die in order to give rise to a new view that sees the underlying unity of All. When the false belief that our finite and infinite aspects are separate dies, we remember our true wholeness.

Wants and Needs

One of the ways we can initiate this deep level of change is by developing an awareness of our needs and how those needs differ from our wants. The two might seem unrelated, but they offer a tangible way of working with Inspiration, which can otherwise feel slippery and abstract. The process is this: By learning how to separate our core needs from our wants, we are in a better position to release attachments to superficial wants that have served as energy-draining distractions. We can then concentrate our efforts on meeting deeper needs that when met, will sustain the work that our soul came here to fulfill. Our individual needs reflect universal human needs; by reconnecting to them, we also reconnect to our shared humanity—our underlying oneness.

While there are different ways of labeling and categorizing universal human needs, I find the Needs Inventory compiled by The Center for Non-Violent Communication to be quite useful. It divides needs into the categories of connection (acceptance, belonging, cooperation, intimacy and love, et cetera), physical wellbeing (food, water, sexual expressions, shelter, touch, et cetera), honesty (authenticity, integrity, presence), play (joy, humor), peace (beauty, ease, equality, et cetera), autonomy (choice, freedom, space, et cetera), and meaning (challenge, contribution, growth, hope, learning, et cetera.)[2] While the list is not meant to be exhaustive, these categories can help us discern our core needs by giving us a frame of reference. If *all* our behavior is an expression of one or more of these needs, it stands to reason that getting more familiar with them will yield rich insights into why we—and

---

2 You can see the full list at https://www.cnvc.org/Training/needs-inventory.

others—do the things we do. Using this list helps us approach the first step in the Inspiration process: identifying our deeper needs.

Next, we learn to discern these deeper needs from more superficial wants. The point of this exercise is not to deny ourselves of everything we want; the point is to devote more effort to meeting the core needs that will leave us feeling more nourished than we would if we focused only on chasing surface-level wants. Let's look at an example. The universal need for contribution, for feeling that we are adding something to an idea, a community, a movement, et cetera can be met in many different ways. I classify the variety of ways this need can be met as wants. We *need* to feel like we're contributing, but we may *want* to do that by volunteering at the local soup kitchen, by getting more responsibility at work, or by joining the stream clean-up team. However, I would argue that the specific act of, say, volunteering at the local soup kitchen is not a need, it's a want. We need to make a contribution, but we want to do so in specific ways. If we conflate the two, then we create the belief that we can *only* make a contribution (i.e., get our deeper need met) by volunteering at the soup kitchen (i.e., fulfilling a surface-level want).

Why does this matter? Well, think of all the circumstances where things didn't go the way you'd hoped: Maybe you didn't get the additional responsibilities at work, or you did and you were overwhelmed and started hating your job, or you did but it also meant you were now working with someone who grates on your nerves, and so on. If you are attached to this specific want being the only way you can get the underlying need for contribution met, now what? You're liable to feel pretty stuck. If you give up the work situation or change it in any way, you risk losing your supposed "one shot" at getting this need for contribution met. Fast forward to retirement—what happens when you aren't working anymore? How will you meet the need of contribution then?

Instead of chasing wants and spending vast amounts of energy trying to force external circumstances to unfold according to our plan, we can look beyond the wants to the underlying need and unlock a multitude of previously hidden options for getting it met. This can also heal perpetual tug-o-wars between what we believe are opposing parties, because if we both want that soup kitchen volunteer position and only one of us can get it, we're setting ourselves up for problems when we believe this position is the only way to meet our core need of contribution. As Lehr writes, "We humans need what we need. Needs aren't luxuries" (Lehr 2016, 201). If our solution to the problem is convincing our "opponent" that they should forego having their needs met, we're going to be waiting a long time for resolution, and the other party is invariably going to react with indignation and anger (see all political issues throughout all of human history for examples). As humans, we all strive to get our needs met as long as we are alive. Expecting other people to forego meeting their needs so we can meet ours is not a viable solution.

If we are willing to loosen our grip on specific wants, we release the sticky attachments that generate suffering (for us and for others) and can focus instead on meeting our *needs*. By doing so, we are able to channel our life force in more effective ways. Think of how much energy we often spend on the pursuit of wants. As an example, a *need* is shelter; a *want* is a specific house that costs $300,000. If we conflate the want for the need, we might feel like we have no choice other than to work a particular job for decades in order to afford the $300,000 house. That decision can result in thousands of hours of our life spent working for a house. If the house truly did satisfy this need and we felt deeply fulfilled by the house, that's wonderful; there isn't anything inherently wrong with this hypothetical house, but rarely do wants like this satisfy a deeper need. In most cases they barely scratch the surface. What's problematic is trading so much of our precious life force for something that doesn't achieve the desired result. This sort of life math just doesn't add up.

When we learn how to identify our true needs, we can spend our time and energy meeting them. And when we meet those needs, we will feel a deeper sense of nourishment that provides the foundation and energy for carrying out the mission our soul came into this life to fulfill. Chances are that your soul did not incarnate to buy that specific $300,000 house. Pardon my French, but I would imagine that your soul doesn't really give a shit about that house. It may have come here to learn how to feel worthy of living in a beautiful and nurturing environment, but there are many, many ways of meeting that need that do not fall apart if you can't afford that particular house, someone else buys it first, or any number of potential situations arise where this specific want could go sideways.

Focusing on our true needs rather than getting overly attached to our wants allows us to get creative, think outside the box, and find satisfaction in different forms than we initially thought possible. This liberates us from the cage of our ego and opens us to a more intimate experience of life as it is, rather than holding back on the sidelines until life is as we want it to be. We let the ego's restrictive rules that dictate how we should use our life force die off, allowing a new world of possibility to be reborn. The Divine Child is freed from false limitations and battle with perceived enemies and we see the world with fresh eyes that find potential where once there were only problems. This awareness allows us to channel our life force more productively in service of meeting our core needs. We share those needs with all of humanity, so channeling in this manner has the power to turn perceived enemies into fellow travelers who are doing the best they know how to get their needs met, just like us.

Exercise Twenty-Six: Free Association of Wants and Needs

Grab a pen and paper or do this exercise in your journal. Write down something you want right now. It can be a physical item, a relationship, or a change in circumstance such as a new job, less arguing with your partner, et cetera.

Spend some time exploring *why* you want this and how you think things will change if you get it. Let your mind free associate as you take notes. You can call on the power of receptive listening to aid and guide you.

When this process feels complete, shift to identifying the underlying need or needs. You might already have some in mind—if so, write those down. I'd recommend looking at the Needs Inventory (page 217) to see if it prompts any additional insights.

When you think about these underlying needs (work with one at a time if you identified multiple needs), do any memories or associations come to mind? When was the first time you remember feeling this need? Was it met, and if so, how? If it wasn't met, do you remember the situation and how you felt? Can you see any parallels between these memories and the present; are there any threads that have woven through your life? You can call on the power of spiritual synthesis to aid and guide you.

If you'd like to do any additional journaling or contemplation, feel free. When you feel ready, take a slip of paper and write down both the want you chose to work with and the associated need(s) you uncovered in as few words as possible. We'll go deeper in our work with these wants and needs through a meditation.

The following meditation is divided into two parts (part two is exercise twenty-eight beginning on page 228). Important: Please do not do the first without doing the second. You end the first meditation leaving your astral self in the earth, so it is very important to complete the process by bringing your astral self fully back into your body. Choose a time when you can perform the meditations roughly three days apart. The three-day interim will allow you to get the most out of the experience. You will be asked during that time to pay extra attention to your dreams, emotions, thoughts, memories, synchronicity, and so on, so it's best to schedule this for a time when external demands will be fairly minimal. You'll do much better if you are able to focus on your internal processes, i.e., you don't have to take time off work but avoid scheduling during a higher-stress period of tight deadlines. If something comes up and you're unable to perform the second meditation three days later, perform it before the three days is up if needed, or as soon as you are able to after the three-day period.

Exercise Twenty-Seven: Transformation of Wants

Retrieve your slip of paper from the previous exercise and read it over a few times to commit the words to memory.

Enter a meditative state (page 26).

Introduce the flow of Reiki (page 125).

Bring your awareness to your inner campfire, focusing on the area of the body where this fire feels most present, perhaps placing your hands there to connect more fully. Conjure the image of the inner fire as you envision approaching its warmth and crackling energy. Sit next to the fire and gaze into the flames.

Look down and see a glass bottle in your hand with a cork stopper. Bring to mind what you wrote on the slip of paper—your wants and needs. Uncork the bottle and envision sending those words and their energy into the bottle. You might see pictures, colored light, or words entering the bottle. Continue until the process feels complete, then cork the bottle.

Feel Reiki traveling down your arm and into your hand. Place your hand over the bottle and use Reiki to seal the cork. The bottle is now hermetically sealed.

Hold the bottle in both hands and begin to merge with the bottle, shifting, shifting, shifting until your body is the bottle in which your wants and needs are contained. Your body is the vessel in which the transformation will unfold. Feel that connection, that strong sense of your body as sacred vessel and the wants and needs contained within.

When this process feels complete, look beyond the campfire's glow to the surrounding forest. You will see a shovel leaning against a tree. Go to it. The earth is rich and fertile, and you use the shovel to dig a large hole.

You, your sacred vessel containing your wants and needs, are now ready to climb into the womb of the earth. Lower yourself into the hole and ask that the Earth gently embrace you as the hole fills with earth, enclosing you in warm soil. Know that you are completely safe, that you can breathe, and that you can easily leave at any time. Be present with any fears or discomfort that arise, and remind yourself, "I am safe."

In your sacred vessel, the energies of your wants and needs begin to break down and reduce to smaller and smaller components no longer associated with this particular want or that specific need. The energies slowly return to a primordial state full of potential, no longer attached to any one state of being. Feel as your internal heat begins to build, like in a compost heap. The primordial energy cooks gently yet thoroughly. Continue to breathe and allow this process to continue.

When the process feels complete, you will come out of meditation but awaken without leaving your earthly womb. Here you will remain for three days, allowing the transformative magic to unfold. Still envisioning yourself in the hole of the earth, warm and safe, return to a normal state of consciousness (pages 26–27). Do any grounding and centering as needed.

During your three-day Inspiration period, be extra intentional with your focus. As you are undergoing this transformation there are numerous reactions occurring that build heat. This heat often feels different than the fires of Illumination you have already experienced; it might build more slowly yet feel more pervasive. Everyone's experience will be unique but the point is to not be alarmed if this three-day period feels intense. Your goal is to build internal heat so that things can break down and be transformed. In order for this work to occur, we need to do our best not to dissipate the energy.

The sacred vessel of your body is more than capable of safely containing this heat, but dissipation occurs when we override this ability and "blow off steam." To aid you in recognizing when this heat dissipation is occurring, imagine that you have a large internal temperature gauge like a numbered thermometer—oversized for good measure. When feelings are mounting, thoughts are churning, or bodily sensations are intense, bring the thermometer to mind and ask, "What is my internal heat level right now?" It's not important to get an exact measure; you're simply looking for a relative indicator: is the heat low, medium, or high? When the gauge is high, we find ways to consciously and subconsciously release heat, most commonly through some form of activity. Think of the action as the opening of a steam valve and ... *ahhh*, the intensity lessens. You might release steam through words—talking about your feelings, hashing out problems, venting, or complaining. You might release steam through physical actions—exercising, constantly having things to do, having sex, eating, or drinking. You might release steam through thoughts—perhaps by telling yourself a story about what happened to feel better, by cycling through habitual thoughts to calm or numb yourself, or even focusing on triggering thoughts and going through the rollercoaster of retriggering yourself, getting a big adrenaline rush, and crashing.

During this three-day period, you want to resist the urge to do these things as much as possible. That said, safety first. If things feel truly untenable, get support. Don't deny yourself talking to a friend or running around the block when you feel like you simply can't handle it any longer. *Do* know, however, that this time is meant to be intense and bring up things that are uncomfortable to see and to feel. Our mind often wants to turn to habitual steam releasers well before we've actually reached our capacity, so while I want you to trust your intuition and take care of yourself if you feel you aren't safe, I also challenge you to pause and see if your mind is convincing you of danger that is less imminent than it appears. Our ego cringes at the first sign of discomfort and jumps into action-mode: *How can I make this discomfort go away ASAP?!* This is one of the habits our entire journey thus far is seeking to release. The constant chasing of relief—even when the discomfort is temporary and carries important lessons—stalls our growth. If we believe that our resiliency is so low that we cannot withstand even the smallest discomforts, our priority will be on securing comfort at all costs, even at the expense of facing difficult things that lead toward transformation and freedom. It's quite possible that our resiliency is actually low if this has been a habit, but this process can help us to rebuild our strength to face life's storms.

When things feel intense, try using some of the tools you've learned from earlier chapters. This is a great way to build habits that are truly in service of your growth over temporary "steam releasers." You can give yourself a Reiki treatment. You can focus on your breath. You can chant the mantras—this is especially great when you're feeling antsy and you need something a little more active. You can walk indoors or out in a meditative fashion (perhaps in a spiral) while chanting. You are doing wonderful things for yourself with these practices and demonstrating to your ego that when things feel wonky, you can return to a sense of safety without reaching for the habitual patterns that serve to distract you or dissipate energy. You are experiencing the power of being fully present with your experience. Additionally, you are activating your spiritual healing abilities in moments when you really need them most by engaging with Reiki, the mantras, or your breath—in short, it's a win-win. Another tool I hope you'll use during this time is journaling. Journal about your dreams (even if they don't make sense right away), your meditations, and daily life experiences including any synchronicity that occurs. Journal the things that resonate with you whether that resonance feels comfortable or uncomfortable. Not only can writing in this manner help you be present with your experience, chronicling this process will allow you to go back and gain additional insights later, perhaps from a different frame of mind. In fact, I urge you to reread your Inspiration entries after your second attunement, which can be seen as a form of Divine Inspiration, to see if your perspective has changed.

Bringing in the New

As with all the steps in self-transformation, there's a great deal of change occurring under the surface with Inspiration. We've been focused here on uncovering our core needs to heal issues associated with attending only to the more superficial wants, but there's another important aspect to identifying our needs. Our True Self is both physical and divine, which means that we have needs that correspond to both our human, finite nature and to our infinite, divine nature. Think of it like this: When we are born to this physical life, a drop of the cosmic ocean "separates" from the whole and is encapsulated in our physical form, giving rise to needs that are unique to physical existence. But our spiritual needs didn't go away either. Our infinite "cosmic ocean" aspect has needs of its own, including regular and nourishing contact with the ocean from whence we came. If our droplet doesn't retain its connection to the greater ocean, it dries up. We need transcendent, spiritual experiences just as much as we need immanent, physical experiences, and in Inspiration is an emphasis on the transcendent aspect. Notice this stage occurs far along in our journey; we didn't skip over the physical experiences just to get to the "good stuff." We still need to pay our bills and do the laundry, just as much as we need to nourish and tend to our spiritual nature. We are activating the awareness that the immanent and the transcendent are two sides of the same coin, neither better than the other. We need both to fully remember our True Self.

The ways in which we experience transcendence will be highly individual, but some common avenues are through meditation, being in nature, intentional or ecstatic movement, prayer or chanting, sex, therapy, vision quests, creating art, and dreaming, among others. It could take the form of an experience that seems supernatural or even a shift in perspective that leaves a deep impression. The methods are many because there are infinite ways to commune with the divine. Even this descriptor shows the limits of language: "Commune" is misleading because it suggests that we weren't already in communion with the divine. (Because we are divine, this is of course fiction.) More accurately, when we commune we are *aware* of our ever-present oneness with the divine, an awareness that is too often forgotten amid the hustle and bustle of daily life.

While these transcendent experiences are vital for many reasons, one that often gets overlooked is that they can paradoxically help us be more grounded. Many of us are desperately seeking these enlightened states, trying this meditation or that vision quest, this drug or that weekend workshop. When we remember our True Self, we see that we don't need to earn our connection to the Divine or go to a special place for it to occur. We realize that we are always connected and have simply forgotten what it feels like, and it's as if our entire being breathes a huge sigh of relief. Those spiritual sayings like "you are what you seek" that seemed annoyingly cliché suddenly make sense. It's not that we will necessarily have this feeling of intense spirituality every moment of our life, but once we experience it we are forever changed because now we know that the feeling is available to us *just by being us*. We don't have to take a course, live in an ashram, or take ayahuasca. It's available while we're hiding out in the bathroom at work to escape a particularly boring meeting just as readily as at a fancy spiritual retreat because we *are* that which we seek. When we carry this awareness within us, we can finally sink fully into groundedness because we know that by doing so, we're not missing any opportunities for transcendence. It's as if we were tiptoeing around before and taking little hops and jumps, constantly trying to take flight into enlightenment because our physicality was seen as an impediment to feeling the transcendence we so craved. We never fully accepted our connection to the ground. We felt scattered, flighty, resentful of work, health issues, and other practical affairs that seemed in opposition to bliss. When we learn how to *embody* our bliss, to experience the True Self that is already both physical and transcendent, we are free of the yearning to be elsewhere than where we are. The True Self is available right here, right now.

The next exercise is part two of the meditation you performed in exercise twenty-seven: Transformation of Wants. Ideally, the second part will be performed roughly three days after the first, but you can adjust to your schedule as needed. In this second meditation, you will come out of the earth womb you entered in part one and ready yourself for inoculation with divine energy: your second Reiki attunement.

Exercise Twenty-Eight: Leaving the Womb

Enter a meditative state (page 26).

Introduce the flow of Reiki (page 125).

Bring your awareness to your inner campfire. Conjure the image of the inner fire as you see yourself approaching its warmth and crackling energy.

Move your awareness a short distance from the fire, where you are resting in your Earth womb. Become one with yourself in the Earth. Smell the fertile scent of the soil, feel its warm embrace. And then, reach up, up, up, as you climb out, climb out, climb out. Find yourself on the surface of the Earth once more, feel the rush of fresh air on your skin and into your lungs. Breathe in and walk toward your inner campfire.

Raise your arms up in a V and welcome Reiki. Feel as the energy showers down through your arms and into your crown, washing over and into you, cleansing you of soil, filling you with light.

When the experience feels complete, begin to release the image of your campfire. Gradually return your awareness back to the physical. Feel yourself fully grounded in your body, in the room, in the here and now as you bring yourself back to a normal state of consciousness (pages 26–27).

Retrieve the slip of paper from exercise twenty-six and check in: how are you feeling toward these wants and needs now? Have any new options arisen for meeting the core needs? Do you feel less attached to the specific wants? What does it feel like to connect to the deeper need and release your attachment, if only slightly, to some of the wants? Journal about your experience.

Your Second Reiki Attunement

The work of this chapter was designed as a prelude to your second Reiki attunement. The night before your attunement, spend some time in contemplation. You may want to go over your journal entries, review your journey thus far, and allow any messages to arise. You might choose to repeat any previous exercises that feel relevant right now. Before bed, call on the power of gestational sleep (or any other powers that feel useful) to aid you on the eve of your second initiation. After your attunement, check in with how you feel. Did the experience feel different than the first attunement? Be sure to journal about your experience.

Before we move on, this is a good time to talk about the increased energy you might experience as a result of Inspiration and your second attunement. Increased energy is generally thought of as a desirable thing, and it absolutely can be wonderful. That said, the energy itself is neutral, neither good nor bad, and it can give more oomph not only to our healthy, desirable pursuits but also to things that are less aligned with our soul. My energy baseline has always been high throughout my life, but I was never taught how to use this energy skillfully. Massive amounts of energy paired with a lack of know-how meant that I experienced life as pretty severe highs and lows. It wasn't until I began to study energy work and magic that I learned how to consciously channel and shape my energy to manifest the desired results. It became clear that I had used addiction to dampen the force of my energy—high energy wielded unskillfully can feel unpleasantly intense. Things like alcohol, pot, and lack of sleep could help dull the intensity, and I'd also create energetic surges and crashes with sugar, excessive exercise, and sex to offload any excess. It isn't coincidental that when I began to meditate regularly and learned how to work with my energy, my desire for drugs and alcohol, among other things, disappeared completely, as did my desire to sugar binge.

We must choose how to channel our life energy. And when our energy flow increases, these choices really come to the fore. Following your attunement and at this stage in your self-transformation work, it's common to feel called to expand and change. If you ignore this call and try to continue with business as usual, the increased energy can become destructive, like water building in a clogged pipe, threatening to explode. If instead you embrace the call to expand and evolve, you will increase your ability to channel ever greater amounts of energy. The more energy you have available to you, the greater your potential impact in this life. It's a beautiful thing and a divine responsibility—wield it wisely.

—10—

BECOMING A REIKI MASTER

In this chapter, we will be exploring the fourth symbol, sometimes called the Master Symbol as it is typically taught in the final/Master level of Reiki instruction. This exploration will prepare you for your Master Attunement. The fourth symbol is believed to help one conduct the energy transmission—that is, perform an attunement—for all three levels of Reiki. This symbol is also said to generate energy, purify self and space (particularly of elements blocking growth and evolution), activate the crown chakra, introduce balance and healing, and connect one with spirit guides. The fourth symbol can be used in all of the ways outlined for the first three symbols, such as tracing it in the air, writing it on paper, et cetera

Drawing Symbol Four: Follow the directional arrows.

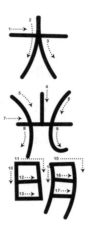

The associated mantra is Dai Kômyô, and it is pronounced die-COE-myo.

Pairing the symbol drawing with the mantra, Dai Kômyô: For the first three lines, intone one syllable per line: Dai-Ko-Myo. Do the same for lines four through six, then repeat for lines seven through nine. You've now said the mantra three times. You will draw the remaining lines, ten through seventeen, without chanting.

Dai Kômyô can be parsed into the following translations, given by Frans Stiene in *The Inner Heart of Reiki:*

Dai—large, great, big

Komyo—hope, glory, bright future

Kô—ray or light

Myô—bright, light, spell, mantra (Stiene 2015, 94)

In some Japanese esoteric schools, the kanji (Sino-Japanese characters) for Dai represents the five elements: earth, air, fire, water, and space or void (compare to the elemental associations for gassho—page 79). Looking at all four symbols, Hiroshi Doi lists the following correspondences: Symbol One represents Earth; Symbol Two, the Moon and Water; Symbol Three, the Sun and Fire; and Symbol Four, the Whole Universe and Wind (Doi 2014, 8). While I am not suggesting that the Reiki symbols were originally intended to be correlated with hermetic teachings, in my own practice I have found it relevant to explore the connections. In the Emerald Tablet, a central Hermetic text, we see all of our major players represented: the Earth, Moon, Sun, Universe, and Wind.

"Its father is the Sun; its mother is the Moon. The Wind carries it in its belly; its nurse is the Earth. It is the origin of All, the consecration of the Universe; its inherent Strength is perfected, if it is turned into Earth" (Hauck 1999, 45).

If we weave this adage together with what we've learned thus far, both about Reiki and self-transformation, one perspective is that the first symbol, which is associated with Earth, represents how you will express your True Self in the here and now, as a being who is able to operate in the physical Earth plane. As beings who are both physical and Divine, we are in a unique position to bring Divine Will into the physical world, channeling it into tangible manifestation. We bring the powerful thought energy of the One Mind into the physical realm where "its nurse is the Earth." When this creative act is in alignment with our True Self, we are, quite literally, em*body*ing the energy and meaning of the first symbol.

The second symbol, associated with the Moon, represents your connection to the unconscious, which we can compare to the One Thing. Throughout our entire self-transformation journey, we have been working to forge a vital bridge between the conscious and unconscious realms of experience by bringing awareness to our projections, the archetypes, active and receptive energies, and so forth, because without this link we are like a puppet, our strings constantly being yanked this way and that by unconscious material. We cannot hope to live as empowered beings without cooperation between the conscious and unconscious forces within.

The third symbol, associated with the Sun, represents your conscious landscape. This relates to how skillfully you wield your conscious awareness, primarily by what you choose to focus on. Energy flows where awareness goes, thus you are directing energy, including your vital life force, toward whatever you choose to focus on—something to ponder when you have the urge to vent and complain! With every ounce of focus you devote to your complaints, you are training more of your life energy on this person or situation you don't like. As my mom once heard a pastor say, "Complaining is praying for what you don't want." The Sun relates to the five divine active powers and the ways in which you relate to the external sphere, including your relationships with others, the work you do in the world, and so forth. Our personal evolution occurs in the context of our relationships with others and the various levels of community in which we participate, from the hyperlocal to the global; we cannot operate in a vacuum. Thus, learning how to effectively relate to the external world is a vital part of our spiritual practice. Your day job is no less spiritual than your meditation sessions, and the more we can operate with this awareness, the more we stay in touch with our True Self, regardless of external circumstances.

And finally, we have the fourth symbol, associated with the Universe. This is where we make deep contact with the truth that everything is one, everything is a dimension of the All. The Moon and the Sun, the receptive and the active, the physical and the spiritual, you and me—we're all, at our core, One. When we are able to hold this awareness even as we move throughout life in our individual meat suits, we bring more wisdom to every encounter, whether that encounter is happening amongst inner aspects of the self or with external "others." When we integrate the truth of Oneness into our very being, it's more difficult to resort to the ego's standard repertoire of fear-based thoughts and behaviors such as competing with and undermining others, ditching self-care to cater to external demands, limiting our potential for fear of failure or success, and so forth. When we rest in the truth, these dysfunctional patterns make less and less sense, and instead we seek responses that express love, not fear. By doing so, our life becomes an expression of our True Self.

The next kanji, *ko*, can be translated as "ray" or "light." Here we are reminded of the uniquely human function of channeling the energy of the elements and transmuting them into the light of spirit, and vice versa—channeling the energy of spirit and transmuting it into the various elements. In less abstract terms, we are able to take pure energy and turn it into things we experience as part of physical existence, things like our job, family, home, and so forth. And in the reverse, we can interact with tangible things and transmute them into pure energy: Think of seeing a beautiful sunset—something tangible—and creating the pure energy of awe and peace from the experience. We possess this ability because we are both physical and divine, and all the ways in which we channel energy add up to create our soul's work in this life. No one else can channel these energies exactly the way you do; your contribution to this Universal cycling of energy is unique and cannot be substituted with another's efforts.

Myô is composed of two separate kanji characters, one representing the sun and the other the moon. Together, the characters speak directly to the union of opposites, the creative dance of receptive and active, inner and outer, conscious and unconscious. Recall our discussion in chapter 6 where we saw how life mastery involves honoring the different strengths of each aspect of our being—the physical, finite aspect and the divine, infinite aspect. You allow the finite to be finite and the infinite to be infinite rather than trying to make either what it is not, and in doing so, you unlock and unite the power of both. Stiene writes, "The sun and moon combined together into one symbol represent the union of absolute truth (Jp. *kutai*) and relative truth (Jp. *ketai*). In the Mahayana Buddhist traditions, kutai is the truth of emptiness, while ketai is the truth of temporariness" (Steine 2010, 97). In other words, we are uniting absolute truth—the emptiness of our infinite, divine nature—with the relative truth: the temporariness of our finite physical nature.

In my own explorations with the fourth symbol, I found myself in a peaceful and silent Times Square in meditation, where I learned that this symbol can help us find the stillness in the noise, the balance in the chaos, our center in the storm. We don't have to leave this physical existence to find peace and stillness; this stillness comes in large part from cultivating the ability to simply be. Just as applying effort is a skill, so too is its conceptual opposite: being. We must learn how to skillfully be just as much as we learn how to skillfully apply effort. Without being, we will be trapped on the never-ending hamster wheel of endless to-dos, but when we balance effort with being, we tap into the awareness that we are already One with all times, places, people, and events—no striving required. It is in the balance of effort and being where we find peace. Eventually, even in the midst of "efforting" we are centered in being, and our efforts take on an entirely different feel and energetic power. Rather than exerting ourselves from a place of force and desperation driven by the fear that we are not enough unless we continuously apply effort, we instead operate from a place of peace and have a sense of being that is unshakable ... and completely independent of our efforts. We can relax on a primal level into the truth that we are already enough, that we don't have to effort our way into earning "enoughness." We simply are. When we're not operating from the misguided belief that we have to earn our right to exist, we make different choices. We're no longer in battle with ourselves and the Universe trying to prove our right to be here, which frees up *so much space and energy* that can now be devoted to living in alignment with our True Self.

Many Signposts, One Destination

Author Barbara Hurd writes about her experience in the Himalayas with a Hindu holy man who said, "The heart is the only real temple. Worship there. Everything else is a distraction" (Hurd 2008, 167). A sage reminder on our journey as we're learning about the various stages of self-transformation and the different Reiki precepts and symbols, for, as Stiene writes, "Mikao Usui put lots of signposts in his teachings, but they all point towards the same thing: rediscovering your True Self. Don't get distracted that there are many different signposts, as they are all pointing to the same place" (Stiene 2015, 101). In a passage mirroring my Times Square meditation, Hurd asks whether this stillness can be found everywhere, "In the middle of Times Square, in a roomful of people? And *in* us? In all of *us*, somewhere, even in the cacophony of emotional confusion" (Hurd 2008, 168). She references a Tibetan word, *shul*, meaning "the hollow that remains after something has moved through," (it's also the Yiddish word for temple): "First emptiness, then form. Probably emptiness again…where we can't see, where the normal constraints, the habits, identities, and the definitions by which we live might lift, disperse momentarily, leave us in enormous space…We stand in the absence, in the clearing, the hollowed-out place and discover, not wisdom or enlightenment, but spaciousness. Room. A *shul*" (Ibid., 170).

The inner stillness and temporary release from preconceived notions speaks to the deeper teachings of the fourth symbol: the willingness to go beyond our attachment to what we think we know, beyond who we think we are. To simply exist in space, to feel the space within us, a space that we too often try to cram full of stuff—physical, mental, and emotional—in an effort to resist this spaciousness, which can feel disorienting, like we're adrift with no tether. When we allow ourselves to ease into this space, to slowly relax, to loosen our grip, to simply *be*, it is here where we remember that we are already one with our True Self.

A Personal Connection to the Symbols

In the next exercise, you will be meditating with each of the first three symbols individually, and after your Master Attunement you can repeat this process with the fourth symbol. The format of this meditation is purposely open, allowing you to develop a very personal connection with the symbols. It also asks that you direct many of the meditation components yourself, preparing you for increasing levels of self-directed spiritual exploration, an important component of Master Level training. You will perform the following meditation three times, either in one sitting or in different sessions, one for each of the first three symbols.

Exercise Thirty-One: Encountering the Symbols

Bring yourself down into a meditative state (page 26).

Introduce the flow of Reiki (page 125).

State your intention to understand the deeper secrets of the symbol you are focusing on. For example, "In this meditation, I seek to know the deeper secrets of Reiki Symbol 1.

On the screen of your mind, call up a door and see the symbol imprinted on the door. Begin chanting the mantra, either aloud or mentally, to open the door.

Step through the door and allow the experience that is correct and good for you to unfold. If you start to feel like your mind is wandering at any point, restate your intention; you can do this as often as necessary. If you feel stuck, try the mantra, "The Way is clear, the Way is clear, the Way is clear," until the stuckness dissolves.

When the experience feels complete, thank any beings you may have encountered, thank Reiki, and thank yourself. Then exit through the same door you entered.

Return to normal consciousness (pages 26–27).

Record your experiences in your journal. I encourage you to do this symbol meditation more than once for each of the symbols to help you see how your conception of and relationship to the symbols is changing over time. You might choose to meditate on the symbols at least once a year to refresh and deepen your connection.

What is a Reiki Master?

As you prepare for your Master Attunement, it's helpful to talk about what it means to be a Reiki Master. As a Master you will be instructed in the ways of attuning others to Reiki on a practical level. You are also in a position to teach Reiki principles and practices, should you choose. Unfortunately, I have met many Reiki Masters who stop studying after they finish their Master level training, which I believe somewhat defeats the purpose of becoming a Reiki Master. The term "master" in and of itself can be a bit misleading, at least in light of our modern interpretation, which seems to connote a sense of completion or an end point. In practice, however, this interpretation couldn't be further from the truth. As a Reiki Master, you are embarking on a personal journey in which you are continually practicing the art of mastery—yes, of Reiki precepts and practices, but more importantly, over the principles and practices of *your life*.

When we covered the process of attunement and why people aren't permanently "fixed" once they receive one, we saw that it is the choices we make following an attunement or Reiki session that determine whether our energy channels remain clear and free flowing or become clogged with energetic ick. Some ick is inevitable to a certain extent, but allowing it to stick around is not; we always have the choice to release obstructions and return to a state of clarity and flow. Thus, as Reiki Masters, as people who have committed to prioritizing the clearing of obstructions in ourselves and to assist others in this process, we are called to walk the talk and practice the daily art of Reiki. We do more than simply give Reiki sessions and talk about Reiki—we are instead *being* Reiki. As Hiroshi Doi writes, "People will give up the easygoing idea that the whole ability is given only by the attunement. They will understand that the attunement opens the door; and that after entering the way of Reiki, they must develop and enhance their true ability on their own" (Doi 2014, 42).

How does one become Reiki? As you might have anticipated by now, there isn't a simple, step-by-step answer to this, but there are guideposts, and we've been covering them throughout our entire journey thus far. Usui left many supports in the form of the Reiki principles and symbols, and other teachings, so for starters, we can meditate on these tools. We can apply them in our daily life. We can mindfully connect to the Reiki that is flowing through all things throughout our day, sensing what this flow feels like in our body, mind, heart, and soul. I'd like to offer something even more concrete, though, something intimately connected to the spirit of what it means to be a Reiki Master. One of the most effective things you can do on your path to (remembering your) oneness with Reiki is to mindfully develop your own practices for reconnecting with this wholeness. Think of this as creating your own user's manual, a collection of practices and teachings that work especially well for you. For myself, this manual takes the form of a journal of techniques and teachings that help me feel more in tune with my True Self. For example, if I don't get outside at least a few times a week (ideally every day), I can feel my energy shift, and not for the better. I'm more foggy and irritable, my body feels less grounded and more rigid, and I'm more prone to pessimistic thinking and complaining. I don't need to go on an epic outdoor adventure to reap the benefits of nature;

even a stroll around the yard is usually enough to get me feeling clear headed and energetically flowing. The same holds true for daily meditation: If I slack, I feel it…and it ain't a good feeling.

If you read a lot of self-help and metaphysical books like me, you know the feeling of being overwhelmed by the number of meditations, chakra clearings, shamanic journeys, and other techniques you could potentially use in any given moment. The truth is that none of these practices are all that useful if we don't *use* them. In that spirit, your mastery journal should be a place where you collect practices that work well for *you* along with commentary that might come in handy later such as notes regarding when a certain meditation is especially useful (e.g., when you're having trouble making a decision or feeling irritable and impatient with people). If you want to get super organized, you can use a binder or index card file that allows you to reorder content as needed, and you can gather practices under tabbed sections that are relevant to you such as "Stress Relieving," "Chakra Clearing," and "Before Healing Sessions," making techniques and other insights easier to find when you need them most.

In addition, I would recommend coming up with a short sequence of things you do every day that you don't have to look up in a book— practices that aren't overly complicated. For example, you might have a few basic stretches you do every morning when you wake up, followed by five or ten minutes of meditation, followed by listing three things you're grateful for. And then boom, you're done. Do that every morning as often as possible (bonus if you have a short sequence you do before bed, too.) This basic sequence becomes the foundation of your daily practice, and you can supplement it at any time with additional practices from your mastery journal. That said, do commit to at *least* doing your basic sequence every day so that you're regularly reconnecting with your True Self. A daily practice also makes it easier to do more advanced practices because you're not starting from scratch every time you decide to crack open your self-care journal; you're building on an already established foundation. If you decide to do a longer chakra balancing meditation this weekend, it will be much easier if you've already built up the habit of meditating ten minutes a day.

While compiling this journal is valuable as a self-awareness and self-care tool, there's another reason this process is useful to your development as a Reiki Master. I view this level of study as primarily self-propelled and self-initiated spiritual growth. Rather than constantly seeking answers from other experts, you are learning how to develop and trust your own wisdom that is rooted in personal practice and experience, not confined to unpracticed theoretical knowledge. As a Master, you are contributing to the body of spiritual knowledge and technology that is Reiki by accumulating your own experience rather than simply absorbing the teachings of those who have gone before. Also remember that you aren't doing your work here simply to fill a book with information; this practice is designed to help you stay aligned with your True Self and to return to alignment when you get off course, as we all do from time to time. This journal will serve as an interactive reminder of your True Self and help you shake out of the trance-like state of going through the motions. As a result, you will be fully, mindfully, vibrantly living.

The Master as Beginner

As with everything else we've been learning, the topic of mastery comes with its own paradox, because while a Reiki Master is self-initiating and self-directed, guided by their True Self rather than constantly seeking answers from without, they are also a dedicated student of the universe. The Master simultaneously knows that all answers can be found within and every situation and being she encounters has something to teach her. The Master also knows she is infinitely wise *and* she barely knows anything. Remember that no matter how much we know, there is still more we can learn from those around us, be they humans, animals, trees, rocks, spirits, or any other type of being. We narrow our minds and constrict the flow of wisdom when we decide that we've "mastered" something and no longer need to receive feedback or insights from others, when we talk much more than we listen, and when we are unwilling to question what we think, believe, say, or do.

Being a student of the universe goes beyond adopting an *attitude* of humility—or even less helpfully, self-deprecation—merely because we believe this is what "spiritual" people are supposed to do. Our humility is not a persona adopted with the aim of looking more "spiritual"; our beginner's mind outlook inspires genuine humility because we are aware that we cannot possibly know all there is to know. When we live from a place of genuine humility, we free up so much energy that the ego's posturing would otherwise consume as it displays and defends what it already knows. It can be challenging to release this habit of demonstrating our knowledge (and I speak from experience) because in its absence we often feel vulnerable and less in control. If we are willing to sit with this discomfort, however, it can be incredibly liberating.

I felt much less pressure in my life when I became more mindful of my motivations for sharing information. I asked myself: "Is this relevant? Is it useful? Am I just trying to show that I know something about this?" I didn't feel the constant need to come off as an expert, even on things that I know a great deal about. It was quite a relief! And while my ego was afraid that my new outlook would lead to people thinking I was incompetent and clueless, I noticed that instead, people came to trust and value my input more when I dropped the posturing. When someone is peacocking or showing off what they know, these interactions often leave the listener with an impression of the speaker's insecurity rather that their wisdom or expertise, the exact opposite of what the speaker is intending. Beyond being a lousy conversational habit, peacocking interferes with the ability to develop and expand our wisdom because it serves as a shield against new information. There's suddenly a lot at stake if we're wrong when the ego is in charge such that our goal in interaction is no longer to enrich and enhance our perspective—it becomes about defending what we think we know. If we relate talking to output and listening to input on an energetic level, we're messing with our flow because we're spewing a bunch of output while relatively little input is permitted. This stagnation can manifest as lack of new ideas and cyclical thoughts and fears; when it precipitates on the physical level, even our bodies start to feel restricted and rigid.

Another component of Reiki mastery is teaching. The more we share our knowledge and experience, the more we change and grow. As a result, we have more knowledge and wisdom to share. That knowledge and wisdom truly are infinite provided we stay connected to Source energy, which we do in large part by practicing self-care. Not only does self-care keep us plugged into Source (the origin of the material we're teaching), it also keeps our channels functioning well so the energy we receive productively flows into and through us, allowing us to effectively transmit the material to others. I have found that the more I write and teach (two of the ways I am called to share), the more information floods to me during meditations, dreams, and daily life that I can then write about and teach. It's like turning on an inexhaustible faucet, and the more committed I am to self-care, the better my energy is able to flow clearly into my writing and teaching.

Committing to the Practice

As you prepare to go deeper with your relationship to Reiki and your True Self by receiving your Master Attunement, take some time to develop a basic self-care sequence you can commit to every day. Write the sequence down, and spend some time thinking about why you've included each component. For example, if meditation is part of your daily sequence, what do you hope to experience? Connection with your True Self? A feeling of calm and renewed clarity? Communion with spirit guides? All of the above? Take time to get clear on why you're doing these things, even if those reasons change over time. When you have this clarity, you're less likely to fall into a rut and simply go through the motions. It can be helpful to write down your reasons so you can look back later if the practice is starting to feel rote. You can always adapt the sequence if it begins to lose its luster, although I challenge you to stick with one sequence for a full month to gain the benefits of mindful repetition and the energetic momentum it carries. If you miss a day or two, no shame or guilt—just return to the practice.

Prior to and following your attunement as you're developing your own ideas on what it means to be a Master, reflect on the following:

"Wisdom is knowledge beyond knowing; the need to know is the shadow side of wisdom" (Milne 1998, 128).

"Life inevitably brings profound quandaries and stress. While they are not necessarily our fault, they may be our responsibility" (Perera 2001, 310).

"Small and large issues alike can feel overwhelming, but often this is a result of trying to solve problems without changing anything about the life that created them" (Bowman 2016, 8).

"Before the creation of humanity and, by extension, sin, God created teshuvah, repentance. Literally, teshuvah means 'return,' implying that when one sins one turns away from one's true nature and true path, and that repentance is returning to that true nature and path" (Shapiro 2009, 42).

"There is a throne. It's there for you. The only person who can enthrone you is you. The throne is your destiny. The throne is waiting for you to be brave enough to be you" (Jagat 2017, 252).

After your Master Attunement, use the following meditation to really feel the power and energy of all four Reiki symbols on all levels of your being.

Exercise Thirty-Two: Meditation with the Four Symbols

Enter a meditative state (page 26), giving yourself as much time as needed to feel fully centered and present.

Chant the Choku Rei mantra in vowel form, chanting on the exhale, pausing as you inhale: O U E I. It will sound like: Ohhhhh oooooo aaaaay eeeeee

Continue chanting as you bring your awareness to the base of your spine or the soles of your feet—whichever is making contact with the earth or the chair—and breathe Reiki in through your base. Feel Reiki arising from the Earth as you chant and allow the energy to rise into your tanden.

Pause the chant as you sink into deeper connection with the grounding sensation of the energy connecting you to the Earth, lending weight and gravity to your inner center of gravity, your tanden. Take a few more breaths in this place.

Shift your awareness to your crown. You will now begin to chant the Sei Heiki mantra in vowel form, chanting on the exhale, pausing as you inhale: E I E I. It will sound like: aaaaay eeeeee aaaaay eeeeee

Continue chanting as you feel your crown chakra unfold. Breathe Reiki down through your crown. Feel Reiki washing down through your central channel, collecting at your tanden. Continue chanting for a few more breaths, allowing the heavenly energy to mix and combine with the Earth energy at your tanden.

Pause the chant as you sink into deeper connection with the union of heaven and earth, above and below, active and receptive. Feel these energies continue to build and blend in your tanden, generating heat as they do so. Allow this heat to build in a way that feels correct and good for you.

Let the heat rise up through your central channel, traveling through your abdomen, heart center, throat, face, and through your third eye until it reaches your crown. This heat begins to melt the heavenly energy at your crown, creating a rain of energy. Feel and perhaps envision this energy dripping down like spring rain into your heart center.

As the rain gently falls into your heart center, chant the Hon Sha Ze Sho Nen mantra: O A SE O NE. It will sound like: oooooh ahhhhh zehhhh oooooh nehhhh

Continue chanting as the heavenly rain waters the garden of your heart, softening your heart center and allowing peace to blossom. Continue to breathe for a few cycles, enjoying this sensation of peace and harmony between heaven and earth, and the flowering of the Intelligence of the Heart.

And now, begin to chant Dai Kômyô: Dyyyye kohhhh myoohhh

Let your awareness expand to take in the rising of Earth energy, the rain of heavenly energy, and the blossoming of the heart. Feel this powerful cycle suffusing your entire being with peace and wellbeing. Feel the steady flow of energy from your tanden to your head, back down to your heart endlessly cycling, the dynamic flow of life. Breathe in the energy of harmony and balance.

When you feel ready, thank Reiki and gently allow any images to fade. Set the intention that the flow of energy will return to a state that is correct and good for you.

Return to a normal state of consciousness (pages 25–26).

Journal about your experience. It's recommended to do this meditation more than once, as it helps you to connect with the deeper teachings of Reiki by embodying them. You might perform this meditation in accordance with a cycle that is meaningful for you, such as every full or new moon. In the next chapter, you will build on the energetic shift of your Master Attunement with the sixth step of self-transformation: Refinement.

— 11 —
REFINEMENT

This step takes the material that we have uncovered and transformed throughout our journey thus far and removes additional traces of the ego's limitations that are preventing us from fully embracing our True Self. With Refinement, we raise our psyche to the highest level possible, to unite with the One Mind. This might sound fine and dandy, but how in the world do we go about this process? Let's put this step into context. In Illumination we began the process of burning away egoic clutter; then in Submersion, we went even deeper by soaking in the waters of our unbconscious mind, uncovering aspects of ourselves that have been buried and rejected, and welcoming them back into the fold so we could reclaim more of our innate wholeness. Polarization heightened our awareness of our internal opposites—in particular, our active and receptive natures. Temporarily separating these powers allowed us to better understand their unique strengths and challenges so that we can more skillfully recombine them in life and in later steps. Merging was the initial union of the polar forces within, the active and receptive, the rational and the unconscious, giving birth to a new form of consciousness and a new way of being. And finally, Inspiration took this product and seeded it with new life, injecting us with divine inspiration.

This brings us to Refinement, a process that centers on becoming even more aware of who we truly are by paradoxically adopting an outlook of life that is much larger than our individual self. You're getting a bird's-eye view of your soul's journey and then applying that big-picture view to the more intimate experiences that constitute daily life. Two of the skills developed in previous stages are particularly relevant here. The first is our work with projections, where we learned how to recognize when we are taking our inner material and projecting it onto the external world, absolving ourselves of responsibility while simultaneously draining our personal power. The second is learning how to sit with emotional energy rather than dissipating it as a means of "blowing off steam." Both of these practices resist the urge to scatter and dissipate our energy and thus help us stay more centered and in possession of our natural state of wholeness.

With Refinement, we now use these skills to look at the events of our life from a bigger perspective, a transpersonal perspective. Transpersonal refers to that which is beyond ("trans") the personal; in other words, beyond the realm of personal identity. For many of us, it might seem odd to consider our life impersonally. While the majority of our conscious moments are spent looking at life through our individual perspective, we have the ability to transcend this view, and the more we practice, the more often and the more readily we are able to do so when needed. Why would we want to transcend our personal perspective? One of the immediate benefits is that it gives us the clarity that is often hard to obtain when we're stuck in our personal identity, which by definition is limited in focus. When we transcend, we are able to see solutions to problems that were previously hidden because they didn't fit with our personal perspective. Here's a practical example: Throughout my childhood and young adulthood, I had no idea that scoliosis was potentially reversible. I had been told by doctors that it was a condition that could at best be managed, or I could have steel rods inserted along my spine. Based on this, I didn't bother to seek out information to the contrary. Many years later, when I began studying massage therapy, I learned that numerous methods exist for reversing the spinal curvature of scoliosis to varying degrees without surgery. I was astounded. All this time, my belief that scoliosis was an irreversible condition limited my ability to see alternatives.

We limit our perspective all the time. Our brain creates shortcuts to help us accomplish more with less conscious thinking to conserve resources, but over time this whittles down our range of possibilities because we start to see our shortcuts as the *only* routes available. We get used to taking a certain way home from work, we get used to relating to our mother in a particular manner, we get used to treating our body in a certain fashion, and on and on it goes. When we transcend our personal database, we open ourselves to a vast store of knowledge and energy that was previously unavailable to our conscious mind.

Now that we understand why we would want to transcend our personal identity, let's look at how to go about doing this. With Refinement, we deepen our ability to take our personal, individual experiences and raise that material to a higher level that allows us to see things with less drama-inducing attachments and other reactions that serve to confuse and constrain us. This process isn't new; in many of the previous exercises such as exercises thirteen and fourteen: Seeing Projections, you developed your ability to separate objective events from the subjective stories of the ego. The difference during Refinement is that we will be creating an even wider separation between objective occurrences and the ego's interpretations using the power of myth. In the space created through this separation, new ways of seeing and thinking can emerge.

How do we use myths to elevate our consciousness? The short answer is by seeing ourselves in the myths, something we already do when we're lost in a good book or film. We identify with one or more of the characters, seeing parts or all of ourselves in them, and the lines between their adventures and our own reality blurs. While this identification often ends with the completion of the film or the book, it can sometimes extend into our everyday consciousness, perhaps inspiring us to do things we wouldn't normally do or see things in new ways. With Refinement, we will consciously identify with figures in myths both ancient or contemporary and use them to activate our transpersonal eyesight. To make the process easier, it's best to choose a specific quality. For example, if we were to choose Hermione Granger, we might focus on the tendency to get caught up in amassing and displaying intellectual knowledge at the expense of fostering connections with others, something that Hermione herself learns on her own journey. We can use this modern myth to help see ourselves more clearly: in what ways are we like Hermione? How is our life affected by those qualities? Are we happy with the effects or are we seeking different outcomes, such as greater intimacy with others or less pressure to prove we are intelligent? We then take the process further by applying this self-inquiry in times of personal challenge. Let's say we're in a work situation where our ego is flaring and our go-to response is demonstrating how much we know in order to feel safe. In the heat of the moment, it can be hard to see beyond the panicking ego as it tries to convince us that something very bad will happen if we don't display our intellect *pronto!* In this state of mind, everything feels extremely personal: our *personal* reputation is at stake, our *personal* authority is being threatened. Through the power of myth, we can see that we are not the only human in history to have faced this challenge. Many others before us—such as Hermione from our example—have felt triggered and have responded by spouting facts and rigidly defending the ego's stance. And many others before us have found that this tactic usually only serves as a temporary fix at best that does nothing to instill a sense of inner safety and stability that is not tied to how smart we appear to others and ourselves.

When we see that this moment in time in which our ego is on the rampage—our personal challenge—is not unique, it's easier to grasp that while this particular moment is one we have the *option* of taking personally, we are neither limited nor obliged to do so. We could instead choose to identify with the transpersonal nature of the situation, to the archetypal, universal scenario of having a bruised ego, something that many others are likely experiencing right now as we speak. In other words, we can see that this occurrence is simply part of human experience, not a personal affront. When we adopt this transpersonal perspective, the rantings of the ego start to recede into the background if only a little, and from this place of greater stillness we can assess the situation from a different vantage point. Perhaps we see our coworker's insecurities that are contributing to the situation and maybe can even empathize with them. Doing so could provide us with a glimpse of an underlying need our coworker is having trouble expressing. We might then pose the question: "It seems like you're feeling rushed on this project and would like more time—is that accurate?" Maybe the conversation goes in an entirely new direction, toward solution rather than standoff. This outcome contrasts to the frame of mind had we taken things personally, of the "How dare they!" storylines that cause us to feel locked into defending ourselves, thereby limiting our options and the ability to see more clearly. Working with myths helps to create space between us and our habitual ways of reacting. In doing so, we tap into a power and awareness that is greater than our individual reserves: archetypal, transcendent wisdom.

The Power of Archetypes

Myths are populated by archetypes; for our purposes, we can think of archetypes as characters that serve as templates or examples of all the different ways we can express our energy. You can imagine the archetypes as filters: As the undifferentiated, divine energy of pure potential makes its way from the great cosmic ocean into a more unique expression in the form of our life, it passes through the filters of the archetypes. As we learned with the ten divine powers, in some circumstances, one power might be just what the doctor ordered, while in others it's less helpful, and in the same way, certain archetypes are ideal in some circumstances but less functional in others.

Let's pull an archetype from the tarot to illustrate how this process works. The Emperor is a card of structure and boundaries, rulership and law. When neutral, universal energy flows through this archetype it becomes temporarily flavored with these qualities. If you wanted to do an unstructured, free-flowing finger painting session, you probably wouldn't want to activate your inner Emperor. However, if you were struggling to carve out time in your schedule for your painting session, Emperor energy could come in handy by helping you to create the structure to support your creativity and maintain boundaries to prevent distractions from encroaching on your creative time.

Archetypal selection is happening throughout our day, although usually without our conscious awareness. We might be in the creative flow and filter energy through the Artist all morning, and then a coworker says something triggering in the middle of a work meeting and—bam—the Judge appears, and we see ourselves and the world around us through this judgmental lens. This simple example might suggest that some archetypes are "good" while others are "bad," but it's all about context; if we're researching which car to buy, for example, the Judge might be helpful. Just like the divine powers, what we really want is to make the process of selection more conscious so we can choose archetypes that best suit our current needs.

There's another layer to our experience of the archetypes: our ability to personalize them, thereby altering their characteristics and by extension the way energy is filtered through them. For example, your experience of your father in childhood might match up in many ways with the archetypal figure of the Emperor, so this archetype is incorporated into your personal repertoire. As you start to internalize this archetype, you add your own twist to it and unconsciously modify it to match up more closely with your dad. While the archetype of the Emperor is connected to rulership and law, in its healthy expression this energy is in service of harmony and stability; it's not punitive. Your father, being human, might express this energy differently—maybe he wielded rules as a way to instill fear and exert undue control over you. As a result, you take this input and model your internal Emperor accordingly. Henceforth, your experience of this archetype will be filtered through your unique "brand" of Emperor, which might be quite different from mine even though we both started with the same Emperor archetype.

By using myths as a tool for self-awareness, we can begin to recognize which archetypes we have internalized and how we may have altered them based on our personal experience. We can then reflect on whether these archetypes are useful to us right now, if they would be more useful if given a "reboot" to return them to their original state (prior to our modifications), or if an entirely different archetype would be more appropriate. Again, the reason we want to bring our archetypal relationships into conscious awareness is because we use the archetypes all the time, whether we're aware of it or not. The archetypes we have chosen and the ways in which we have modified them based on our life experiences dictates how we channel the energy of the greater cosmic ocean into the day-to-day stuff of our life. If we're channeling energy

through archetypes that aren't suited to the situation or have been modified in dysfunctional ways, the energetic blueprint of our life will be
out of whack. By healing our archetypal relationships, our efforts are
directed to the source of the issue, not the symptoms.

These archetypes are the bridge from our individual consciousness
and the greater cosmic consciousness, so it's to our advantage to use (and
choose) them wisely. They enable us to channel more energy than we
can contain in our personal reserves, and because energy is information,
we'll have access to information that might otherwise be unavailable to
our personal awareness field. For example, when we embody the Healer
perhaps in the archetypal form of the Greek god Asclepius, we might
see previously hidden options and solutions or receive intuitive insights
that propel our healing forward by leaps and bounds. Our perspective
is broadened and we enter the realm of transpersonal consciousness by
channeling archetypal energy. In this space, we are no longer limited
by our personal identity and the associated beliefs, thoughts, and other
trappings that may be dampening our connection to our True Self.

Your Personal Grail Quest

In addition to giving us access to greater stores of energy and information, we can also apply the power of myth on a grander scale. By pulling
back and looking at our life or at stages of our life through myth, we
can gain a clearer sense of our soul's quest. One of the reasons I think
many of us are drawn to past-life exploration is because it gives our life
a sense of scale that is much larger in scope than a one-life-and-you're-
done perspective. It feels more epic, like a grand quest with a purpose.
When life feels a little too sloggy and directionless and we can't see
the forest for the trees, it's natural to hunger for something more,
something bigger than hitting the snooze button for the third time
and getting stuck in rush-hour traffic on our way to work. And here is
where the power of myth comes in handy, for not only can we refine
our momentary struggles, we can also refine the sum total of our lives.

We can raise our life story to the level of myth and thereby infuse the morning battle with the alarm clock and the slow inching of traffic with spiritual purpose. Remember that all the work we've been doing is not designed to make the alarm clocks and the traffic jams of the world disappear; it's meant to reveal the divine nature of even the seemingly mundane.

The ability to see the magic in the mundane and unite our human and divine nature has been a major focus of our transformational work. We are not physical beings by accident. We did not incarnate simply to learn how to "rise above" our physical nature. Our soul has chosen life in a physical body to learn what it means to be flesh given spirit, embodied spirit, to be we who have resided in the purely spiritual realms and descended to earth, uniting the powers of the above and the below. Learning to embrace the full glory of *both* our physical and our spiritual nature is why we are here. When we do this, we are able to unite the big-picture, transpersonal vision of spirit with the fleshly vessel through which we are able to carry this vision into the world. How you as a unique being use transpersonal energy to make an impact here on earth—*that* is your soul's quest, your *raison d'être*. In other words, the ways in which you embody spirit are synonymous with your soul's purpose, for no one else on earth will embody spirit quite like you.

In the book *The Maiden King,* Jungian analyst Marion Woodman writes: "Many people are undermined by a loss of connection to *their own life energy in their own body.* [emphasis mine] Patriarchal judgment in both mothers and fathers has cut them off, leaving a trail of wounding in both sons and daughters. If their natural desires were met by a constant "No," they gradually disconnected from their own "I desire" in the survival chakra in order to please. ... As adults, they look at other people who seem to love life and wonder why they themselves do not. They pretend, even as children, to be reaching from their own desire ... [but] because their bodies are not expressing desires that come from natural instincts, they fall into unnatural desires, driven desires that overwhelm them with stupor and manifest as addictions. They crave food that brings them no nourishment, drink that brings them no spirit, sex that brings them no union...The drive that remains hidden is compulsion; the drive that is revealed is freedom" (Bly and Woodman 1999, 130).

When our self-reflection and process of self-growth does not encompass our dual nature, physical and spiritual, we are the person who is "undermined by a loss of connection to their own life energy in their own body," a disconnect that often manifests in very tangible ways—in our health, finance, and livelihood issues, as well as in spiritual ways such as lack of purpose and clarity and a feeling of separation from our intuitive powers. These disconnects from various parts of our life combine to produce a sort of malaise we try to mask through addiction and all the other ways in which we numb the pain of being out of touch with our wholeness, such as staying busy, depression and anxiety, being hypercritical of self and others, and so on.

When we are disconnected from our soul's purpose, it can be easy to fixate on external situations that trigger worry, fear, anger, and judgment, which brings us right back to our work with projection: It's painful to look at our internal disconnect, so we project it onto the world and see external situations and people to blame for the way we feel. I believe this fixation is rooted in the following dynamic: When we don't have an intimate connection with our soul's purpose, our entire being experiences a nagging uneasiness, a feeling of dis-ease. We know something is amiss, but when we can't bear to own this seeming emptiness, we project it onto the world around us and become fixated on all of the awful things we see in the news, the things that aren't working in our own and other people's lives, and the things that leave us feeling angry and helpless. From the ego's point of view, it is far better to live in a hopelessly messed up world and spend our time complaining about that state of affairs than it is to take responsibility for re-creating intimacy with our soul. Why? The ego hasn't a clue how to accomplish the latter, but it does know how to complain, worry, rage, and obsess.

We are given the choice in each moment to feed the ego by complaining, fixating on our fears and worries, being hypercritical of ourselves and others, and outlining all the reasons something won't work before we even try. Alternatively, we could choose to be the witness to the ego and stay centered in our True Self amidst the ego chatter with compassion and self-love, abstain from complaining, replace "I'm worried that…" with "I wonder if…," and forgive ourselves and others. We can trust that ruminating over worst-possible scenarios does not make us more prepared. We can continually open ourselves up to the soul's possibilities rather than stay locked in the ego's false certainties. One of our most powerful tools for this process of nourishing the True Self instead of feeding the ego is myth; we can use it to refine our personal experiences and raise them to the level of the transpersonal, thereby freeing ourselves from the trap of the ego, which by definition is confined to the personal level.

Recall our discussion of the Emperor and how we internalize and modify this archetype based on our life experiences, thereby affecting how we channel energy through the Emperor and into our life. Depending on our modifications, the energy could be more that of stifling hierarchy and patriarchy, harsh punishment and rigid discipline, and negation of intuition—the shadow side of the Emperor—and this can lead to a dysfunctional relationship to structure and authority. We might routinely find ourselves at war with authority figures, making work a source of constant stress, or we might throw the baby out with the bathwater and reject helpful structure altogether, making it difficult to prioritize things that are important to us such as healthy eating or time for creative pursuits. This is why we encounter Refinement only after having done a great deal of self-transformation work. The previous steps helped us work with these archetypal energies in a way that is less clouded and cluttered by ego chatter and other filters, and now as we learn how to apply myth to our lives, we can experience the resultant energy in a more powerful way.

At its heart, myth is a way of making meaning from the forces and complexities of life. We are making meaning from the events we experience all throughout life, internally and externally. We can allow the ego to take charge of this meaning-making process, in which case we often end up with interpretations like, "Kyle is such a jerk, and if I don't fixate on what he's doing and how it's a personal attack, then I won't be safe!" The problem with this storyline is that it traps us in misery, powerlessness, and unappealing choices, but it's also an inaccurate reflection of reality. The ego's story is *never* the whole story. It might contain fragments of truth (or it might not), but it can never capture the full depth of meaning. The ego boils things down into a simplistic portrait of black and white, us versus them, this or that; in doing so, it loses 99 percent of the picture. In contrast, myth expands our view, bigger than any one interaction with Kyle "the jerk"—bigger than any individual, personal life. Myth expands the level of meaning we're able to access.

The Expansion of Acceptance

Life is complex and ultimately a mystery, but the ego wants none of that; it wants to file everything away in orderly and labeled boxes to be stored in one of two closets: Good or Bad. In order to achieve this goal, it throws anything that doesn't fit into these boxes into the unconscious, and our lives are whittled down to a slim shadow of their full potential. It's no wonder we feel "less than" and struggle with fears that we're not enough. These fears don't point to an actual not-enoughness we must fix by striving for perfection or more orderly labeling and shoving into closets—they point to the truth that we are only accepting a mere fraction of our total selves. There is so much more to us than meets the ego's eye, and by raising our life experiences above the narrow lens of the personal—by Refining them—we gain a vantage point from which we can take in and remember more of our True Self.

This expansion serves to bring more of our abilities and hidden powers to the forefront, because with the ego busily throwing away everything that doesn't match up with its simplistic stories, we're left with a paltry subset of our true skills and original wisdom. Through Refinement, we throw open the doors to previously locked rooms and unearth the treasures within. This process isn't all cupcakes and unicorns, but the difficult material—our secret shames and deep wounds—is not separate or different from our gifts. The two are one and the same. We must resist the ego stepping in and shoving this material back into the closets. It will try to convince us that we should pick through the boxes and only take out the pretty things, but once more, the ego's perspective is limited and inaccurate, for the parts of us that are beat up, tarnished, and looking a little worse for the wear are *precisely* where our magic lies. Within our wounds is the very cure for what ails us, but we must be willing to meet them face to face, heart to heart. We must accept them. We must stop running, hiding, and trying to hack off parts of ourselves in search of healing and wholeness.

> Every dark thing one falls into can be called an initiation. To be initiated into a thing means to go into it. The first step is generally falling into the dark place and usually appears in a dubious or negative form…The shamans say that being a medicine man begins by falling into the power of the demons; the one who pulls out of the dark place becomes the medicine man, and the one who stays in it is the sick person (Von Franz 1993, 64).

Myth can help lift us out of our dark places while retaining the wisdom these places contain by showing us unconscious aspects of ourselves, things we can't see through the ordinary eyes of consciousness.

The Refinement Process

Myth serves as a translator, a go-between for our unconscious to communicate with our conscious mind, enabling us to choose archetypes that help us connect with our True Self, and there are two primary ways to kickstart this process. One is to immerse yourself in myths. Deliberately expose yourself to these potent stories. Read myths from different cultures. Read different tellings of the same myth. Research interpretations of the myths. Watch films based on myths. As you do so, you deepen your ability to "speak" Myth. You hone your ability to see beyond the literal, to think symbolically, to think mythically. This practice increases your contact with the transpersonal and your ability to tap into this mode of consciousness at will. When you are in a challenging situation, this will help you access new perspectives more readily. Think of these perspective shifts as your ticket aboard the transpersonal express, the train from the limited confines of personal identity to a more expansive vantage point where you'll have access to new ways of responding, new choices, and new ideas. Every time you tap into this, you are breaking out of ruts that might be very deep indeed, what yogic philosophy calls samskaras, the mental and emotional habits that keep us trapped.

The second way to kick start this process is to pay attention to the stories that resonate with you, and this resonance needn't be restricted to the pleasant variety. When you're reading the news, watching movies, lost in a novel, looking at a painting, and so on, pay attention to the stories that make you uncomfortable, that push your buttons, that fill you with emotions. When you find yourself drawn to a particular story, pay attention—it's pushing your buttons for a reason. If you follow the breadcrumbs, you'll be led to an interior space that your conscious mind might not be able to find on its own. The more I expose myself to myths, the larger my mythical "vocabulary," and the easier it is for me to see the mythic aspects in my own life. The more I pay attention to the stories that engage me on a deep level, the more I am led to areas of myself that are yearning to be accepted, understood, and refined, thereby releasing trapped, stagnant energy and bringing me back to my True Self.

In addition to these two approaches, here are other ways to engage with mythic elements:

- Choose a myth and develop your own interpretation beyond the literal meaning. Be sure to write it in your journal; your take on a story might change over time in telling ways.

- Meditate on a myth—go into the story in your mind and see what happens. What do the characters say to you? Are you one of the characters, and if so, which one? What does it feel like to be this character? What kinds of thoughts, desires, and emotions do you have? Does your participation alter the story?

- Read the myths before bed and pay attention to your dreams. Write them in your journal the following morning.

- Retell the myth to others, activating the energetic potential of these stories.

- Act the myth out when you're feeling stuck. How does this energy feel in your body, mind, and soul?

- Approach a situation you're struggling with as a character from myth. What would Apollo do? What would Little Red Riding Hood do? What would Kali do?

- Tell the story of your current situation in the form of a myth, perhaps translating into a bedtime story or fairy tale format. Look beyond the literal events, beyond the he-said, she-said, and search for symbolic meaning. Losing your voice could mean a struggle to speak your truth, an argument that took place in the kitchen could suggest a conflict around being nourished by life, and so on. How does this reframe alter your perspective? Can you see anything now that was previously hidden?

- If a particular symbol in a myth is speaking to you, like a golden apple or ruby slippers, meditate on what the symbol represents. Look it up. Journal about it. Make a piece of art in response to the golden apple, wear red shoes to work. How does this change your perspective?

Regardless of the method you choose, the aim is to continually expand your perspective. Think of your ego mind like a plot of soil. When you keep walking back and forth over the same area, the soil becomes compacted, dense, and difficult to work with. It's hard for anything but the toughest of vegetation to grow here. Every time you engage the transpersonal mind, you are breaking up another clod of soil, allowing it to become more breathable and receptive to life. You're introducing compost, new organic matter, new ideas, new ways of being. We always have the choice to become more set in our ways or continually seek expansion, growth, and possibility.

The ego tries to establish fixed ways of reacting to simplify reality. When someone does something we don't like, we respond in predictable ways—so predictable, in fact, that it can feel like we don't have a choice. If someone says something rude, we *have* to get mad, right? That's a "normal" response. We tell our friends how rude the person was, they agree with our anger, and our belief that we responded in the right way is solidified. However, we always have a choice. While everyone else is busy getting angry, you can take a transpersonal view and see what is hidden in plain sight; what is everyone else missing because they're content with the react to rudeness with anger, rinse, wash, and repeat formula? While others complain about the specifics of their work situation, you can pull back and take a less personal view, a more mythic view. What might you see if you weren't limited to seeing only through your eyes? What options present themselves and routinely get ignored, drowned out by the din of habitual reaction? What pearls of wisdom are hiding in plain sight that people kick out of the way to pave the road for the safe certainties of the ego?

Exercise Thirty-Three: Tapping Into the Power of Myth

Choose a myth to focus on for this exercise. My recommendation is to seek intuitive guidance beforehand and ask for the myth that is correct and good for you at this time to make itself known. Then make a trip to the library and choose a book that resonates with you. Check in with your intuition again and ask to be led to the story you most need to hear right now.

Once you've selected your myth, read it. Soak it in. What impressions come to you while reading or looking at the pictures? Write them down in your journal. Then go back over the story and look at individual details more closely. Don't worry about interpreting them "correctly."

Now take a situation in your life about which you'd like to have more clarity. Assume that the myth contains exactly what you need in order to shift your perspective; the wisdom is hidden in plain sight. Free write or speak aloud ways that the myth addresses your situation. What comes up for you?

Reflect on how the information presented in the myth can usher in a new way of thinking about and responding to your situation. How would various characters in the story behave in your shoes? What advice would they give you? Imagine yourself responding in these different ways. How does it feel? What sensations do you notice in your body? What emotions arise? Keep journaling. Capture the threads. Seek what is hidden in plain sight.

Come up with at least one way to take this new information and apply it to your life. Commit to taking this new action this week. What happens? How does it feel? Does it change how you interpret the myth? How you interpret your life situation?

The more familiar you are with the language of myth, the more likely you are to see the hidden reality of your life and the more readily you can interpret the literal to extract a higher level of meaning that goes far beyond the ego's limited, reactionary meanings, such as, "When I'm threatened, I need to respond defensively or people will take advantage of me." "When I don't have an answer, people lose respect for me so it's better to say *something* even if it's not true." "When people cross my boundaries, they're deliberately trying to hurt me, and I'm justified in punishing them." We might read these ego statements now and consciously disagree, but these are often the very beliefs we fall back on when we're actually in challenging situations. If things go sideways, we often don't stop to question the efficacy of our approach…we just do it harder! Using myth to dial down the intense feeling of being personally attacked allows us to pause before the reactionary storm. The more we become accustomed to creating this reflective pause, the longer it lasts, and eventually the storm is no longer inevitable. We no longer experience what we believed were external phenomena over which we have no control. We see that the storms were always chaos of our own making, perhaps ways we justified lashing out in anger, feeling self-righteous and hopping on our soapbox, being controlling and critical, wallowing in victimhood, overstepping people's boundaries, or indulging in addictions. We can now choose to create clarity and calm instead. We can call back our projections and take responsibility for the way we see the world. When we take responsibility in this way, we feel our power gather and build rather than dissipate as we search for something—anything—to quell the storm within.

The work we are doing helps us release the drive to look for answers externally, which is something we believe we need when we become fixated on trying to figure out what's going on in someone else's head ("Why didn't he call?" "Why did my boss say that to me?" "Why is she being such an ass?") or when we equate solving a problem with changing the scenery: ("I just need to find another job, another house, another girlfriend, another…and *then* things will be different," "If work wasn't such a madhouse, I wouldn't be so anxious," "If my mom would stop nagging me, *then* I'd be happy."). Instead we see, feel, and *know* the axiom "as above, so below; as within, so without." The way we experience the world is a direct reflection of our relationship to our self. Changing the scenery isn't the answer. Changing other people isn't the answer—and we couldn't even if it was because people only change by their own initiative. Changing how we relate to ourselves is *everything*.

Take the specifics of your life, the physicality and the literalness of it all, and rather than allowing this to become a prison of matter, imbue this physicality, this literalness, with spirit in the form of myth. Unite the above and the below; bring out the best in both. Take the glorious mess of human life—the ups, the downs, the bitter and the sweet, the heartwarming and the heart wrenching. Take it all. Don't throw any of it out; it's all gold. Lift this beautiful mess to the heavens, let it be transformed in the mythic realms of spirit, and then embrace it wholeheartedly as it returns to earth, here and now, in your morning commute, in your lover's embrace, in the harsh words of a coworker, in the smile of a stranger. Let it penetrate all of life. Every last bit. In this state of accepting the full range of yourself and the full range of the world, nothing gets left out. You and the world are as you were always meant to be—*whole*. Every fiber of matter is perfused with spirit. The receptive dances in step with the active. Your intuition partners with intellect. Your darkness breaks bread with your light. Your life is a daily practice of em*body*ing the divine, and you remember your True Self. You *become* Reiki.

—12—
INTEGRATION

We have come to our final step of self-transformation: Integration. What a journey it has been! We have been illuminated, submerged, polarized—you name it—all in preparation for our climax: bringing it all home. This phrase is apt: by integrating what we have learned on our journey, we are coming home to ourselves, embodying the spirit of Reiki. We are remembering our True Self. Throughout our journey, we have been working with the concept of opposites in various forms both helpful and harmful. We have explored projection, in which we cast aspects of ourselves onto other people, creating the perceived opposition of us versus them. This process generates internal opposition in which we categorize aspects of our selfhood into acceptable versus unacceptable. In this state of fragmentation, we seek ways to distract ourselves from the pain of feeling disconnected from our natural wholeness, and these distractions often come in the form of habitual responses and addictions.

We also learned about our internal polarity of receptive and active forces and how this polarity can generate a great deal of energy, which can then be channeled into productive pursuits. We had our first taste of the beneficial side of opposition, which is important because society generally teaches us to view opposition as something to be eradicated. However, the more we seek to wipe out the "other," the stronger its subconscious hold over us. We become locked in a never-ending struggle. Neither side can win in a scenario of the absence of opposition, so we must seek another way out of this quandary—embracing paradox. If we go back to the Hermetic creation story, things began when the All chose to separate into the One Mind and the One Thing, but in spite of this separation, both the One Mind and the One Thing are still the All. They're separate *and* they're one. In the same way, you and I are separate *and* we're one, and you can continue this pattern for all of existence. Here is another signpost on our path: In order to evolve, we must reach a point where we can fully embrace paradox in all areas of our life. The more we are able to do so, the more we remember our wholeness, our True Self.

In *The Maiden King*, authors Bly and Woodman speak of a progression from thinking about things literally to psychologically to mythologically. We worked with this a great deal in chapter 11 but it bears another look here: When we are stuck in literal thinking, we cannot get past the gate of the ego. We cannot see past the literal events of a situation and our ego's narrow, literalistic interpretation of them. Here is where we take everything personally. Each time we encounter a person who says something unkind to us, we respond in predictable ways: we interpret their behavior as a personal attack and react from a place of habit. The ego can do this repeatedly, it never tires of it. At a certain point, *we* get tired of it, though, and then we begin to shift to a more psychological viewpoint—we begin to think about what might be motivating the other person to act in this way and are more open to that reason not having much, if anything, to do with us. We begin to think about what's motivating *us* and why we tend to react in the same manner in these situations and reach a point where we are sometimes (maybe even frequently) able to choose a different response. If we decide to take our work even further, we tap into a mythological perspective: we start to see the overarching themes and archetypal energies at play. Things become less about "Brian acting like a controlling asshole" and more about seeing how our soul is curious to learn how to relate to authority in different, more enlivening ways. From this mythical, transpersonal (that is, "beyond personal") perspective, we are better able to take in the rich complexity that is life.

If we are stuck to reducing everything to an egoic level of simplicity, we are forgetting the nature of the True Self, for the truth is always more complex than we can ever see from our finite point of view. In our current state of consciousness, as far as I can tell, we are never privy to all possible factors contributing to a situation; there are simply too many moving parts. And while we don't need to see all of these factors in order to move through life, we *will* benefit from acknowledging their existence even when we can't see them. We do this by admitting that no matter how certain our ego is, the truth is always bigger. No matter how strong our opinion, other people are allowed to feel differently, and it doesn't automatically make them wrong. No matter how well something works for us, it doesn't mean it's right for everyone. And on it goes.

Now, we don't have to agree with everything and everyone, and we can certainly take a stand on issues that are important to us. Above all, we have to be big enough and expand into our true fullness so that we are able to hold space for the *reality* of differences. When we are overly identified with the ego, who we believe ourselves to be is relatively small. Let's use the analogy of a house. You are this house, and your ego is only aware of the first floor. The basement and the upstairs are a complete unknown to the ego. As you start filling in the first floor with all of the things the ego knows, such as your opinions and beliefs, it starts getting pretty crowded; if someone comes along with a different opinion, the ego is loath to make space for it. Its *modus operandi* is to slam the door and stay inside, surrounded by its familiar opinions and beliefs. We can think of this shutting-down process as coming from a lack of metaphorical space. There isn't enough room to accommodate both your and someone else's opinions, so you're faced with an all too familiar scenario: shut the person out, try to change their mind, and/or view them as "the other" while warily watching them from behind curtained windows.

But what if you could make more room? The True Self is aware of your entire house, a structure that is infinite in reality. There is no limit to how much you can expand, but to do so you must be willing to step outside of the ego's familiar territory. When you do, there's more room to acknowledge—even if you don't agree with—other people's opinions. Your goal here isn't really about agreement; it's about having enough space that both can exist without constantly stepping on each other's toes. When there's enough space, there's less need to eradicate the opposition because you both can live comfortably. In practical terms, you are able to acknowledge that someone else feels differently without this difference stirring up so much internal discomfort in your crowded house that you must rush to change their mind or shut them out. This doesn't necessarily mean that you won't feel discomfort; it simply means that in your infinite house, there is enough room for the differing of opinions *and* the discomfort that arises as a result. There's room enough for all of it—good, bad, and neutral. There's a place at the table for all of your parts to sit, and there is no need to cast off aspects of yourself and project them onto other people, whom you fervently try to keep locked outside. This is what we mean by bringing it all home: You allow all parts of yourself *to be a part of you*. And the secret is that even if the ego wasn't allowing them to be a part of you, they're here just the same but are stuck in the basement of the unconscious where they can wreak far more havoc than if they were invited to the table.

Reflecting our work with projection, part of the motivation for keeping our windows shuttered and our doors locked is the belief that we contain acceptable parts and unacceptable parts. The latter get shoved into the basement of the unconscious and projected onto the external world. The illusion that these things only exist somewhere called "out there" feels safer; it keeps us from having to see that all these parts exist inside our house as well. As long as we're attached to this illusion, the harder we will work to keep these forces "out." This effort and strain manifests as being rigidly tied to our beliefs and opinions and responding to differences by either trying to convert people to our way of seeing or shutting them out. Our work with Integration is therefore all about gathering the pieces together—what we call good and bad, as well as the neutral—and making space for all of them to exist.

This gathering of pieces parallels a metaphysical process that occurs when our soul enters physical existence (i.e., when we are born). When we incarnate, the singleness of spirit is split into the four elements that give rise to physical reality. Think of this process like the white light (spirit) refracted into a rainbow of colors. Our soul is aware that underlying the presentation of different colors exists a single source, the white light of spirit. As we live in the physical world, it's often easier to identify with the colored lights—the matter—than it is to connect with the cohesive white light of our spiritual essence. Transformation is not about negating the existence of the colored lights—they're here, we can see them all around us, and they're a facet of reality we must accept—it's about being able to hold in our awareness the existence of both the rainbow *and* the white light, the matter *and* the spirit, and to understand that they are ultimately One. We do not have to leave our physical experience to unite with the divine; our physical experience *is* divine.

Jump into the experience while you are alive!

Think…and think…while you are alive.

What you call 'salvation' belongs to the time before death.

If you don't break your ropes while you're alive

Do you think

Ghosts will do it after?

The idea that the soul will join with the ecstatic

Just because the body is rotten—

That is all fantasy.

What is found now is found then.

If you find nothing now,

You will simply end up with an apartment in the City of Death.

If you make love with the Divine now, in the next life you will have the face of satisfied desire.

—Kabir (1977, 8)

In the next exercise, you will explore your current relationship with the four elements. In order to fully remember our True Self, we must be comfortable embodying all of the elements, but in practice, we tend to favor one or two. This exercise will show you which elements need more attention in your life, allowing you to consciously welcome those elements back home, gathering the refracted colors into the white light of spirit, your True Self.

Exercise Thirty-Four: The Quaternio

Enter a meditative state (page 26).

Introduce the flow of Reiki (page 125).

Create an image in your mind of the quaternio as if it were painted on or etched into the ground.

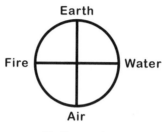

The Quaternio

See the four directions: north and south, east and west. See yourself standing in the center of the quaternio, facing north.

Starting with the north, feel the presence of earth in front of you. Notice sensations in your body. Do any images, thoughts, or emotions arise? Allow the experience to unfold naturally as you connect with the earth of the north.

In your mind's eye, turn to the left, facing west. Feel the presence of water in front of you. Notice sensations in your body. Do any images, thoughts, or emotions arise? Allow yourself to connect with the water of the west.

In your mind's eye, turn to the left, facing south. Feel the presence of air in front of you. Notice sensations in your body. Do any images, thoughts, or emotions arise? Allow the experience to unfold as you connect with the air of the south.

In your mind's eye, turn to the left, facing east. Feel the presence of fire in front of you. Notice sensations in your body. Do any images, thoughts, or emotions arise? Allow yourself to connect with the fire of the east.

Turn so you are once more facing north, and this time, tune into the energies of the four elements surrounding you without turning to face each one. Feel the energy of earth in front of you, the presence of air behind you, water to your left, and fire to your right. See if you can hold awareness of all four elements at once, perhaps shifting from one to the next to the next, again and again, until they begin to flow together.

Now, ask your True Self to indicate where you are right now in relationship to the elements. Are you emphasizing one or more of the elements? If so, you will feel a shift and perhaps see yourself being pulled toward one side of the quaternio. Don't resist, allow the shift to occur.

If you have shifted, where have you shifted to? Are you solidly situated near one element or part way between two? If you're between two elements, are you a bit closer to one or the other? Ask your True Self any questions you have at this time. You might ask to see what underlies your elemental imbalance and how you can return to a more unified state.

The elements around you begin to glow with the colors of the rainbow, and you are surrounded by a circle of rainbow lights. Take a few breaths to connect with the image and feel a sense of the rainbow lights encircling you.

Shift your awareness to your heart and feel your heart energy begin to expand. Your heart energy pushes outward, moving beyond your skin on all four sides. It moves outward further, reaching the limits of your aura. Continue expanding your heart, using the breath to guide this expansion. Each breath expands a bit more. See as your heart energy expands large enough to encompass the entire circle of rainbow colors… as it does so, they are transformed to pure white light. Rest in the presence of this pure white light for a few minutes.

When you feel ready, gradually bring your heart energy inward, allowing it to return to a state that feels comfortable and natural for you. Once more you are standing within a circle of rainbow colors, but you retain the awareness that they are simultaneously the white light of Spirit, just as they are the rainbow spectrum of matter. *You* are simultaneously the white light of spirit, just as you are the rainbow spectrum of matter. You have the ability to transform energy at will, transmuting it from spirit to matter, from matter to spirit. Hold this awareness in your entire being as you breathe in and out, in and out, feeling your flesh and blood animated by the breath of spirit.

When this process feels complete, thank your True Self, thank each of the four elements—earth, fire, air, and water— and spirit. Begin to release the image of the quaternio from your mind and bring your awareness back to your breath.

Return to a normal state of consciousness (pages 26–27).

Journal about your experience, making note of any insights you received from your Higher Self. What did each of the elements feel like to you? When you asked to see your current elemental relationship, what happened? Which element(s) were you pulled towards, and what information did you receive about the underlying cause of this shift? Following this exercise, begin to research the associations for each element. A great place to start is with a book on the tarot. The portion of the deck known as the minor arcana is divided into four suits that are associated with—you guessed it—the four elements. You can think of each suit as a map, what Penzcak describes in *The Witch's Coin* as "a sacred quest, a journey we undergo several times in our lives in a desire to pierce the four mysteries." (p 86) If the elements are the building blocks of life as the Hermetic creation story explains, learning how you uniquely channel these energies to create your life is immensely useful. By looking at the flow of these energies, you can see areas where you tend to get stuck or areas that come more naturally to you. Together, you'll have a richer picture of the reason your soul came into this particular body in this particular lifetime. Jung believed that the archetypes of the four elements are so central to our human experience that we all seek (often unconsciously) to balance these elements throughout our lives. We have an innate sense of harmony and unity amongst the elements, which I believe is a memory of our pre-physical existence as a whole and self-contained white-light being before the light separated into the four elements, signaling our entrance into the physical world. We seek to return to that state of wholeness and unity. How much easier would our task be if we had insights as to where we might be out of sync with a particular element or elements?

Exercise Thirty-Six: The Hieros Gamos

For your final exercise, I offer you inspiration. What you do with it is entirely up to you. As the master of your own destiny, you are the sovereign of your life. To honor your remarkable passage into selfhood, perform a marriage ceremony: a coagulation of the inner opposites, a melding of spirit and matter, One Mind and One Thing, active and receptive. This union is what Hermeticists referred to as the Hieros Gamos or divine marriage. The specifics of the ceremony I leave to you; this is a deeply personal transition deserving of an equally personal ritual celebration. I once read of a woman who hiked out to a remote lake, donned a wedding gown, and submerged herself in the water, baptizing herself that she may be born anew, whole. A friend spent three days on a solitary vision quest that culminated in a naked ritual, and danced beneath the moon and stars. Remember the tools and skills you have acquired along the way—meditation, calling back your projections, the Reiki precepts, the symbols, the mantras. Perhaps some or all of these are meant to be part of your ceremony. Take your time; let your intuition and your intellect partner in the creation of your rite of passage. Do it solo or invite some of your fellow travelers on this path. Allow the creation and the act of this ritual to be an expression of your True Self. And, as always, record it in your journal. This is one experience you won't want to forget.

Becoming the True Self

And now, we reach the end…which is of course also the beginning. Where to from here? That is up to you, my fellow traveler, for only you can know your True Self. You have many tools at your disposal and many signposts to guide your path. Use them well. Use them often. Remember that they are tools and signs, they are not the truth to which they lead. Use them when they serve your continual evolution and unfolding, but don't allow them to constrain the expansion of your soul. You are a divine being beautifully woven into a physical tapestry. Embrace your dual nature that is One, embrace the paradox. Remember your True Self.

Conclusion

You've made it—you're here! To the end and the beginning, all rolled into one. And what better way to send you off than with the timeless wisdom of Dr. Seuss:

Congratulations!

Today is your day.

You're off to Great Places!

You're off and away!

You have brains in your head.

You have feet in your shoes.

You can steer yourself

any direction you choose.

You're on your own. And you know what you know.

And YOU are the [one] who'll decide where to go (Seuss 2011, 1).

You've come a long way, shedding the light of awareness into the hidden hallways and boarded-up windows of the unconscious, all in service of remembering your birthright: your True Self. Throughout this journey, you've gathered valuable tools and knowledge to help you stay aligned with this self and to return when you wander, as we all do from time to time.

These practices and principles are designed to help you find wholeness and happiness amidst the messiness of daily life, for, as you've discovered, you don't need to retreat to a mountaintop to find them. And even the word "finding" is inaccurate—this wholeness, this happiness was never truly lost, merely obscured by egoic clutter. In any moment, no matter where you are, what you're doing, or whom you're with, you can choose to remember who you really are: you are luminous divine energy inhabiting a miraculous physical body. Embrace *both* aspects of your nature—the physical and the spiritual—for they equip you with wonderful abilities that neither can achieve in isolation.

The way that you as a unique being learn to live as both physical and divine *is* your soul's calling expressed through your work, relationships, health, hobbies—through every aspect of your life. No one else will express this duality quite the way you do, and the world needs your unique contribution. The time is now. Reclaim your inner throne. No one else can fill this throne; it is waiting for *you*. Rule yourself with compassion: seek out your hidden aspects, your rejected aspects, and welcome them home through acceptance. Trust that all of your parts are worthy of this acceptance, not just the shiny and pretty ones. The more you are able to accept your internal diversity and internal paradox, the less you will seek to eradicate differences in the people and in the world around you. You will realize that your True Self is big enough to contain all paradox, and you can walk away from the endless ego battle that no one can win toward vibrant, soul-led living.

Remember also that you have the support of the Reiki practices and precepts, the guideposts Usui left us so that we can always find our way when times get dark and the path is hard to see. Use them often; make them a part of your daily life. The more you connect with Reiki, the easier it is to remember that you *are* Reiki, and your thoughts, words, and actions will spring from this place of wisdom and clarity, giving birth to a life that is in alignment with your soul. When you feel stuck, return to the stages of self-transformation: Which step seems to resonate with you most right now? Return to that stage and engage the practices; go through the exercises, ask for and open to receive guidance. *You are never alone on this journey.* All of the beings who have traveled this path before and who are traveling it with you now have left footprints of light, marking the way. Use the practices in this book to reconnect with your own light of awareness, and the path will emerge from the shadows, and you, too, will add your footprints on the collective journey toward remembrance of the True Self.

Bibliography

Andrews, Ted. *Animal-Speak: The Spiritual & Magical Powers of Creatures Great & Small.* St. Paul, MN: Llewellyn Publications, 2005.

Beattie, Melody. *Codependent No More: How to Stop Controlling Others and Start Caring for Yourself.* Center City, MN: Hazelden Publishing, 2016.

Bly, Robert, and Marion Woodman. *The Maiden King: The Reunion of Masculine and Feminine.* Shaftesbury, UK: Element Books, 1999.

Bowman, Katy. *Movement Matters: Essays on Movement Science, Movement Ecology, and the Nature of Movement.* Sequim, WA: Propriometrics Press, 2016.

Campbell, Joseph, and David Kudler. *Pathways to Bliss: Mythology and Personal Transformation.* Novato, CA: New World Books, 2004.

Campbell, Joseph, and Evans Lansing Smith. *Romance of the Grail: The Magic and Mystery of Arthurian Myth.* Novato, CA: New World Library, 2015.

Chia, Mantak. *Chi Nei Tsang: Chi Massage for the Vital Organs.* Rochester, VT: Destiny Books, 2007.

Dale, Cyndi. *The Subtle Body: An Encyclopedia of Your Energetic Anatomy.* Boulder, CO: Sounds True, 2009.

Doi, Hiroshi. *A Modern Reiki Method for Healing.* Southfield, MI: Vision Publications, 2014.

Estés, Clarissa Pinkola. *Women Who Run with the Wolves: Myths and Stories of the Wild Woman Archetype.* New York: Ballantine Books, 1997.

Fleming, Nic. "Plants talk to each other using an internet of fungus." BBC Earth. November 11, 2014. http://www.bbc.com/ earth/story/20141111-plants-have-a-hidden-internet.

Von Franz, Marie-Luise. *The Feminine in Fairy Tales.* Boston: Shambhala, 1993.

Grice, Keiron Le. *The Archetypal Cosmos: Rediscovering the Gods in Myth, Science and Astrology.* Edinburgh, Scotland: Floris Books, 2010.

Hauck, Dennis William. *The Emerald Tablet: Alchemy for Personal Transformation*. New York: Penguin Compass, 1999.

Hendricks, Gay. *The Big Leap*. New York, NY: HarperCollins, 2009.

Huffington, Arianna. *Sleep Revolution: Transforming Your Life, One Night at a Time*. New York: Harmony Crown, 2017.

Hurd, Barbara. *Entering the Stone: On Caves and Feeling Through the Dark*. Athens, GA: University of Georgia Press, 2008.

[Anonymous] Three Initiates. *The Kybalion: A Study of the Hermetic Philosophy of Ancient Egypt And Greece*. New York: TarcherPerigee, 2017.

International House of Reiki, *Self-Published Manuals 1, 2, and 3*. http://www.ihreiki.com/ 2010.

Jagat, Guru. *Invincible Living: Practical Yoga for Every Body*. San Francisco: HarperElixir, 2017.

Johnston, Anita A. *Eating in the Light of the Moon: How Women Can Transform Their Relationships with Food through Myths, Metaphors & Storytelling*. Carlsbad, CA: Gúrze Books, 2000.

Jung, Carl Gustav. *The Collected Works of C. G. Jung*, vol. 13. Princeton, NJ: Princeton University Press, 1967.

Jung, Carl Gustav. *Memories, Dreams, Reflections*. Edited by Aniela Jaffe, translated by Clara Winston and Richard Winston. United States: Random House, 1989. First published 1963 by Pantheon Books, New York.

Jung, Carl Gustav. *Mysterium Coniunctionis*. Translated by Gerhard Adler, and R. F. C. Hull. Princeton, NJ: Princeton/ Bollingen Press, 1977. First published 1963 by Bollingen Foundation, New York.

Kabir, and Robert Bly. *The Kabir Book: Forty-Four of the Ecstatic Poems of Kabir*. Fitzhenry and Whiteside, 1977.

LaPorte, Danielle. "Cheap easy, quality easy, and the Myth of Endurance." From "White hot truth sermons on life." March 27, 2016. http://www.daniellelaporte.com/what-is-easy/.

LeGrice, Keiron. *The Archetypal Cosmos*. London: Floris Books, 2011.

Lehr, Jennifer. *ParentSpeak: What's Wrong with How We Talk to Our Children—and What to Say Instead*. New York: Workman Publishing Co., 2016.

Lübeck, Walter, Frank Arjava Petter, William Lee Rand. *The Spirit of Reiki: The Complete Handbook of the Reiki System*. Twin Lakes, WI: Lotus Press, 2001.

Milne, Hugh. *The Heart of Listening: A Visionary Approach to Craniosacral Work*. Berkeley, CA: North Atlantic Books, 1998.

Nedergaard, Maiken, and Steven A. Goldman. "The Brain's Waste-Disposal System May Be Enlisted to Treat Alzheimer's and Other Brain Illnesses." *Scientific American* March 2016, 46–49.

Ozeki, Ruth L. *A Tale for the Time Being*. Toronto, Ontario, Canada: Penguin, 2014.

Penczak, Christopher. *Foundations of the Temple: A Witchcraft Tradition of Love, Will and Wisdom*. Salem, NH: Copper Cauldron Publishing, 2014.

————. *The Inner Temple of Witchcraft: Magick, Meditation, and Psychic Development*. St. Paul, MN: Llewellyn Publications, 2002.

————. *The Witch's Coin: Prosperity and Money Magick*. Woodbury, MN: Llewellyn Publications, 2009.

Perera, Sylvia Brinton. *Celtic Queen Maeve and Addiction: An Archetypal Perspective*. York Beach, ME: Nicolas-Hays, 2001.

Pollack, Rachel. *Seventy-Eight Degrees of Wisdom: A Book of Tarot*. London: Thorsons, 1997.

Rosenberg, Marshall B., and Arun Gandhi. *Non-violent Communication: A Language of Life*. Encinitas, CA: PuddleDancer Press, 2015.

Ruiz, Miguel, and Janet Mills. *The Four Agreements*. Thorndike, ME: Center Point Publishing, 2008.

Shapiro, Rami M. *The Angelic Way: Angels Through the Ages and Their Meaning for Us*. New York: BlueBridge, 2009.

Sōhō, Takuan, and William Scott Wilson. *The Unfettered Mind: Writings of the Zen Master to the Sword Master*. Tokyo: Kodansha International, 2007.

Sneed, Brandon. *Head in the Game: The Mental Engineering of the World's Greatest Athletes*. New York: Dey St., an imprint of William Morrow, 2017.

Stiene, Bronwen, and Frans Steine. *The Reiki Sourcebook*. Lanham, UK: O-Books, 2010.

Stiene, Frans. *The Inner Heart of Reiki: Rediscovering Your True Self*. Winchester, UK: Ayni Books, 2015.

Seuss, Dr. *Oh, the Places You'll Go!* London: HarperCollins Children, 2011.

Thomas, Scarlett. *The Seed Collectors*. Edinburgh, Scotland, UK: Canongate Books, 2015.

Valiente, Doreen. "The Charge of the Goddess" via www .doreenvaliente.com/Doreen-Valiente-Doreen_Valiente _Poetry-11.php#sthash.5e0jVaG0.Ba2wRYCX.dpbs.

GET MORE AT LLEWELLYN.COM

Visit us online to browse hundreds of our books and decks, plus sign up to receive our e-newsletters and exclusive online offers.

- Free tarot readings • Spell-a-Day • Moon phases
- Recipes, spells, and tips • Blogs • Encyclopedia
- Author interviews, articles, and upcoming events

GET SOCIAL WITH LLEWELLYN

Find us on  @LlewellynBooks

www.Facebook.com/LlewellynBooks

GET BOOKS AT LLEWELLYN

LLEWELLYN ORDERING INFORMATION

 Order online: Visit our website at www.llewellyn.com to select your books and place an order on our secure server.

 Order by phone:
- Call toll free within the US at 1-877-NEW-WRLD (1-877-639-9753)
- We accept VISA, MasterCard, American Express, and Discover.
- Canadian customers must use credit cards.

 Order by mail:
Send the full price of your order (MN residents add 6.875% sales tax) in US funds plus postage and handling to: Llewellyn Worldwide, 2143 Wooddale Drive, Woodbury, MN 55125-2989

POSTAGE AND HANDLING

STANDARD (US):
(Please allow 12 business days)
$30.00 and under, add $6.00.
$30.01 and over, FREE SHIPPING.

INTERNATIONAL ORDERS,
INCLUDING CANADA:
$16.00 for one book, plus $3.00 for each additional book.

Visit us online for more shipping options.
Prices subject to change.

FREE CATALOG!

To order, call
1-877-
NEW-WRLD
ext. 8236
or visit our
website

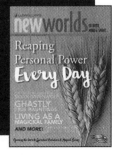

A Modern Master's Approach to Emotional,
Spiritual & Physical Wellness

the

Healing Power

of

Reiki

Foreword by Mehmet C. Oz, MD

RAVEN KEYES

The Healing Power of Reiki
A Modern Master's Approach to Emotional, Spiritual & Physical Wellness
Raven Keyes

The ancient art of Reiki has the power to heal our minds, bodies, and spirits in ways few of us can imagine. The first Reiki Master to practice in an operating room under the supervision of Dr. Mehmet Oz, author Raven Keyes has brought Reiki to the defining events of our time. With engaging prose, Keyes tells moving stories of giving Reiki to rescue workers at Ground Zero, PTSD survivors, professional athletes, trauma patients, and those suffering from crippling emotional pain. Keyes offers inspirational experiences of connecting with angels and spirit guides, and shares the joys and pains of working with patients, their loved ones, and their communities. Through stories and meditations, readers are filled with hope and a sense of good will. Helpful exercises and meditations are included to invite healing and provide the opportunity to engage with Reiki energy more deeply.

978-0-7387-3351-7, 288 pp., 5 ¼ x 8   **$16.99**

Focused Energy for Healing, Ritual & Spiritual Development

MAGICK OF

Reiki

CHRISTOPHER PENCZAK

Magick of Reiki
Focused Energy for Healing,
Ritual, & Spiritual Development
CHRISTOPHER PENCZAK

What is Reiki? How has this Japanese healing tradition evolved over the years? How are modern magick practitioners using Reiki energy in their spells and rituals?

Christopher Penczak answers these questions and more in his groundbreaking examination of Reiki from a magickal perspective. The history, mythos, variations, and three degrees of Reiki are discussed in depth. Penczak also suggests way to integrate Reiki and magickal practice, such as using Reiki energy for psychic development and with candle magick, crystals, herbs, charms, and talismans.

Winner of the 2005 COVR Award (Best Alternative Health Book)

978-0-7387-0573-6, 288 pp., 7 ½ x 9 ⅛   **$19.99**

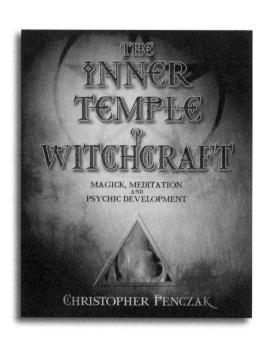

THE INNER TEMPLE OF WITCHCRAFT

MAGICK, MEDITATION
AND
PSYCHIC DEVELOPMENT

CHRISTOPHER PENCZAK

The Inner Temple of Witchcraft
Magick, Meditation and Psychic Development
Christopher Penczak

Explore your Inner Temple—your personal sacred space where there are no boundaries and all things are possible. With study, dedication, and practice, the lessons and exercises in this book will empower you to transform the repetitive rigors of the daily grind into a witch's web of magickal experiences.

The Inner Temple of Witchcraft is a thorough course of education, introspection, meditation, and the development of the magickal and psychic abilities that are the birthright of the witch. Four introductory chapters present the history, traditions, and principles of witchcraft, followed by thirteen lessons that start with basic meditation techniques and culminate in a self-initiation ceremony equivalent to the first-degree level of traditional coven-based witchcraft.

978-0-7387-0276-6, 352 pp., 7 ½ x 9 ⅛ **$24.99**

The Witch's Coin
Prosperity and Money Magick
Christopher Penczak

Along with quick-fix money spells, this timely book explores the consciousness of prosperity and how to transform poverty into abundance through magick, meditation, affirmations, and astrological timing. The Witch's Coin offers a materia magicka of the most powerful correspondences in wealth spellwork, including gods, stones, metals, herbs, and coins. Unlike most money magick books, it builds upon a foundation of real-world financial principles. Penczak also discusses offering magickal services professionally, including how and when to charge for readings and healings.

978-0-7387-1587-2, 288 pp., 6 x 9   **$17.95**

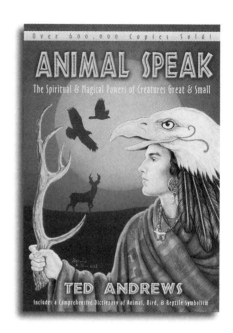

Animal Speak
The Spiritual & Magical Powers of
Creatures Great and Small
TED ANDREWS

Open your heart and mind to the wisdom of the animal world.

Animal Speak provides techniques for recognizing and interpreting the signs and omens of nature. Meet and work with animals as totems and spirit guides by learning the language of their behaviors within the physical world.

978-0-87542-028-8, 400 pp., 7 x 10   **$22.99**